D1344367

CONSTRUCTION AND THE BUILT ENVIRONMENT

PEARSON

Published by Pearson Education Limited, Edinburgh Gate, Harlow, Essex, CM20 2JE.

www.pearsonschoolsandfecolleges.co.uk

Text © Pearson Education Limited 2013.
Typeset by Phoenix Photosetting, Chatham, Kent, UK
Original illustrations © Pearson Education Limited 2013
Illustrated by Phoenix Photosetting, Chatham, Kent, UK
Cover design by Pearson Education Limited and Andrew Magee Design
Picture research by Caitlin Swain
Front cover photo: © Shutterstock.com/Darryl Sleath
Indexing by Torquil Harkness

The rights of Simon Topliss, Syed Aftab Mohyuddin, John Murray-Smith and Ashley Stokes to be
identified as authors of this work have been asserted by them in accordance with the Copyright, Designs
and Patents Act 1988.

This edition published 2013

17 16 15 14
10 9 8 7 6 5 4 3 2
British Library Cataloguing in Publication Data
A catalogue record for this book is available from the British Library
ISBN 978 1 446906 46 0

Printed in Italy by L.E.G.O. S.p.A.

Copies of official specifications for all Pearson qualifications may be found on the website:
www.edexcel.com

A NOTE FROM THE PUBLISHER

In order to ensure that this resource offers high-quality support for the associated BTEC
qualification, it has been through a review process by the awarding organisation to confirm
that it fully covers the teaching and learning content of the specification or part of a
specification at which it is aimed, and demonstrates an appropriate balance between the
development of subject skills, knowledge and understanding, in addition to preparation for
assessment.

While the publishers have made every attempt to ensure that advice on the qualification
and its assessment is accurate, the official specification and associated assessment guidance
materials are the only authoritative source of information and should always be referred to for
definitive guidance.

BTEC examiners have not contributed to any sections in this resource relevant to examination
papers for which they have responsibility.

No material from an endorsed book will be used verbatim in any assessment set by BTEC.

Endorsement of a book does not mean that the book is required to achieve this BTEC
qualification, nor does it mean that it is the only suitable material available to support the
qualification, and any resource lists produced by the awarding organisation shall include this
and other appropriate resources.

Contents

Picture Credits

The publisher would like to thank the following for their kind permission to reproduce their photographs:

(Key: b-bottom; c-centre; l-left; r-right; t-top)

Alamy Images: David R. Frazier Photolibrary, Inc. 38, Jeffrey Blackler 39t, Photofusion PIcture Library 40b; **Comstock Images:** 196; **Construction Photography:** Buildpix 245 (Banner), 272, David Potter 15, 256; **Corbis:** 203; **Digital Vision:** 4 (Banner), 39b, 245, 262; **DK Images:** Andy Crawford 133cr, Kate Davis 200b, Steve Gorton 52, 214 (Wheel cutter); **Fotolia.com:** auremar 244, 253, Carson Liu 42, david hughes 275, kotomiti 218t, simmittorok 176b; **Harris:** 194 (Shears); **Imagemore Co., Ltd:** 216 (Spanners); **Pearson Education Ltd:** Studio 8 202 (Boots), 202 (Gloves), 202 (Goggles), 202 (Mask), 213, 214 (Tube cutter), 222t, 222b, 226, 230b, Ben Nicholson 149, 150 (Banner), 160, 169, 170 (Banner), 180, David Sanderson 8, 114, 176l, Gareth Boden 5, 102, 150 (Bevel), 150 (Combi-square), 150 (Marking gauge), 150 (Mortise gauge), 150 (Tri-square), 151 (Block plane), 151 (Chisel), 151 (Level), 151 (Mallet), 151 (Pincers), 151 (Saw), 151 (Smoothing plane), 152 (Auger bit), 152 (Bradawl), 152 (Nail punch), 152 (Screwdrivers), 153t, 153c, 153b, 156 (Nails), 156 (Oval nails), 156 (Pins), 156 (Plugs), 158, 170b, 171 (Blocks), 171 (Iron), 171 (Jointing trowel), 171 (Pins), 171 (Recess jointer), 171 (Walling trowel), 172t, 172c, 172b, 190t, 190tc, 190b, 190bc, 191t, 191tc, 191bc, 192t, 193bl, 193bc, 193br, 194 (Brush), 194 (Knife), 194 (Level), 194 (Plumb line), 195t, 195b, 197, 200t, 200c, 202 (Overalls), 214 (Pipe cutters), 215 (Hand bender), 216 (Hammer drill), 216 (Pipe grips), 216 (Pipe vice), 217t, 218b, 220, 224, 230t, 230c, 232, 238 (Electrician's pliers), 238c, 239 (Hacksaw), 239 (Screwdrivers), 292, HL Studios 64 (Banner), Joey Chan 268, Jules Selmes 152 (Twist drill bit), 178, 215 (File), 239 (Cable strippers), 239 (Side cutters), 239 (Testing), 246, 252, 299, Naki Kouyioumtzis 103, 151 (Tape measure), 170c, 194 (Tape measure), 208, 215 (Tape measure), 238 (Tape measure), Sophie Bluy 40t, Trevor Clifford 150 (Steel rule), 215 (Hacksaw), 240; **PhotoDisc:** 45, 214 (Banner), 216 (Wrench), 222c, 289, Neil Beer 122; **Photos.com:** Abhishek Aggarwal 166, Alistair Forrester Shankie 242, Ansar Mahmood 234, Ben Blankenburg 125, Bertold Werkmann 101, Carl Millar 48, Cathy Yeulet 233, Charles Daniel Howell 2, ChrisMilesPhoto 29, Comstock 62, 216b, darren wise 59, David Dawson 259, Dean Mitchell 126, Dejan Ristovski 168, Diane Diederich 304, Dmitry Kalinovsky 185, 209, Dobresum 186, DragonImages 146, DutchScenery 287, 288 (Banner), Errol Brown 99, 100 (Banner), Hemera Technologies 128, Hongqi Zhang 36, Jupiter Images 129, Lev Kropotov 279, LuminaStock 188, 190 (Banner), Nomadsoul1 237, Pelham Mitchenson 191b, Rick Lewis 257t, Ridofranz 95, Ronald Hudson 257b, Ryan Morrison 133bl, Sanjay Deva 286, Shelly Perry 210, Tjui Tjioe 98, Tracy Fox 298, viki2win 34, Vladimir Tarasov 176c, Witthaya 192; **Shutterstock.com:** Ant Clausen 35, Arcady 211, benicce 266, Bruce Raynor 285, Derek Abbott 116, dotshock 127, kxdbzxy 61, meunierd 288l, pjhpix 167, R Nagy 37 (Banner); **Sozaijiten:** 14, 133tl, 133tc, 133tr, 133bc; **SuperStock:** Corbis 235, fStop 147, Ingram Publishing 187, Juice Images 3, Westend61 255; **Veer/Corbis:** 350jb 130 (Banner), Adrian Britton 241, Andresr 46, arekmalang 60, 148, Babar760 273, CandyBoxImages 63, daviddear 263, diego cervo 307, Greg Epperson 165, hansenn 117, Henri Ensio 284, irin-k 9, laguna35 173, MarFot 20, Monkey Business Images 96, nolan77 238 (Banner), Patrick Lane 236, Sarah Allison 259, stocklite 145, Wavebreakmediamicro 212, Wong Sze Fei 254; **www.imagesource. com:** 97

Cover image: Shutterstock.com: Darryl Sleath
The publisher would also like to thank Damian McGeary for his kind permission to reproduce the drawings on pages 54 and 56.

All other images © Pearson Education

Picture Research by: Caitlin Swain

Every effort has been made to trace the copyright holders and we apologise in advance for any unintentional omissions. We would be pleased to insert the appropriate acknowledgement in any subsequent edition of this publication.

Authors' acknowledgements
Simon Topliss thanks his wife Linda for supporting him in his endeavours, as well as Paul Monroe, his friend, mentor and guiding hand.
Syed Aftab Mohyuddin thanks his family and the team at Pearson for their support during the writing of this book.
John Murray-Smith thanks his wife Evelyn and grandson Noah for their support when writing his contribution to this book.
Ashley Stokes thanks Mark Doyle for his time and advice, and also his family for their unwavering support.

This book is designed to help you through your BTEC First in Construction and the Built Environment, and covers 15 units of the qualification.

About your BTEC First in Construction and the Built Environment

Choosing to study for a BTEC First in Construction and the Built Environment is a great decision to make for lots of reasons. This qualification will prepare you for virtually any career in the construction sector. It will introduce you to key roles you may be interested in exploring, key skills such as painting and decorating or plumbing, and key topics like sustainability. It will also build your confidence in the science and maths that you will need to use in a career in construction.

About the authors

Simon Topliss has worked at the Grimsby Institute of Further and Higher Education for the past 17 years, delivering BTECs in Construction and the Built Environment. His extensive publishing for Pearson includes more than 18 technical books and guidance documents. He is also a member of the Institute for Learning and an associate of the Chartered Institute of Educational Assessors.

Syed Aftab Mohyuddin has years of experience working in design and construction, maintenance, quantity surveying and teaching, both in the UK and abroad. He is a member of the Chartered Institute of Building and the Institute for Learning, and is particularly interested in technology, sustainability, mathematics and science.

John Murray-Smith has worked in several colleges and schools in the south east and London. He is currently Curriculum Manager for Schools Construction and BTEC Level 2 Construction. He has considerable practical site experience and has worked as far afield as West Africa on construction projects.

Ashley Stokes worked as a professional decorator doing high class domestic work for over 15 years. During this time he ran his own business and employed apprentices and qualified decorators. Since 1998, Ashley has worked at York College in the Construction Department where he teaches full time decorating students from Level 1 to Level 3, as well as Intermediate and Advanced Apprentices.

This book is designed to help you use your skills and knowledge in work-related situations, and assist you in getting the most from your course.

These introductions give you a snapshot of what to expect from each unit – and what you should be aiming for by the time you finish it.

How this unit is assessed

Learning aims describe what you will be doing in the unit.

A learner shares how working through the unit has helped them.

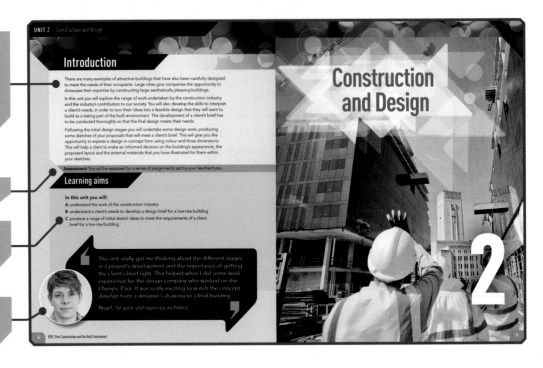

▶ Features of this book

There are lots of features in this book to help you learn about the topics in each unit, and to have fun while learning! These pages show some of the features that you will come across when using the book.

Learning aim and topic references show which parts of the BTEC you are covering.

Key terms are important words or phrases that you will come across. Key terms appear in blue bold text and are defined within the topic or in a key terms box on the page. Also see the glossary.

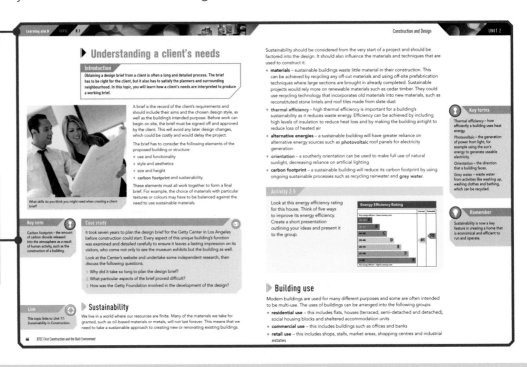

Activity 11.5

Nandita is an architect and is involved in designing a housing project. Her client wants the project to be sustainable.

Explain why Nandita might include two named features in a sustainable house.

> Activities will help you learn about the topic. These can be completed in pairs or groups, or sometimes on your own.

Assessment practice 1.5

The grid below shows a number of locations and different types of insulation. Match the location to the appropriate type of insulation.   [3]

Proposed location	Type of insulation
A music studio in a drummer's garage	Triple glazing
A conservatory on the flight path to Heathrow	Heavy-density blockwork
A house next to a busy main road	Acoustic ceiling

> A chance to practise answering the types of test questions that you may come across in the paper-based examination. (For Unit 1 and Unit 11 only.)

Assessment activity 8.1

Your employer has given you the following information about a job:

1 An exterior panel door is to be painted. It is in sound condition with the exception of the bottom two panels, which are flaking in places.

2 A hallway that has been previously painted is dirty and has some small cracks. It is to be finished in vinyl matt paint.

Produce a tool list for these jobs and explain why you have selected them.

Tips

- Name the tools and equipment needed to complete the job and why you have chosen each. You could also write a specification for all the materials needed for the preparation and painting tasks.
- Explain how you would safely use the tools, materials and equipment, and how they should be stored.

> Activities that relate to the unit's assessment criteria. These activities will help you prepare for your assignments and contain tips to help you achieve your potential. (For all units **except** Unit 1 and Unit 11.)

Just checking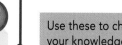

1 What type of work would be undertaken by a civil engineering company?

2 In a short paragraph describe what you understand by the word 'infrastructure'.

3 List four kinds of leisure-related building activity.

> Use these to check your knowledge and understanding of the topic you have just covered.

Someone who works in the construction industry explains how this unit of the BTEC First applies to the day-to-day work they do as part of their job.

WorkSpace

▶ Ellie Wise

Junior design engineer

I'm a junior design engineer working for a local consultant firm. My job involves designing structural elements of buildings such as beams, columns and roofs. I get to work on lots of different projects and I also meet lots of different people. It is an interesting job as every project is different and challenging. I am involved in all stages of designing from client meetings to designing a whole project. In time, I hope to become a design engineer and take responsibility for a project of my own.

Having a good knowledge of mathematics and science is really valuable in my job. Mathematics helps me to do all the calculations such as areas and volumes as well as applying trigonometry, especially for roof structures. Without a good knowledge of science and construction materials as well, I wouldn't know what materials to choose for various parts of the structure as all materials have different properties.

All this knowledge has helped me to talk confidently to our clients and to explain technical details. It gives them confidence in me too!

Think about it

1 Why do you think it is important for everyone who works in the construction industry to know about mensuration?

2 How do you think the information about the properties of materials could benefit Ellie in her job?

3 What sorts of characteristics do you think a design engineer needs to have?

4 Is this a job you would be interested in? If so, why?

95

This section also gives you the chance to think more about the role that this person does, and whether you would want to follow in their footsteps once you've completed your BTEC.

▶ BTEC Assessment Zone

You will be assessed in two different ways for your BTEC First Construction qualification. For most units, your teacher/tutor will set assignments for you to complete. These may take the form of projects where you research, plan, prepare, and evaluate a piece of work or activity. The table in this BTEC Assessment Zone explains what you must do in order to achieve each of the assessment criteria. Each unit of this book contains a number of assessment activities to help you with these assessment criteria.

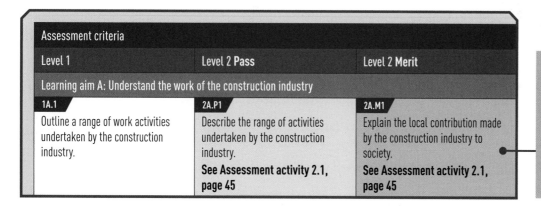

Assessment criteria		
Level 1	Level 2 Pass	Level 2 Merit
Learning aim A: Understand the work of the construction industry		
1A.1	**2A.P1**	**2A.M1**
Outline a range of work activities undertaken by the construction industry.	Describe the range of activities undertaken by the construction industry. **See Assessment activity 2.1, page 45**	Explain the local contribution made by the construction industry to society. **See Assessment activity 2.1, page 45**

The table in the BTEC Assessment Zone explains what you must do in order to achieve each of the assessment criteria, and signposts assessment activities in this book to help you to prepare for your assignments.

For Unit 1 and Unit 11 of your BTEC, you will be assessed by a paper-based examination. The BTEC Assessment Zone for these units helps you to prepare for your test by showing you some of the different types of questions you will need to answer.

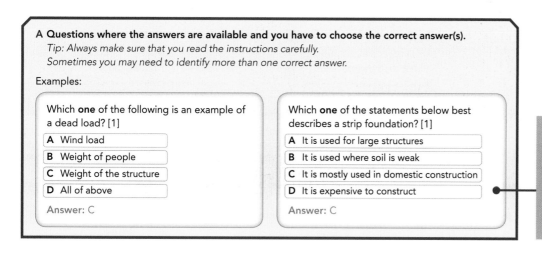

A Questions where the answers are available and you have to choose the correct answer(s).
Tip: Always make sure that you read the instructions carefully.
Sometimes you may need to identify more than one correct answer.

Examples:

Which **one** of the following is an example of a dead load? [1]

A Wind load
B Weight of people
C Weight of the structure
D All of above

Answer: C

Which **one** of the statements below best describes a strip foundation? [1]

A It is used for large structures
B It is used where soil is weak
C It is mostly used in domestic construction
D It is expensive to construct

Answer: C

You will find examples of the different types of questions you may need to answer, as well as sample answers and tips on how to prepare for the paper-based examination.

Study skills

Planning and getting organised

The first step in managing your time is to plan ahead and be well organised. Some people are naturally good at this. They think ahead, write down commitments in a diary or planner and store their notes and handouts neatly and carefully so they can find them quickly.

How good are your working habits?

Improving your planning and organisational skills

1 Use a diary to schedule working times into your weekdays and weekends.
2 Also use the diary to write down exactly what work you have to do. You could use this as a 'to do' list and tick off each task as you go.
3 Divide up long or complex tasks into manageable chunks and put each 'chunk' in your diary with a deadline of its own.
4 Always allow more time than you think you need for a task.

Sources of information

You will need to use research to complete your BTEC First assignments, so it's important to know what sources of information are available to you. These are likely to include the following:

Textbooks
These cover the units of your qualification and provide activities and ideas for further research.

Internet
A vast source of information, but not all sites are accurate and information and opinions can often be **biased** – you should always double-check facts you find online.

Sources of information

Newspapers and magazines
These often cover construction topics in articles about construction.

People
People you know can be a great source of opinions and experience – particularly if you want feedback on an idea.

Television
Programmes such as *Grand Designs* can give you an insight into the world of construction.

▷ Organising and selecting information

Organising your information

Once you have used a range of sources of information for research, you will need to organise the information so it's easy to use.

- Make sure your written notes are neat and have a clear heading – it's often useful to date them, too.
- Always keep a note of where the information came from (the title of a book, the title and date of a newspaper or magazine and the web address of a website) and, if relevant, which pages.
- Work out the results of any questionnaires you've used.

Selecting your information

Once you have completed your research, re-read the assignment brief or instructions you were given to remind yourself of the exact wording of the question(s) and divide your information into three groups:

1 Information that is totally relevant.

2 Information that is not as good, but which could come in useful.

3 Information that doesn't match the questions or assignment brief very much, but that you kept because you couldn't find anything better!

Check that there are no obvious gaps in your information against the questions or assignment brief. If there are, make a note of them so that you know exactly what you still have to find.

▷ Presenting your work

Before handing in any assignments, make sure:

- you have addressed each part of the question and that your work is as complete as possible
- all spelling and grammar is correct
- you have referenced all sources of information you used for your research
- that all work is your own – otherwise you could be committing **plagiarism**
- you have saved a copy of your work.

Key term

Plagiarism – If you are including other people's views, comments or opinions, or copying a diagram or table from another publication, you must state the source by including the name of the author or publication, or the web address. Failure to do this (so you are really pretending other people's work is your own) is known as plagiarism. Check your school's policy on plagiarism and copying.

Introduction

How much do you know about how a building is designed and constructed? You have probably thought about it before choosing to take this course, but you may not have realised how important this knowledge is to every job in the construction industry.

Different parts of buildings serve different purposes and so they need to perform in different ways. A roof, a floor and a wall all need to be strong and stable, but they have different jobs and so they must be designed to resist different forces.

In modern construction, sustainability is also a key feature of any design. This ensures new developments do not have a negative effect on the environment.

Whether you are a plumber, an architect, a groundworker or a site manager, it is vital to understand the processes in the construction of buildings. This unit is the foundation of your understanding of the built environment.

Assessment: You will be assessed using a paper-based examination lasting one hour.

Learning aims

In this unit you will:

A understand the structural performance required for low-rise construction

B explore how sub-structures are constructed

C explore how superstructures are constructed.

The unit has made me think more about how buildings are designed and constructed. I really enjoyed doing the sketches as they helped me to understand the different processes and materials that can be used. I'd never even thought about them before!

Andy, *15-year-old aspiring electrician*

Construction Technology

Performance requirements

Introduction

A building has to be designed and constructed to fulfil certain **performance** requirements. It has to be strong and **stable**, but it also needs to able to do other things, such as resist fire and bad weather. People should be comfortable in the building whether it is a house or a workplace. Buildings should also now reach goals of **sustainability** in materials and construction when they are built.

Key terms

Performance – how well a building provides a comfortable, safe environment for its occupants.

Stable – when a structure can keep its balance without moving.

Sustainability – preserving resources for future generations and minimising the impact of construction activities on the natural environment.

 ## Link

Sketching is a good way to improve your understanding of how a building performs. For more about sketching and construction drawings, see *Unit 2: Construction and Design* and *Unit 5: Construction Drawing Techniques*.

Strength and stability

Loads are the various forces acting on a structure such as a building. A building structure is made up of walls, floors, roofs and foundations. These are called the elements of a building and need to be strong enough to support various loads. If they are not, the building may fall down. There are three types of loads:

1 **dead** – this is a load that does not move, such as the weight of the building itself

2 **dynamic** – these are loads that can change during the use of a building, such as the load from people and furniture

3 **impact** – this is when something hits a building or falls on it, such as a heavy object.

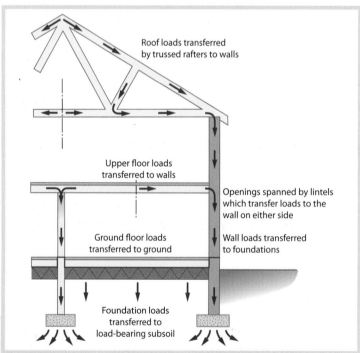

Figure 1.1 A dynamic load is transferred from the roof to the foundations through the walls and floors

The loads depend upon the location of the building. These loads are transferred from the roof to the foundations through walls and floors as shown in Figure 1.1. A building has enough strength if it can resist these loads and remain stable.

Discussion

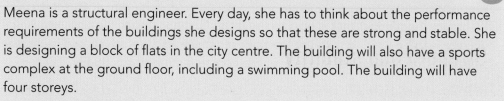

Think about the building you live in. Working in groups, answer the following questions.

1 Which parts of this building are holding it together?

2 Are you putting any load on the building? What type of load is this?

Case study

Meena is a structural engineer. Every day, she has to think about the performance requirements of the buildings she designs so that these are strong and stable. She is designing a block of flats in the city centre. The building will also have a sports complex at the ground floor, including a swimming pool. The building will have four storeys.

1 Why does Meena have to think about the performance requirements of the different parts of a building at the beginning of the design process?

2 Meena is making a list of all the loads this block of flats would have. What sort of loads should she think about when she is designing the building?

3 Are the loads you have mentioned live, dead or dynamic?

Slump testing on a building site. What do you think will happen if the water : cement ratio is too high or too low?

Testing and grading materials

The strength and stability of a building depends on the materials used to construct it. These materials are tested to make sure they have the needed strength.

Concrete is commonly used in foundations and floors, so its strength is crucial. Before concrete is used, tests are carried out on site to make sure it is strong enough.

- Slump testing checks that the **ratio** of water and cement in wet concrete is correct. If wet concrete loses its shape or 'slumps' too easily, the balance is not right.
- Compressive strength testing checks that the hardened concrete is strong enough to withstand loads.

Timber is used in structures such as frames of buildings or roof trusses, as well as in doors and windows. The strength of various types of timber is tested. Timber is then sorted into various groups. This process is called stress grading or strength grading.

Mortar testing is performed by making cubes of mortar to check how much water can pass through it, or if there are any gaps causing leakage.

Specifying and grading materials

For any building, the designer tells the construction team clearly about the type of materials to be used. This is called material specification.

The materials selected will comply with either British Standards or European Standards. These are standards that ensure the quality of materials used in all sorts of industries, including construction. It is important to use materials that meet these standards because this makes sure the building has the right strength to support the loads.

Key term

Ratio – the proportion of one thing to another. For example, if a ratio of water : cement is 1 : 2, there is twice as much cement as water.

Remember

A British Standard starts with the letters BS. The document tells us that the material meets the minimum standards needed in Britain. A European standard starts with the letters EN, which means that the document has details about materials meeting the standards needed in Europe. A standard containing 'BS EN' shows that both British and European standards have been met.

The material specification will also confirm the strength of material needed. Most materials are graded or classified according to their strength.

The strength of a material is calculated by working out how much pressure it can take. This pressure is measured in Newtons per square millimetre (N/mm^2), which means the amount of pressure that a piece of the material measuring 1 mm by 1 mm can resist. So if the strength of a concrete mix is 30 N/mm^2, a piece of that concrete measuring 1 mm by 1 mm could withstand 30 Newtons of pressure before it broke. The strengths of different materials are as follows.

- **Concrete** – available strengths of concrete range from 8 N/mm^2 to 60 N/mm^2. When specifying materials, concrete with a strength of 25 N/mm^2 is written as C25. The higher the number that is next to the letter C, the stronger the concrete is. If concrete is to be used to take the load of a structure, its strength should be at least 25 N/mm^2. The standard that is relevant to concrete strengths is BS EN 206-1.

- **Timber** – timber strength ranges from 14 N/mm^2 to 70 N/mm^2. When it is being specified, the letter C (**coniferous**) means softwood and D (**deciduous**) means hardwood. This means that timber is classified from C14 to C50 and D30 to D70. A D30 timber is a hardwood with a strength of 30 N/mm^2. The strength class is stamped on the timber.

Activity 1.1

You are working on a house that will be built using a wooden frame. The designer has specified a C30 timber for the frame and a D30 timber for the wooden floor. What sort of timber do you need to buy?

- **Bricks** – these are classified according to their strength and the amount of moisture that they can absorb. All bricks should have a minimum strength of 5 N/mm^2. The relevant standard for clay bricks is BS EN 771.

- **Hardcore** – this is used to provide an even base under the floors. It is a mix of gravel, sand, broken bricks and crushed concrete, and is also known as **aggregate**. It is classified based on the size of the pieces of material in the mixture. The higher the number in the classification, the larger the pieces are.

- **Mortars** – these provide a bond between layers or courses of brick and block work. These are classified according to where they will be used. For example, a commonly used mortar in masonry is called G, which means it is for general purpose. The other classification is based on how these are made – for example, factory-based or site-based. BS EN 998 is the relevant standard.

Just checking

1 What does BS stand for? What does it indicate?
2 What are the two standard tests used to check the strength of concrete?
3 How is the strength of a material calculated?

Cavity walls

Cavity walls are walls constructed as two halves, called skins or leaves. The gap between the two skins is called a cavity, which is normally filled with insulating material above ground level. Below ground level, it is filled with concrete to make it both stronger and more stable.

As a cavity wall is constructed in two halves, **wall ties** are provided to connect these together. This makes sure the wall will stay in place and will not move. Wall ties should be provided every 900 mm horizontally and every 450 mm vertically as shown in Figure 1.2. These wall ties make sure a cavity wall provides both strength and stability or composite strength and stability.

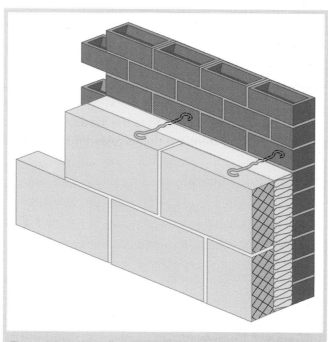

Figure 1.2 Cavity walls are provided with wall-ties to make them stable. What do you think might happen if a cavity wall did not have any wall ties?

Key term

Wall tie – a component used to join the two halves or skins of a cavity wall.

Remember

Sketching does not mean that you have to produce a perfect drawing. It just means that you have to represent an object, whether that is a brick wall or a whole building.

Research

- Find out which Building Regulations affect work on buildings no taller than 12 m.
- Find out the maximum height, length and thickness of a cavity wall for a two-storey building.

Activity 1.2

Sketch a diagram showing the transfer of loads from the walls into the foundations.

Assessment practice 1.1

Complete the sentences below.

1 A timber classified as C45 is: [1]

☐ **A** a hardwood   ☐ **C** a softwood

☐ **B** planed all round   ☐ **D** deciduous.

2 Wall ties are provided: [1]

☐ **A** so that the wall looks good   ☐ **C** only horizontally for stability

☐ **B** for no particular reason   ☐ **D** both horizontally and vertically for stability.

Fire resistance

Fire-resistant buildings can save lives and damage to property. Fire resistance can even make sure a building stays standing after a fire.

Fire-resistant materials

When building a new structure, it can be best to build using fire-resistant materials. These include:

- plasterboard
- concrete
- blockwork
- **intumescent paint** applied to an existing structure to improve its fire resistance.

Fire-resistant design

The design of a building can also affect its fire resistance. Buildings are usually divided into sections called fire compartments, so that a fire in one compartment will not affect the others. These compartments are separated by features known as fire barriers. These include fire walls and separating floors made out of concrete, door closers which stop doors being left ajar, and fire-resistant doors that are steel, painted with intumescent paint. This stops the spread of fire and makes it easier for firefighters to put out the fire.

Equipment for fire resistance

Other features can also be used to stop fires occurring or spreading, or to make a building safer if a fire does break out, such as:

- fire escapes – these allow people to reach safety without using stairs or lifts inside a building. Fire escpes are often attached to the sides of buildings
- refuge areas – these are fire-resistant areas inside a building, designed to be used by less able bodied people, or people with reduced mobility
- cavity fire barriers – these are used to stop the spread of fire through cavities in a building, such as in a wall or ceiling
- fire alarm systems and smoke detectors – these help to alert people to the fire as soon as possible, making it easier to get everyone out of a building quickly and safely
- sprinkler systems – these help to put out fires, especially small fires. They are located in the ceiling and switch on automatically when a fire is detected.

Why is a fire escape necessary even if there are internal stairs and a lift?

Assessment practice 1.2

1 Carry out a survey of your college building and identify two fire-resistance measures that have been provided. [2]

2 Explain the functions of: [2]
- fire barriers
- sprinkler systems.

Thermal insulation

Buildings have to be heated to make them comfortable to live in. However, buildings are not airtight, so they lose heated air through gaps in their structure or in the materials used to construct them. This is why buildings need thermal insulation.

A poorly insulated building will use more energy to maintain a comfortable temperature inside. This means that the energy costs will be higher. A well-insulated building uses less energy and so is cheaper to heat.

U-values

A U-value is used to measure heat loss from any element of a building. A lower U-value means that the building element is well insulated. The Building Regulations Approved Document L specify the U-values for various elements of a building. These are shown in Table 1.1 below.

Can insulation be made of sustainable materials?

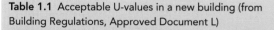

Table 1.1 Acceptable U-values in a new building (from Building Regulations, Approved Document L)

Element of building	Highest acceptable U-value
Roof	0.20 W/m²K
Wall	0.30 W/m²K
Floor	0.25 W/m²K
Windows	2.00 W/m²K

Activity 1.3

A house has recently been built and you have been asked to check whether it has the right U-values. Using Table 1.1 above and the following information, comment on whether the U-values below are acceptable.

- Floor 0.22 W/m²K
- Windows 1.98 W/m²K
- External walls 0.70 W/m²K

Types of insulation

There are lots of different kinds of insulation and it is important to choose the right one for the job. This is done by using the right type of insulation.

Table 1.2 Some different types of insulation

Type	Made from	Advantages	Disadvantages
Sheep's wool	Wool	• Can be reused and recycled • Absorbs extra moisture	• Has some non-renewable material • Thermal conductivity can increase if compressed
Glass fibre or glass mineral wool	Recycled glass and silica	• Fire resistant • Does not rot • Can be recycled	• Made from silica, which is not a renewable material • Carbon emissions during its production

continued

Table 1.2 continued

Type	Made from	Advantages	Disadvantages
Rock mineral wool	Rocks	• Fire resistant • Does not rot • Can be recycled	• Production is not environment friendly • Can cause temporary skin irritation
Cellulose	Recycled newspapers	• Made from recycled material • Can be reused and recycled	• Paper dust during installation • Can release gases from the printing inks on the recycled paper
Foam	Crushed glass	• Can be recycled • Has good compressive strength	• Production is not environmentally friendly

Research

Select a building, such as your house or your school or college. Find out the type of insulation used in:

• the walls
• the roof.

Think about why this insulation might have been used in this location.

Assessment practice 1.3

1 Explain the difference between sheep's wool insulation and foam insulation. [4]
2 Identify two materials that would give good roof insulation in a terraced house. [2]

Thermal resistance

Buildings can also be constructed from materials that resist the movement of heat. This means that less heat escapes through them and so they need less insulation. These materials have **thermal resistance** and they include:

• aerated lightweight concrete blocks – these can be used to construct walls. The blocks are made of aerated concrete, which is concrete with a lot of air in it. Air is very insulating when it is trapped between solid layers – for instance, when it is cold and you put on an extra jumper, you trap a layer of air between layers of clothing, which insulates you from the cold. So aerated concrete blocks provide better insulation

• timber – this can be used to create features such as window frames and doors. It can also be used to construct timber-framed buildings

• lightweight **screed** – this is made with lightweight aggregates. These contain more air, so lightweight screed gives good insulation.

Key terms

Thermal resistance – this is measured as an R-value. This shows the ability of a material to reduce heat loss because it resists the movement of heat through it. Increasing the thickness of a material increases its R-value.

Screed – this is made from cement and sand to provide a level surface before a floor is laid.

Location

Some areas of a building are more likely to lose heat than others. Table 1.3 shows which types of insulation are best for different parts of a building.

Table 1.3 Different kinds of insulation are needed in different locations

Location	Appropriate insulation
Cavity walls	The cavity in a cavity wall can be filled with an appropriate insulating material such as cellulose or mineral wool.
Solid walls	Plasterboard can be used to line solid walls and help reduce heat loss.
Roof	Mineral wool insulation could be used between joists.
Floors	Sheep's wool insulation could be used under floors.
Windows and doors	• **Double glazing** improves a building's U-values by stopping unnecessary heat loss. • Draught strips can be applied to door frames to improve the air-tightness of doors by stopping draughts.

Assessment practice 1.4

Chris is designing a house for a client who is interested in sustainability and wants to keep their future energy costs as low as possible.

1 Name two areas or elements of the proposed building that are most likely to lose heat. [2]

2 For each area or element named in question 1, suggest a suitable insulation material. Give reasons why you have chosen that material. [4]

Sound insulation

A building should be insulated to resist letting sound through its structure. This means that people living in one house are not disturbed by noise from their **adjacent** neighbour. Good sound insulation is important in improving quality of life by reducing external noise into the building, such as traffic or the sound of overhead aircraft. It also ensures privacy, so that your next-door neighbour cannot overhear your conversations!

When sound travels inside a building, it bounces off the walls, ceilings and floors. Sound can also travel in from outside, from passing vehicles or passers by. This sound can travel inside through windows, doors or external walls. This creates **noise** and thus affects the human comfort of the people using the building – that is, it makes it less enjoyable for people in there.

Discussion

Why do you think a roof and a floor might need different kinds of insulation?

Key term

Double glazing – this is a technology used to make windows less likely to lose heat. A double-glazed window is made of two panes of glass with a narrow gap in between them. The air is sucked out of this space to create a vacuum. It is difficult to transfer heat through a vacuum, so a double-glazed window loses less heat.

Key terms

Adjacent – next to or touching something. For example, the houses either side of a terraced house are adjacent to it.

Noise – this is any unwanted sound. Noise should be avoided wherever possible.

Types of sound insulation

Buildings therefore have to be insulated against this noise. Like thermal insulation, there are a lot of different types of sound insulation. These include:

- **triple glazing** – used in doors and windows
- **heavy density blockwork** – used to construct sound-resistant walls between adjacent rooms and flats
- **sound insulation quilt** – usually used in floors and cavity walls as well as in ceilings and under floors
- **plasterboard layers** – generally used in insulating both solid walls and cavity walls
- **flooring mats and carpeting** – these can be an effective form of sound insulation as they absorb noise. If no carpets are provided, the sound will bounce off the walls and floors, resulting in noise
- **acoustic ceilings** – made up of special materials that absorb sound and are used where good sound transmission is required, such as in theatres, music rooms or home cinemas.

When designing a building, it is really important to locate sound insulation appropriately. You should think about the likely uses of rooms and the potential noise levels of each room.

Activity 1.4

You are planning a new arts and drama building for your local college or school. The building is going to have:

- a music studio
- two drama performance studios
- six practice rooms for music practice, including one room for a drum kit
- a dance studio.

What sort of sound insulation are you going to need? Where will it be needed? Remember to give reasons for your answers.

Provision of sound insulation

Good sound insulation can be achieved by:

- increasing the density of a material. This means that the speed of sound trying to pass through these materials is slowed down
- using robust design details. A robust detail is a set of drawings or sketches that makes sure buildings have the right sound insulation, according to Part E of the Building Regulations. This ensures that all buildings have the correct insulation built into their design
- dividing the building structure in a way that sound from one part does not travel into the other part. This is called sound isolation of a structure. For example, in larger buildings, one part can be detached from another
- using machinery silencers. These help to reduce the noise from machinery used in the construction process. This is especially important when working on a site adjacent to other houses.

Discussion

- Why do you think that noise in buildings from either people or machinery can be a problem?
- Think about a time when you were disturbed by other people's noise. Do you agree with the term 'noise pollution'?

Assessment practice 1.5

The grid below shows a number of locations and different types of insulation. Match the location to the appropriate type of insulation. [3]

Proposed location	Type of insulation
A music studio in a drummer's garage	Triple glazing
A conservatory on the flight path to Heathrow	Heavy-density blockwork
A house next to a busy main road	Acoustic ceiling

Research

Find an appropriate robust detail for a masonry wall. Sketch and label the detail.

Weather resistance

Buildings are designed and constructed to provide a comfortable environment for their occupants. This means that they should protect people from weathering elements, such as heat, cold, humidity and rainwater.

These weathering elements can also damage the building and its finishes. For instance, if rainwater can enter a building through the roof, this will not only stain the walls but also damage them, reducing the building's **useful life**.

How are buildings made resistant to the weather elements? There is a variety of waterproof and **impervious** materials available to the construction industry. These include:

- **using materials such as PVC** to make guttering, **soffits** and window frames. PVC is a plastic and is very weather resistant, particularly against water. Mastic can be used to keep ventilation ducts weatherproof, as it stops the water penetrating through
- **rubber weather seals** and **sealants** – these are applied to doors and windows to stop water entering into the building. Seals and sealants do so by either blocking the entry or letting it drain
- **weather stripping** – these are strips of vinyl that are used to close the gaps in a door or window so that building is weatherproof. Draught strips are also used so that the building is airtight and does not lose heat
- **falls** – these are slopes provided on outer frames of doors and windows as well as on sills so that these can easily shed the water off
- **overhangs** – overhanging eaves above the window also protects it from weathering elements
- **flashings** – these are metal sheets, usually made of lead, used to cover the joins between the roof and a feature protruding from the roof, such as a chimney. This makes the structure weatherproof.

Key terms

Useful life – the length of time that a building fulfils the needs of the people who live or work in it.

Impervious – not allowing water to pass through.

Soffits – the undersides of eaves.

Discussion

Why do you think a sloping exterior sill could be considered a weather-resistant feature? Should the sill slope towards the window or away from the window?

Take it further

Explain why you have chosen the measures that you have picked.

Assessment practice 1.6

Identify four measures you could take to make a house weather resistant. [4]

Sustainability

A sustainable building is designed and constructed to make as small an impact on the natural environment as possible. **Sustainability** aims to:

- achieve reduction in building energy use – this not only reduces energy costs but also reduces the impact of fossil fuels on the environment
- conserve **finite resources** – natural resources such as water and timber are limited or finite. These need to be used carefully so that there is enough for future generations, so wastage of these resources should be avoided
- reduce carbon emissions to the atmosphere – when **fossil fuels** are burned (for instance when a car uses petrol or a power station burns coal), carbon dioxide is released into the atmosphere. Over time, this causes the Earth's temperature to rise, causing issues such as rising sea levels and droughts. It also causes air pollution.

Methods of sustainable construction

In order to construct a truly sustainable building, sustainability must be part of its initial design. This can be as simple as making sure that the building is facing the right way! To achieve sustainability, the following things should be done.

- Reuse **brownfield** sites. This reduces the number of **greenfield** sites that are used for construction and so keeps a maximum amount of green space. As brownfield sites have usually already been built on, it may also mean that less energy would be needed to develop sites.
- Achieve maximum sunlight through building **orientation**. A building in the UK that faces south will get the maximum amount of natural light. This can reduce the amount of electricity the building uses.

Why is it so important to consider the orientation of a building? Why might this affect the fitting of solar panels?

Link

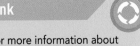

For more information about sustainability, see *Unit 11: Sustainability in Construction*.

Key terms

Sustainability – meeting the needs of the present without giving up the needs and rights of future generations.

Fossil fuels – non-renewable fuels such as coal, oil, gas or peat.

Brownfield – sites that have already been used.

Greenfield – sites that have never been used before.

Orientation – the direction a building faces.

Prefabricated – 'pre' means 'before' and 'fabricated' means 'made'. The term describes the parts of the building made in a factory and brought to site for assembly only.

Embodied energy – the energy needed to produce a material from extraction to its point of use. It is also known as embedded energy, as it is the energy contained by or embedded in each brick, tile or piece of timber.

- Reduce time and wastage by using local suppliers, ordering the right quantities of materials and using **prefabricated** materials.
- Recycle site waste by separation and reuse. Site waste is separated as people put domestic waste into different bins so that it can be easily recycled. Material can be reused as well, such as reusing old bricks and crushing waste concrete.
- Recycle waste materials. Instead of throwing away old items, such as copper tubing, you can reuse and recycle these. These recycled materials use less energy to be produced and thus have low **embodied energy**. They are more sustainable than those made from all-new raw materials. Another example is aluminium, which is found in earth but can also be reused by melting the old aluminium.
- Use sustainable materials that are from renewable sources in construction activities. For example, sheep's wool insulation is a sustainable material because the wool needed to make it can be regrown and so is renewable.

Discussion

Discuss in groups why prefabrication reduces wastage. Give two reasons.

Why do you think it is so important to use sustainable materials as much as possible?

Sustainable materials

Using sustainable materials is an important part of the construction industry today. They ensure that we do not waste our natural resources.

Research

Using the internet, find out why construction with hemp is called carbon-negative.

Key terms

Render – a type of plaster finish used on external as well as internal walls. It can improve a building's insulation.

Cladding – a covering or coating on the outside of a structure.

Table 1.4 Sustainable materials and their uses

Material	Sustainability
Hemp	This is a widely grown plant and has excellent insulation properties. Hemp can be mixed with lime to make insulation products.
Lime	This is a natural, renewable substance used to make mortar. Unlike cement mortar, lime-based mortar can be removed when a structure is knocked down, which means that bricks can be recycled. Lime can also be used in **rendering**.

continued

Table 1.4 continued

Material	Sustainability
Cedar	This is a type of wood used for **cladding**. It has natural resistance to moisture and humidity, and gives excellent insulation.
Softwoods	These are used to construct timber-frame buildings, softwoods include the Douglas fir and pine. These softwoods can be grown quickly in a sustainable way.
Straw	Straw bales can be used to build walls and even entire houses.
Sheep's wool	This can be used as insulation. It is more sustainable than most artificially made insulation materials.
Aluminium	This is a soft metal that is easily melted down and recycled. It can be used instead of PVC to make guttering and downpipes.

Just checking

1 List two ways to make a window weather resistant.
2 How does a cavity wall give both strength and stability?
3 List three methods to give sound insulation in a building.

Assessment practice 1.7

Identify any four elements of a sustainable building.   [4]

TOPIC A.2

▶ Common structural forms for low-rise construction

Introduction

In this topic, you will learn about the most common parts or structural forms of low-rise buildings. You will learn the terminology (industry-specific words) associated with each part or component, as well as their advantages and disadvantages.

Link

Sketching is a really good way to learn about the different elements in buildings. See *Unit 5: Construction Drawing Techniques* for more about drawings in construction.

▶ Traditional cavity wall construction

In a traditional cavity wall construction:

- the walls and foundations are usually the loadbearing elements of the construction

- the external walls are normally constructed as cavity walls while internal walls are solid or partition walls
- the external cavity walls have an outer skin of brickwork and an inner skin of blockwork
- the outer skin can also be rendered to provide extra insulation.

Assessment practice 1.8

Sketch and label the cross-section through an external cavity wall. [4]

Cross-wall construction

In cross-wall construction, the front and back of the building is constructed as non-loadbearing, while loadbearing walls are at right angles to these walls. This leads to the name cross-wall. The floor between these cross-walls is connected to all four walls and provides **lateral restraint**.

This form is suitable for blocks of flats or apartments, as it is ideal for creating similar floors. They are quick to construct as components such as whole walls can be made off-site.

However, there can be problems where the non-loadbearing claddings and the cross-walls meet, as these junctions might not be weatherproof.

Structurally Insulated Panels (SIPS)

These are insulated timber panels that are strong enough to take loads. They have a central layer of insulation, with a plywood face on each side. SIPS construction is similar to timber-framed construction but is faster and large panels can be made to speed up the process. The method provides a lighter frame, is thermally efficient and helps to reduce site waste. Because the panels are wooden, fire resistance could be an issue.

Finishes can be applied directly to the panels. These include exterior brickwork, blockwork, tiling and rendered finishes, as well as more sustainable finishes such as timber cladding and hemp rendering.

Research

Using the internet, research the use of SIPS. Look out for:
- the advantages and disadvantages of using SIPS
- different types of buildings that have used SIPS.

Timber-framed construction

Timber framing is commonly used in houses. The frames are made of softwood and faced (or covered) with plywood. Loadbearing timber walls are made up of small timbers called studs. Short timber pieces called noggins are placed between them to give stability.

Discussion

Why do you think cavity walls are used as external walls?

Key term

Lateral restraint – when movement of building elements is stopped sideways.

Did you know?

If both walls and floors are made using reinforced concrete, series of 'boxes' are formed. This is called box frame construction.

Link

For more about sustainable finishes, see *Unit 11: Sustainability in Construction*.

Key terms

uPVC cladding – a covering made of uPVC (unplasticised polyvinyl chloride).

Shingles – a roofing material, generally made of cedar wood.

Timber-framed construction is a sustainable form of construction. It can be constructed with a high level of accuracy and in less time than traditional construction. Frames provide space for the services and are thermally efficient. Timber frames are finished using a variety of secondary finishes, including brickwork, rendered blockwork, cedar cladding, tile hanging, **uPVC cladding** and **shingles**.

The most common parts of timber-framed buildings and their functions are:

- damp-proof course – moisture can penetrate the building from the foundations or under the floors. A damp-proof course (dpc) stops moisture coming in from the foundations, while a damp-proof membrane (dpm) is provided under the floors for the same purpose.

- finishes – timber-framed buildings can be finished like any other type of building and can even be given the look of a traditional building with a brickwork finish. These finishes are attached to the timber frame using flexible wall ties.

- insulation – insulation is provided between the timber studs. Insulation is tied to these studs so that there are no gaps.

- lintels – where openings are provided for windows and doors, a small beam called a lintel is used to direct rainwater away from the opening. Timber studs are also placed around these openings to add strength.

- studs – the timber frame is made of a number of upright timbers called studs.

- moisture resistance – a polythene sheet, called a vapour check, is built in between the internal wall and the insulation to stop moisture penetration.

- plywood sheets – these are attached to the external walls to provide bracing.

Case study

Hui is a joiner's apprentice and is helping to build a timber-framed construction house. He is thinking of important features of timber-framed construction, as well as how to reduce waste using this form of construction.

1 Identify three features of timber-framed construction.

2 List two ways in which waste can be reduced in timber-framed construction.

Assessment practice 1.9

Identify two advantages and two disadvantages of SIPS construction.   [4]

Pre-construction work

Introduction

Lots of activities have to be done before work can begin on site. This topic will explore why these are carried out, what has to be provided on a site and how this is done. Sketching is a good way of learning about pre-construction work. Some activities are provided in this section for you to practise sketching.

Desk-based pre-construction

Before work starts on site, a range of activities need to be carried out.

- Some legal requirements have to be fulfilled, such as a construction health and safety plan, method statements and risk assessments. The Health and Safety Executive (HSE) may also need to be informed.

- A scaled site layout plan is prepared. This needs to show site accommodation such as site offices and material storage, and welfare facilities such as toilets and storage accommodation. It also needs to show security fences and temporary roads and services. Fire precaution measures are also considered at this stage.

- A document showing the programme of work or schedule of activities is produced. This schedule should also plan out the delivery of resources and materials.

- Resources and materials are bought.

- Safety signs are set out and statutory notices are organised. This includes telling people in the local area about any footpath closures.

- Road crossings for plant and deliveries and traffic management are planned.

Link

For more about health and safety in the construction industry, look at Units 6, 7, 8, 9 and 10.

Pre-construction work on the site

This includes all the works carried out on site before construction works can start.

First, the site is cleared of vegetation and trees. Any existing structures are knocked down. Then any existing services (water, gas, electricity) are protected from damage by the building work.

Next, access and egress (exit) routes into and out of the site are constructed.

Finally, the site is set up, providing site accommodation and temporary services including temporary lighting. Temporary roads and hard standing are put in place. Security arrangements are also installed at this point, including fencing and gates.

 ### Link

If you want to know more about pre-construction works, see *Unit 4: Construction Processes and Operations*.

Activity 1.5

You are setting up a site near a town centre, for a block of flats to be built. Identify:

- two welfare facilities you would need to provide
- three security measures you would need to take
- two factors you would have to consider when planning for materials storage.

Sub-structure groundworks

Introduction

Sub-structure works include activities done below ground level. In this section, safe construction of sub-structures is discussed, including potential hazards. Control of water encountered during groundworks is also looked at. Foundations and floor construction will then be explored.

Sub-structure involves all the construction works below floor level, including the foundations and associated activities. A very important operation at this stage is excavation. This means digging the ground so that foundations can be constructed.

Hazards associated with groundworks

There is a range of potential hazards when groundworks are carried out. Table 1.5 lists these hazards as well as how they can be controlled.

Why do you think it is so important that people working on foundations follow safe working practices?

Table 1.5 Hazards associated with groundworks

Hazard	Risk	Control measure
Gas	Injury or death	Avoiding services such as gas mains.
Collapse of the sides of the excavation (could be due to soil type)	Injury or death	• Trench supports such as timbering is provided to hold back the sides of the excavation. • Physical barriers can be put in place to stop machinery or people putting pressure on weak ground near the edge of the excavation. • A different method could be used, such as trenchfill foundation, which lets foundations be excavated and poured immediately, giving the soil no time to loosen.
Presence of ground water	Flooding or drowning	Pumping out excess water.
Confined space	Crushing or **musculoskeletal** injuries	Using appropriate PPE and reducing the amount of work done in confined spaces.
Existing services such as gas mains, water pipes or electricity cables	Injury, flooding, death or power outages	Locate and protect all existing services before work begins.
Proximity of excavation plant	Injury or death	Barriers stop moving machinery from going too close to excavation.

Key term

Musculoskeletal – to do with the human frame and muscles that function to give movement.

Did you know?

• A hazard is something that has the potential to cause harm, such as the collapse of the sides of an excavation.
• A risk is the result of any accident or event that happened because of that hazard, such as a broken arm resulting from the collapse of the excavation.

Control of water

Sub-soil water is the water present below ground. It is also known as groundwater. When designing and constructing sub-structure, by law sub-soil water must not be allowed to enter the building and damage it. There are two different ways of controlling water, one temporary and one permanent.

Depending on the site, sub-soil water and surface water might just need to be controlled temporarily during excavation. This is called simple sump pumping, because the water collects in a sump or pool and is then pumped out.

Some sites might need permanent control of sub-soil water. This is known as land drainage. There are several methods of land drainage.

 # Earthwork support

This is the support of the sides of excavation. There are different methods of earthwork support depending on the needs of the site and the type of soil you are excavating, including:

- steel trench sheets
- timbering
- hydraulic trench supports
- aluminium walling.

 # Foundations

The function of a foundation

A foundation is designed and constructed to safely transmit the loads of the building to the ground or sub-soil. They should be able to support the loads of the building for its lifespan.

Different kinds of foundation

Various types of foundation are used in low-rise construction. The kind of foundation used depends on the load, type of structure, site requirements and the type of soil. Table 1.6 overleaf shows the advantages and disadvantages of different foundations.

 Link

Foundations are discussed in more detail in *Unit 4: Construction Processes and Operations.*

 Remember

Foundations provide stability by spreading the building load over a larger area.

 Research

Research technical drawings of strip and deep strip foundations. Use the information on page 22 or use other books and the internet. Then create your own sketches, remembering to annotate (label) each part of these foundations.

Table 1.6 Advantages and disadvantages of different types of foundation

Type and uses	Advantages	Disadvantages	Structure
Strip – commonly used in low-rise construction such as houses where the soil has the right strength.	<ul><li>Traditional method understood by site staff</li><li>Involves doing brick and blockwork in trenches</li><li>Cheap</li></ul>	<ul><li>Might take longer</li><li>Can be hazardous as the soil can get loosened</li><li>Might need trench support</li></ul>	
Deep strip or mass fill – used for similar types of buildings, quick to construct.	<ul><li>No brick or blockwork needed in trenches</li><li>Faster methods of construction</li></ul>	<ul><li>Could be more expensive</li></ul>	
Raft foundation – used where soil does not have the same strength or where heavy loads are expected. These are used for commercial or industrial buildings.	<ul><li>Provides good foundation where soil is variable</li><li>Can be used as a floor</li><li>Can be used to fit in services</li></ul>	<ul><li>Expensive to construct</li><li>Can crack if not constructed correctly</li><li>Needs formwork</li></ul>	
Short bored piles	<ul><li>Provides foundations when the soil is weak</li><li>Quick to construct</li></ul>	<ul><li>Expensive</li><li>Construction causes lot of noise</li></ul>	
Pad foundations – used for columns.	<ul><li>Provides foundations for heavy loads</li><li>Quick to construct</li></ul>	<ul><li>Needs formwork</li><li>Can move if loads are not balanced around it</li></ul>	

▶ Ground floors

A ground floor is the floor of the lowest level of a building. Ground floors can be either solid or suspended.

A **solid floor** bears directly onto the ground from which it gains its support. It is usually made of solid concrete. Solid floors are made up of:

- hardcore to provide a strong base
- sand blinding – a layer of sand to even off the surface of the hardcore
- damp-proof course (dpc)
- damp-proof membrane (dpm) – this stops moisture transfer from the ground into the building by the overlapping of sheets, the taping of any joints, linking to dpc and by having a certain thickness of membrane
- insulation – this should have good compressive strength.

A **suspended floor** is one that is suspended above the ground. It rests on beams spanning between supporting walls. In the modern construction industry, suspended floors are generally built using the beam-and-block method.

Beam-and-block floor

This is a type of suspended floor. It uses precast concrete beams with lightweight concrete blocks as an infill. The method is becoming very popular as it is quick to construct and ensures a high quality.

These floors do not need any preparation and put less of a load on the foundations. As they are precast, they can be laid in bad weather.

Link

Floors are also discussed in *Unit 4: Construction Processes and Operations.*

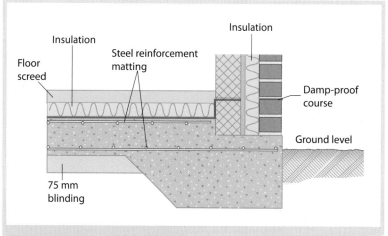

Figure 1.3 Typical solid floor details.

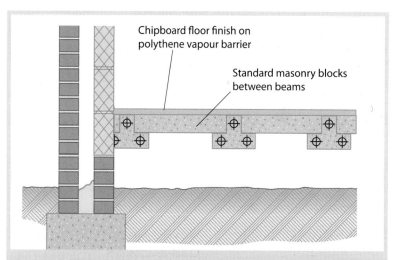

Figure 1.4 A beam-and-block ground floor. The wall below the DPC, often includes an airbrick. This ventilates the empty space below the suspended floor.

Just checking

1 Name three kinds of earthwork support.
2 List two advantages of deep strip foundations.
3 What sort of soil might need a short bore pile foundation?
4 Why might a beam-and-block floor be better than a solid floor?
5 Describe how a damp-proof membrane (dpm) stops moisture entering a building.

A sub-structure engineer needs to identify the component parts of a foundation drawing.

1 Label the components of the foundation cross-section shown opposite. [7]

2 What is the name given to the foundation in the cross-section shown in Figure 1.5? [1]

☐ **A** Deep strip   ☐ **C** Ground beam

☐ **B** Raft   ☐ **D** Mass fill

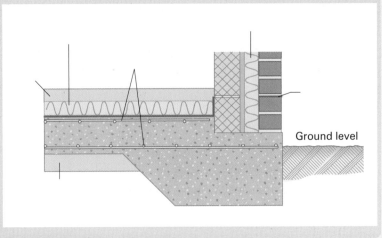

Ground level

Figure 1.5 Foundation cross-section.

▶ Superstructure – walls

Introduction

The superstructure is everything in a building above ground level. In this topic, you will learn about the construction of walls, the materials used and the finishes applied.

Link

More details on the superstructure can be found in *Unit 4: Construction Processes and Operations*.

A wall performs a number of functions such as:

- resisting heat transfer
- reducing sound transmission
- transferring loads to foundations
- providing shelter and security.

▶ Detailing a wall

This is the process of producing a drawing that contains all the details about the construction of a wall, such as the materials to be used and the wall's size.

Internal partitions are constructed to divide the floor area of a building into smaller and more useful spaces such as an en-suite bathroom. Internal walls can be constructed as timber stud walls, which are similar to timber-framed construction. Internal walls can also be constructed in solid blockwork where concrete blocks are laid in layers or courses. Partitions can also be provided using metal stud walls, generally made of aluminium frame, with glass panes, doors and windows as required.

See pages 7 and 16 for more information on cavity walls.

Materials used

While finishing a wall in brickwork, care must be taken that the colour and appearance of the brickwork does not vary too much, so that the finished look is as pleasing as possible.

Mortar is a mixture of sand and lime, or sand and cement with or without lime. Lime makes the mortar more workable but as it is more porous (letting moisture through), it allows frost to penetrate and cause damage.

Thin joint masonry is a faster method of constructing walls. As the name suggests, the joints between various layers are thin compared with traditional methods. These joints are 2 to 3 mm thick. A fast-setting mortar is used, which can give the required strength very quickly. This masonry depends on the accuracy of block sizes. Generally lightweight blocks are used, which also provide good thermal efficiency.

 Did you know?

The most common kind of mortar is general purpose masonry mortar (indicated by the letter G). This may be factory-made or site-made.

 # Wall finishes

Rendering blockwork is a process similar to plastering, though render can be given different textures.

Facing brickwork usually has various types of joints with **pointing**. Joints improve the weather-proofing and the appearance of the brickwork. Weather-struck and bucket handle joints provide better weather resistance, as water can run off and will not penetrate through the brickwork. Flush and recessed joints give a better appearance.

Wall openings

Openings have to be included in walls to provide:

* ventilation – the circulation of fresh air in a building
* sunlight
* **aesthetics** – the attractiveness of a building.

 Key terms

Pointing – filling the joints in brickwork with mortar to improve appearance and weather proofing.

Aesthetics – the appreciation of beauty or the appearance of something.

Table 1.7 Components of wall openings and their functions

Component	Function
Lintel	A horizontal support across the top of a wall opening, such as over a door or a window.
Sill	A piece of material below a door or window to allow rainwater to run off, away from the opening.
Threshold	A strip of material forming the bottom of a doorway.
Cavity tray	A damp-proof course inside a cavity wall, which funnels moisture out of the cavity through weepholes.
Cavity closer	This closes off the cavity around a wall opening, reducing heat loss.
Weep hole	A small opening in brickwork which allows moisture to escape.

Assessment practice 1.12

1 Identify three components of a wall opening.   [3]
2 The function of wall openings is to provide: [1]

☐ **A** ventilation, fresh air and water   ☐ **C** aesthetics, light and weep holes

☐ **B** ventilation, light and aesthetics   ☐ **D** a view of the landscape.

▶ Superstructure – floors

Introduction

In this section, you will learn about construction of floors in terms of materials used. Finishes applied are also discussed. This topic is covered in more detail in Unit 4.

Link

For more details on floors, see *Unit 4: Construction Processes and Operations.*

Floors are horizontal surfaces that are designed to provide a level surface. They make our buildings able to be lived in and functional. They also reduce sound transmission within a building and transfer loads to the walls.

As discussed on page 23, floors can be constructed as solid floors or as suspended floors.

▶ Materials

Floors are constructed using a wide range of materials. These include:

- concrete – beam-and-block floors use pre-cast concrete beams with lightweight concrete blocks as an infill
- timber – suspended floors can be constructed using different types of timber joists, which are like beams and support the floor load. These can be made of natural timber or man-made timber products. Some joists are not solid and have open areas providing space for services. These are eco-joists and use less timber
- engineered timber – newer buildings may have floors made of applied finishes such as laminate and engineered timber. These need less maintenance and are also less likely to be affected by moisture and defects such as rot.

▶ Floor finishes

Solid floors can be finished in screed, which provides a level and even surface. Additional floor finishes such as carpets can be laid on top of this.

Floors could be finished using ordinary chipboard, moisture-resistant chipboard or softwood. A wooden board called a skirting board is provided along the bottom of the wall. This is used to make the joint between the wall and the floor look more attractive and protects the wall base as well.

▶ Floor components

The floor is made up of joists or beams suspended between supporting walls which support the load from the floor. Joists are supported by the walls. They can either rest on the wall or be connected using special components called hangers. These are attached to the side of a wall and receive the joists.

▶ Superstructure – roofs

Introduction

In this section, you will learn about the construction of roofs, the materials used and the finishes applied.

▶ Function of a roof

Roofs are designed and constructed to be able to support their own weight as well as resist loads due to their finishes and other loads such as snow and wind. A roof should also be able to:

- discharge rainfall away from the building, usually through overhanging eaves and guttering
- make the structure waterproof
- provide a recreational area in the case of green roofs (roofs covered with grass and plants)
- be aesthetically pleasing, through the use of attractive roof tiles and finishes
- provide extra accommodation or space.

Link

You can learn more about roofs in *Unit 4: Construction Processes and Operations.*

▶ Details of roofs

A roof can be constructed as flat or pitched. Types of pitched roofs can include lean-to, mono pitch, double pitch, gable end and hipped-end.

As there are lots of different types of roofs, it is important to consider the performance requirements of the building before deciding on which kind of roof to construct. Table 1.8 shows the advantages and disadvantages of flat and pitched roofs.

Table 1.8 Advantages and disadvantages of flat and pitched roof types

Type	Advantages	Disadvantages
Flat roof	<ul><li>Aesthetically pleasing</li><li>Provides parapet feature in the building</li><li>Ease of maintenance</li><li>Forms recreational areas</li></ul>	<ul><li>Water run-off may be difficult, causing puddles on the roof</li><li>Solar reflective paint required, which needs to be maintained</li><li>Extra hardwearing surfaces might be needed</li></ul>
Pitched roof	<ul><li>Aesthetically pleasing</li><li>Creates more floor space or storage space</li><li>Better water run-off</li><li>Less maintenance needed</li></ul>	<ul><li>Initial cost higher than flat roof</li><li>Takes longer to build</li><li>Difficult to access for maintenance</li></ul>

Roofing terminology

Different parts of a roof have names. It is important to know this terminology. Figure 1.6 shows the components of a roof and their names.

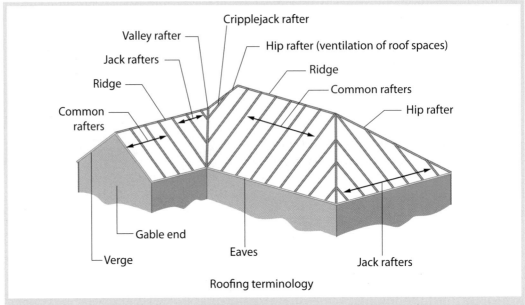

Roofing terminology

Figure 1.6 Different parts of a pitched roof. What advantages do you think a pitched roof has over a flat roof?

Components and materials

A roof is made of components that support the load or weight of the structure. These can be made of timber, concrete or steel. Insulating materials and materials to provide resistance to moisture are also used. Pitched roofs are finished using a variety of tiles such as natural slates, clay and concrete tiles.

A flat roof is finished using waterproofing materials. Both flat and pitched roofs drain rainwater away through a system of drainage pipes.

Assessment practice 1.13

1 Describe one advantage and one disadvantage of two kinds of pitched roof. [4]
2 Identify four components of a pitched roof. [4]

WorkSpace

▷ Dom Goodwill

Trainee quantity surveyor

I'm a trainee quantity surveyor with a firm of chartered surveyors. At first, my job involved estimating quantities of materials, but soon I got involved in all sorts of activities, from the submission of tenders to variations and claims. In a normal day, I will use my knowledge of construction technology to prepare estimates and price work to be done.

My supervisor and mentor is a professionally qualified senior surveyor. She helps me to think about my future career in quantity surveying, so now I know what I need to do in order to reach my goals.

Sketching is really important in my job. It really helps you to understand how something is constructed. I often use it in front of clients to explain technical details which would be difficult to explain in words. My job also involves interpreting drawings and sketches, so I need to keep up to date with Building Regulations, new materials and methods.

If you think you know what career you want in the construction industry, then construction technology may not seem relevant right away. However, knowing how buildings are constructed will be useful in any job in the construction industry.

Think about it

1 How do you think having a mentor helps Dom?
2 How do you think understanding drawings helps Dom to prepare estimates and price work?
3 Which job roles need knowledge of construction technology?

How you will be assessed

You will take a paper-based examination. The examination paper will have a maximum of 50 marks. The number of marks available for each part of a question will be shown in brackets, e.g. [2], with the total for each question being shown at the end of the question.

There will be different types of question in the examination:

Disclaimer: These practice questions and sample answers are not actual exam questions. They are provided as a practice aid only and should not be assumed to reflect either the format or coverage of the real external test.

A Questions where the answers are available and you have to choose the correct answer(s).
Tip: Always make sure that you read the instructions carefully. Sometimes you may need to identify more than one correct answer.

Examples:

Which **one** of the following is an example of a dead load? [1]

A	Wind load
B	Weight of people
C	Weight of the structure
D	All of above

Answer: C

Which **one** of the statements below best describes a strip foundation? [1]

A	It is used for large structures
B	It is used where soil is weak
C	It is mostly used in domestic construction
D	It is expensive to construct

Answer: C

B Questions where you are asked to produce a short answer worth 1 or 2 marks.
Tip: Look carefully at how the question is set out to see how many points need to be included in your answer.

Examples:

Construction materials are tested before their use in a building. State two such tests performed on **two** different construction materials. [2]

Answers: Concrete – slump test. Timber – stress grading.

Name **two** pieces of equipment used to provide fire resistance in buildings. [2]

Answers: Smoke detectors and sprinkler system.

C Questions where you are asked to provide a longer answer – these can be worth up to 8 marks.
Tips: make sure that you read the question in full, and answer all of the parts of the question which you are asked. It is a good idea to plan your answer so that you do not forget anything and remember to check your answer once you have finished.

Example:

A construction firm is planning to construct fifty houses and a sports centre near a large industrial estate. The firm wishes to use construction methods which will have the least impact upon the environment.

Advise the construction firm regarding sustainable construction methods, giving reasons for your suggestions. [8]

Answer: The company's choice of site is important. They could construct on brownfield sites. This will save green areas and will also save the energy required to develop greenfield sites. They should also use the site so the buildings will get maximum sunlight, which can reduce the amount of electricity the buildings use.

Materials also need to be thought about in a sustainable way. Using local materials will reduce transportation costs and carbon emissions. Ordering the right quantities of materials will help reduce wastage of materials. Another way of reducing waste is using pre-fabricated components, because the materials do not need to be cut on site.

The company could also make sure that they use materials from renewable sources, like FSC-certified timber. This means that we will not run out of resources in future.

Recycling and reusing materials reduces waste as well as saving the energy required to make new materials. Using materials which have consumed less energy during their production also helps ensure that the buildings are constructed using the least energy possible.

Finally, the company could make sure that the buildings are well insulated. This ensures that the buildings will use less energy when in use.

Hints and tips

Use the time before the test – make sure that you have got everything you will need. Check that your pen works and that you read the instructions on the front of your examination paper. Try to make yourself feel comfortable and relaxed.

Keep an eye on the time – the examination will last one hour. You should be able to see the clock in the examination room so that you will know how long you have got left to complete the paper. Allow roughly one minute for every mark on the paper, so that a question worth 5 marks takes you about 5 minutes to answer.

Read the questions fully – it is easy to misread a question and then write an answer which is wrong. Always check you are doing what you have been asked to do.

Plan your answers – when answering longer questions, spend a minute or two writing down the key points that you want to include in your answer. If you are being asked to evaluate, remember to include positive and negative points in your plan and answer.

Check your answers – once you have answered all of the questions on the paper, you will probably have a few minutes to spare. Use this time to check your answers, especially the longer ones. Fill in any blanks which you have left. Try to answer every question on the paper.

Make sure you have completed the front of the paper – once the examination has finished, check that you have written your name and candidate number on the front of the paper.

How to improve your answer

Read the two student answers below, together with the feedback.
Try to use what you learn here when you answer questions in your examination.

 Question

> You are working in a construction firm which is currently working on a housing project. The architect has suggested using beam and block floors instead of solid floors and you agree.
>
> Your manager wants to know the reasons for your preference. Describe **three** advantages of beam-and-block floors. [6]

 Student 1's answer

Advantage 1 – no curing required

Advantage 2 – lightweight

Advantage 3 – can be built in bad weather

Feedback:
Although the advantages listed are correct, there is no attempt to explain them. This student would get 1 mark for mentioning each advantage, for instance because beam and block floors are lightweight. However, no reason is given to back up these advantages, for instance why a lightweight floor is an advantage. This means that this student will achieve 3 marks in total rather than 6 marks.

 Student 2's answer

Advantage 1 – No curing period is required for beam and block floors. This means that they can be built straight away and hence reduces the construction time.

Advantage 2 – These floors are lightweight which means that they will put less load on the foundations

Advantage 3 – Because beam and block floors are pre-cast, these can be constructed even when weather conditions are bad.

Feedback:
This student has identified three advantages of beam and block floors and backed up these advantages with clear reasons why this is an advantage over solid floors. This student will achieve 6 marks in total.

Assess yourself

▐▶ Question 1

Which **one** of the following will provide stability to a cavity wall? [1]

- A Damp proof course
- B Mortar
- C Wall ties
- D Damp-proof membrane

▐▶ Question 2

A site plan is made before construction work starts. It contains details of accommodation, welfare facilities and security arrangements.

List **two** welfare facilities a site plan should have. [2]

▐▶ Question 3

An architect is designing a large office building. She is trying to decide which type of roof should be used.

Evaluate whether she should choose a flat or a pitched roof. [8]

For further practice, see the Assessment Practice questions on pages 7, 8, 10, 11, 13, 16, 18, 21, 24, 26, and 28.

Introduction

There are many examples of attractive buildings that have also been carefully designed to meet the needs of their occupants. Large cities give companies the opportunity to showcase their expertise by constructing large aesthetically pleasing buildings.

In this unit you will explore the range of work undertaken by the construction industry and the industry's contribution to our society. You will also develop the skills to interpret a client's needs, in order to turn their ideas into a feasible design that they will want to build as a lasting part of the built environment. The development of a client's brief has to be conducted thoroughly so that the final design meets their needs.

Following the initial design stages you will undertake some design work, producing some sketches of your proposals that will meet a client's brief. This will give you the opportunity to express a design in concept form using colour and three dimensions. This will help a client to make an informed decision on the building's appearance, the proposed layout and the external materials that you have illustrated for them within your sketches.

Assessment: You will be assessed by a series of assignments set by your teacher/tutor.

Learning aims

In this unit you will:

A understand the work of the construction industry

B understand a client's needs to develop a design brief for a low-rise building

C produce a range of initial sketch ideas to meet the requirements of a client brief for a low-rise building.

" This unit really got me thinking about the different stages in a project's development and the importance of getting the client's brief right. This helped when I did some work experience for the design company who worked on the Olympic Park. It was really exciting to watch the concept develop from a designer's drawing to a final building.

Nigel, *16-year-old aspiring architect*

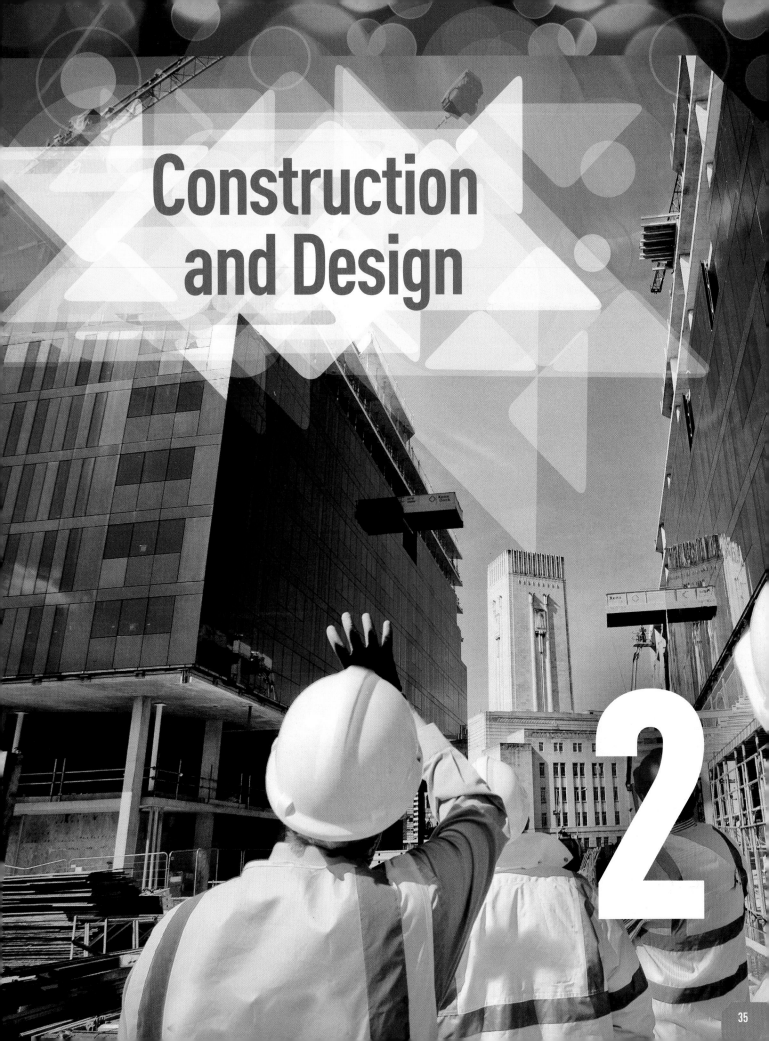

Construction and Design

2

BTEC
Assessment Zone

This table shows what you must do in order to achieve a **Pass**, **Merit** or **Distinction** grade, and where you can find activities in this book to help you.

Assessment criteria

Level 1	Level 2 **Pass**	Level 2 **Merit**	Level 2 **Distinction**
Learning aim A: Understand the work of the construction industry			
1A.1 Outline a range of work activities undertaken by the construction industry.	**2A.P1** Describe the range of activities undertaken by the construction industry. **See Assessment activity 2.1, page 45**	**2A.M1** Explain the local contribution made by the construction industry to society. **See Assessment activity 2.1, page 45**	**2A.D1** Evaluate the local and national contributions made by the construction industry to society. **See Assessment activity 2.1, page 45**
1A.2 Outline a contribution that the construction industry makes to society.	**2A.P2** Describe the contribution that the construction industry makes to society. **See assessment activity 2.1, page 45**		
Learning aim B: Understand a client's needs to develop a design brief for a low-rise building			
1B.3 **English** Identify client's needs for a given project scenario.	**2B.P3** **English** Describe client's needs to develop a client brief for a given project scenario. **See Assessment activity 2.2, page 54**	**2B.M2** **English** Analyse needs and constraints to develop a client brief for a given project scenario that prioritises the design requirements. **See Assessment activity 2.2, page 54**	**2B.D2** **English** Prioritise needs and constraints to develop a client brief for a given project scenario that examines ways of complying with design requirements and constraints. **See Assessment activity 2.2, page 54**
1B.4 Identify constraints on design for a given project scenario.	**2B.P4** **English** Describe the constraints on design to develop a client brief for a given project scenario. **See Assessment activity 2.2, page 54**		
Learning aim C: Produce a range of initial sketch ideas to meet the requirements of a client brief for a low-rise building.			
1C.5 Produce initial sketches for a minimum of two concept ideas that meet the requirements of a client brief, with support and guidance.	**2C.P5** Produce initial sketches for a minimum of two concept ideas that meet the requirements of a client brief. **See Assessment activity 2.3, page 58**	**2C.M3** Produce initial sketches for a minimum of three fully annotated concept ideas that meet the requirements of a client brief. **See Assessment activity 2.3, page 58**	**2C.D3** Produce initial sketches for a minimum of four fully annotated concept ideas that fully comply with all the requirements of a client brief and are influenced by different design styles. **See Assessment activity 2.3, page 58**
1C.6 Review concept ideas against a client brief with support and guidance.	**2C.P6** Review concept ideas against the requirements of a client brief. **See Assessment activity 2.3, page 58**	**2C.M4** Refine a concept idea following client feedback. **See Assessment activity 2.3, page 58**	

English ⟩ Opportunity to practise English skills

How you will be assessed

This unit is internally assessed by two or three assignments set by your tutor/teacher. These will cover a range of assessment criteria for this unit. The assignments will contain a scenario to help you focus on what to include in your written evidence. Within this unit you will be partly assessed on your design portfolio. This is a series of freehand sketches produced from a client's design brief.

The assessments will give you the opportunity to work towards the Merit and Distinction levels, but you will need to extend many of the topic areas in order to achieve these levels. Make sure that you meet the assessment deadlines in order to receive useful feedback from your assessor. The unit specification will give you additional guidance as to the evidence requirements for each of the grading criteria.

▶ The work of the construction industry

Introduction

The construction industry is a worldwide industry, so the range of construction activities is vast. These activities include the design and planning, construction and maintenance of a building throughout its lifecycle. These construction activities contribute to our society economically and socially. If you think about the built environment around you, you will see that buildings that are attractive and well designed contribute to our sense of wellbeing.

Discussion

In groups or pairs, take a 30-minute walk around either your local school or college environment or your neighbourhood. Do you like what you see and feel around you?

Key terms

Built environment – the buildings and other structures constructed by humans.

Aesthetics – the appreciation of beauty or the appearance of something.

Sustainability – meeting the needs of our future generations by preserving the resources that are available.

▶ Designing structures and buildings

Buildings can improve the quality of our lives and enhance our **built environment**. We can create functional buildings that are also amazing and attractive. This is achieved by:

- designing for appearance and **aesthetics** – creating an attractive, innovative and outstanding design for the external and internal spaces of a building
- designing for **sustainability** – using green technology and materials to reduce the harmful impact of a building on the environment
- designing for functionality – creating a lasting environment that will not need major changes or refurbishments to extend its useful life for its occupants
- designing for occupant and public safety – allowing safe access for everyone who uses the building and its facilities.

Designing for sustainability can be expensive but may save future maintenance costs such as electricity bills.

Case study

The Shard in London was a bold venture, constructed by Irvine Seller and designed by Renzo Piano on the back of a menu during lunch. It represents a shard of glass rising out from the City of London and is entirely clad in external glazing. During its planning and design, many hurdles had to be overcome before it was allowed to be constructed.

Research the construction of the Shard and then discuss the following questions:

1 What makes this unique building an icon?

2 What effect has the Shard had on its surroundings?

3 What features make the building sustainable?

4 What features within the internal design offer a variety of functions for the occupants?

5 How has the design ensured that the building is safe for all occupants?

▐▶ The contribution to infrastructure

There are many different ways in which the construction industry contributes to our society. Not only does it provide us with well-designed buildings, but it also creates and maintains the **infrastructure** required by modern society.

This can include:

- transport networks – such as road, rail, airports and motorways

- drainage – the provision of waste connections to houses, offices and other commercial buildings like shops

- provision of services – the supply of water, gas, electricity and communications to our houses and towns

- flood defences – provision of defences to protect our buildings from flooding by rivers and rising sea levels.

What examples of transport networks can you see?

Key term

Infrastructure – the basic structures needed for the operation of a society, including roads, buildings and power supply.

Research

The summer of 2012 was the wettest summer in 100 years, and this caused a lot of flooding. Do you live in a flood risk area? Have a look at local flood management in the area closest to you and see what is being done to help areas most at risk.

Activity 2.1

Pick one of the elements of infrastructure listed above and think of five ways in which it impacts on your daily life.

Discussion

Discuss what might happen if the community was not involved in a project to build a new housing estate on the outskirts of a busy town.

Including the community

The plans for any new building project should include the needs of the local community. This means that the buildings constructed fulfil the needs of the community as well as its occupants and owners.

Community involvement starts at the design stage, shaping the planning, shape, form and layout of a project. The needs of the community can influence the following elements of a development:

- housing – including low-cost affordable homes within the overall number of planned homes
- green spaces – including social green spaces in construction projects. These spaces provide space for socialising and play, as well as improving the community's sense of wellbeing
- transport hubs – these are points where several modes of transport such as buses and trains meet. Well-planned transport hubs allow the community to travel to work easily and efficiently
- employment – the construction industry itself provides a range of opportunities, from professional positions to on-site general operative roles. It also provides the offices and buildings needed by other companies and their employees
- security – designing better layouts such as open green spaces and including facilities such as adequate lighting means that the community can live in a safe, comfortable environment. Using good-quality components such as secure windows and doors also adds to the community's security.

What are the benefits of including green space in a new development?

How can involving the community improve a development's sustainability?

Case study

Haboakus is a collaboration between Hab Housing, the company established by Kevin McCloud of Channel 4's Grand Designs, and the housing group GreenSquare. Haboakus is a sustainable residential development company, creating purpose-built community projects containing many aspects of community involvement within the design, to pioneer house designs that focus on the residents, neighbourhoods and communities that they house.

Visit their website to look at the projects that have been constructed, as well as those which are in the development stage. Now answer the following questions:

1 What aspects of the designs enable neighbours to get to know each other?
2 How do they deal with cars in their designs?
3 Is the land use brownfield or greenfield?
4 How is the green space incorporated?
5 Are the homes affordable?
6 What do you think makes them attractive to live in?

Economic and social benefits of construction

The construction industry brings a wide range of economic benefits to individuals, companies and nations. For instance, many job opportunities exist in the development of land, the construction of buildings to live and work in, and the maintenance of buildings during their useful life.

Construction also contributes to our society by making our built environment a pleasant place to live in.

Table 2.1 gives some examples of the economic and social benefits of construction.

Table 2.1 Economic and social benefits of construction

Type of benefit	Specific benefits
Economic	Employment in the construction industry and other related industries – this puts money into the local community through local businesses, taxes and council spending. It also encourages spending and growth in the national economy.
	Creation of wealth and jobs through property development – the growth of **buy-to-lets** has developed new businesses and created jobs in refurbishment and property maintenance.
	Home ownership – the value of homes increases, meaning that homeowners get a good return on their initial purchase.
	New developments attract further commercial opportunities – this brings further economic wealth into an area after the initial development is complete.
	Economic migration – a booming construction industry attracts workers from other countries. This then allows more construction to take place.
Social	Inner city regeneration of run-down areas – unsightly buildings are demolished and replaced, regenerating an area and injecting new growth.
	Lower crime – better planning and construction makes an area attractive and safe.
	Affordable housing – planners now have to include this type of housing in any new housing development. This allows people to own their own homes more easily.
	Reduction in pollution – the inclusion of alternative transport, trams, buses and light railway networks reduces reliance on cars.

Did you know?

The construction industry in the UK employs just over 2 million people, which is around 6 per cent of the UK's workforce.

Key terms

Buy-to-let – when someone buys a property to rent out rather than to live in themselves.

Affordable housing – low-cost properties that are built within a development that buyers (particularly first-time buyers) can afford to purchase or rent.

Activity 2.2

Take a look at some of the inner-city regeneration projects that have been undertaken in Manchester, Birmingham and Glasgow. Using the internet, research and then discuss the effect of these projects on the local community. Think about both economic and social benefits.

▶ Who benefits?

The benefits in Table 2.1 affect three different parts of society: the built environment, the local community and the UK as a whole. Sometimes they can contribute to all three.

Benefits to the built environment

The benefits to the built environment can be enormous. The construction industry regenerates old and run-down urban centres as well as constructing attractive and efficient new buildings and developments.

Benefits to the local community

The local community benefits from the regeneration of the built environment and employment opportunities in the local area. They also benefit from improved transport networks and the creation of green open spaces. Another benefit is that an attractive city or an area with good transport networks draws in tourism, which boosts the local economy.

Benefits to the UK as a whole

The construction industry provides approximately 2 million jobs in the UK. It contributes about 7 per cent of our gross domestic product (**GDP**). This creates jobs and encourages spending and growth in the UK's economy.

Key term

GDP – this is the value of the total amount of goods and services produced by a nation in one year. .

Activity 2.3

In a group, look at Table 2.1 and decide whether each of the benefits it lists is a benefit to the built environment, the local community or the UK nationally. Remember, these benefits might apply to more than one category.

TOPIC   A.2

Construction activities

Introduction

There are many different activities that are included under the umbrella of the construction industry. In this topic you will learn about the range of activities undertaken by the construction industry.

▶ Thinking about categories

Because there are so many different kinds of construction activities, you can group them in different ways. You can think about these groups or categories in terms of:

- the kinds of jobs that people do in the construction industry – this includes jobs in construction, civil engineering, **building services** or maintenance
- the kinds of building constructed and their functions – this includes educational buildings like schools and colleges, healthcare buildings such as hospitals and health centres and leisure buildings such as swimming pools and stadiums
- the kind of activities that take place in the construction industry – this includes the design of buildings and structures, refurbishment of existing buildings, repairs and maintenance, estates management or facilities management.

Key term

Building services – the services of water, gas, electricity and communications that have to be designed for a building.

Discussion

Analysing the activities of the construction industry can be daunting at first because there are so many activities. In groups, discuss the following questions:

1 Can you name five construction activities in the built environment?

2 Can you classify these activities?

3 How do these activities contribute to society's wellbeing?

Construction

Construction covers many different types of work, from taking on projects for private individuals through to commercial property development. There are many different types of construction, including:

- industrial – factories, industrial workshops, industrial estates and industrial units
- residential – private houses, flats, apartments, housing association properties and social housing
- commercial – retail units, shops, offices and business parks
- retail – shop refurbishment, public house refurbishment, shopping parks and retail centres
- health – hospitals, community care centres, retirement homes, clinics and medical centre developments
- education – construction of new schools, further education facilities, universities and training centres
- leisure and recreation – cinemas, sports facilities, all-weather facilities and football stadiums.

Activity 2.4

Using a web-based interactive map application, zoom in on your local area and look at the different types of construction that are taking place. See if you can classify them using the categories above.

Civil engineering

Another category of construction is civil engineering. Civil engineering covers the construction of public infrastructure such as roads and railways. It often involves the use of large volumes of concrete and structural steelwork. Typical civil engineering works may include many of the following activity areas:

- railways – the construction, improvement and maintenance of railways, such as the electrification of the East Coast Main Line
- roads – the maintenance and construction of motorways, bypasses, trunk roads and new housing estate side roads
- bridges – the construction of road bridges and railway bridges
- air travel – the construction of runways and airport terminals
- sea defences – the construction of sea and flood defences such as the Thames Barrier in London
- river and harbour works – the construction of port facilities
- renewable energy projects – the construction of resources such as wind turbines, wave power stations and tidal power plants.

Most civil engineering projects do not contain many architectural elements that would feature in commercial or residential buildings.

How might climate change affect a civil engineer's job?

Just checking

1 What type of work would be undertaken by a civil engineering company?
2 In a short paragraph describe what you understand by the word 'infrastructure'.
3 List four kinds of leisure-related building activity.

Assessment activity 2.1

You have been asked to produce a promotional leaflet for the construction industry national conference. Your booklet should be divided into three sections as follows.

1 The first section must include details of at least three activity areas within the construction industry in the UK. For each area you should include at least one example of the type of work involved. For example, a construction activity could be house construction.

2 The second section will describe the different ways in which the construction industry contributes to society nationally. You should include one economic contribution and one social contribution.

3 The third section will discuss the impact of out-of-town retail developments on local communities. Focus on both the positive and the negative aspects of this sort of development, and include evidence and examples for the statements you make.

Tips

- Try to explain the contribution in local terms that construction makes to society, using your own local area to answer this with examples of real buildings and positive contributions.

- To push yourself even further, you should expand any local contributions to show what construction can offer society nationally. You will need to examine aspects such as the economic contribution of construction, and the benefits of inner city improvements, housing estates and employment.

Take it further

Imagine that you are a member of the local community group that sits on the enterprise board of the local council. You have been asked to evaluate the impact of a proposed out-of-town shopping centre on the local community.

Understanding a client's needs

Introduction

Obtaining a design brief from a client is often a long and detailed process. The brief has to be right for the client, but it also has to satisfy the planners and surrounding neighbourhood. In this topic, you will learn how a client's needs are interpreted to produce a working brief.

What skills do you think you might need when creating a client brief?

A brief is the record of the client's requirements and should include their aims and the chosen design style, as well as the building's intended purpose. Before work can begin on site, the brief must be signed off and approved by the client. This will avoid any later design changes, which could be costly and would delay the project.

The brief has to consider the following elements of the proposed building or structure:

- use and functionality
- style and aesthetics
- size and height
- **carbon footprint** and sustainability.

These elements must all work together to form a final brief. For example, the choice of materials with particular textures or colours may have to be balanced against the need to use sustainable materials.

Key term

Carbon footprint – the amount of carbon dioxide released into the atmosphere as a result of human activity, such as the construction of a building.

Case study

It took seven years to plan the design brief for the Getty Center in Los Angeles before construction could start. Every aspect of this unique building's function was examined and detailed carefully to ensure it leaves a lasting impression on its visitors, who come not only to see the museum exhibits but the building as well.

Look at the Center's website and undertake some independent research, then discuss the following questions.

1 Why did it take so long to plan the design brief?
2 What particular aspects of the brief proved difficult?
3 How was the Getty Foundation involved in the development of the design?

Link

This topic links to *Unit 11: Sustainability in Construction*.

Sustainability

We live in a world where our resources are finite. Many of the materials we take for granted, such as oil-based materials or metals, will not last forever. This means that we need to take a sustainable approach to creating new or renovating existing buildings.

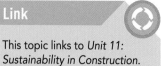

Sustainability should be considered from the very start of a project and should be factored into the design. It should also influence the materials and techniques that are used to construct it:

- **materials** – sustainable buildings waste little material in their construction. This can be achieved by recycling any off-cut materials and using off-site prefabrication techniques where large sections are brought in already completed. Sustainable projects would rely more on renewable materials such as cedar timber. They could use recycling technology that incorporates old materials into new materials, such as reconstituted stone lintels and roof tiles made from slate dust

- **thermal efficiency** – high thermal efficiency is important for a building's sustainability as it reduces waste energy. Efficiency can be achieved by including high levels of insulation to reduce heat loss and by making the building airtight to reduce loss of heated air

- **alternative energies** – a sustainable building will have greater reliance on alternative energy sources such as **photovoltaic** roof panels for electricity generation

- **orientation** – a southerly orientation can be used to make full use of natural sunlight, decreasing reliance on artificial lighting

- **carbon footprint** – a sustainable building will reduce its carbon footprint by using ongoing sustainable processes such as recycling rainwater and **grey water**.

Key terms

Thermal efficiency – how efficiently a building uses heat energy.

Photovoltaic – the generation of power from light, for example using the sun's energy to generate useable electricity.

Orientation – the direction that a building faces.

Grey water – waste water from activities like washing up, washing clothes and bathing, which can be recycled.

Activity 2.5

Look at this energy efficiency rating for this house. Think of five ways to improve its energy efficiency. Create a short presentation outlining your ideas and present it to the group.

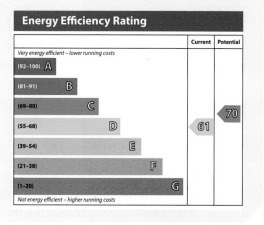

Remember

Sustainability is now a key feature in creating a home that is economical and efficient to run and operate.

Building use

Modern buildings are used for many different purposes and some are often intended to be multi-use. The uses of buildings can be arranged into the following groups:

- **residential use** – this includes flats, houses (terraced, semi-detached and detached); social housing blocks and sheltered accommodation units

- **commercial use** – this includes buildings such as offices and banks

- **retail use** – this includes shops, stalls, market areas, shopping centres and industrial estates

- **industrial use** – this includes factories and buildings containing engineering and fabrication works.

Size and height

A building's size is often dictated by the amount of land that can be purchased and the size of the plot that can be built on. The planning department will often have restrictions on a building's size. The **building line** that they have set will also affect the size and shape of your building.

When considering a building's size, make sure you think about its function as well, as this can influence the decision. You need to consider:

- the number of rooms or amount of floor space required, particularly for hotels and offices
- the building's internal dimensions – for instance, a football stadium must be built to accommodate a pitch that is the minimum FA pitch size
- the building's function – for example, a sports facility with squash courts will have different size requirements to a facility with a swimming pool
- the amount of circulation space – a shopping centre will need a large central circulation space with shops either side, while a factory will need less circulation space as it contains a process line that manufactures a product and does not need many operators
- the number of floors required and the floor-to-ceiling height. These heights are used to make occupants comfortable and to leave sufficient space for services to be hidden above ceilings and below floors.

The Scottish Parliament building is striking and attractive.

Style and aesthetics

A building's appearance is often the most important feature in a client's initial plans for a project. Clients usually want a building that is attractive. This is especially true if it is a commercial building such as a shopping centre, which needs to make people want to visit it. The way in which a building interacts with its surroundings is also very important, particularly when the plans are reviewed by the statutory planning authorities.

Planning a building's aesthetics is not limited to its external appearance. It can also cover the internal appearance. The Scottish Parliament building in Edinburgh shows that internal and external appearance can be designed to work together. It is also a great example of a building being both functional as a workplace and attractive for visitors.

The costs of making a building attractive often have to be weighed against any future income made from rents or leases once the building is complete. However, beautiful or iconic buildings are more likely to attract people who will spend money in the building.

Developments like shopping outlets usually prioritise the **front-of-house design**. This means that most of their budget is spent on what people can see, while less is spent on the corridors and service areas.

You may also have to help a client decide whether to follow a traditional style or whether to take a more modern, contemporary aesthetic.

The final decision is often down to the local planning policies and the decisions made by the planning officers. Planners usually want to see what the 'street scene' looks like and how a new building fits into this scene. This is because they want to ensure that it will not spoil the appearance of the existing built environment. As a result, they often focus on the choice of colours and the type of external materials, as these will make the greatest impact on passers-by.

Often, designers create a mood board. This is a sketch of the design along with different colours and themes painted or stuck on to demonstrate textures and colours.

Research

Are there any restrictions on how tall buildings can be? Find out what the next tallest building being planned is. What will it look like?

Just checking

1 List three of the differences between the requirements of a private house and the requirements of a sports centre.

2 What is the building line? How might it affect a planned development?

TOPIC   B.2

 # Understanding the constraints on design

Introduction

Not every design can be constructed exactly as first planned. Compromises often have to be made because of **constraints** on budget and time, or local planning policies.

▶ Resources

Without the correct resources, it would be impossible to construct a building to meet the client's requirements. It is important to take time at the design stage to consider the resources that will be needed to complete the project. This is often called the **'feasibility** phase'.

Key terms

Constraints – limiting factors.
Feasibility – the possibility of being able to do something.

Activity 2.6

In groups, discuss whether you would spend more on materials at the start of the project to save on future repairs and maintenance costs. What sort of sustainable materials could you choose to save costs on future maintenance?

Budget

The client's budget is one of the most important considerations at the design stage. The sketch designs that are produced for a client will need to include estimates of cost so the client can make informed decisions when approving or rejecting designs. It is very important to consider every possibility and give an accurate picture of a project's final costs. This will help avoid surprises later on in the project that may exceed the client's budget and lead to cutbacks on the final result.

The budget can be split into three different cost areas:

- initial capital costs – this includes the cost of borrowing money to finance the project, the initial design costs, the cost of acquiring the land to build on and the costs of obtaining planning permission.
- the cost of construction – this includes the actual building costs, worked out after the **tendering** process once a contract has been awarded to the successful bidder. This is the stage where the materials in the specification are priced at the specified quality level by the contractor. Where these costs exceed the client's budget, materials are often replaced by cheaper alternatives to save money.
- lifecycle costs – the whole lifecycle costs of a building during its useful life. This includes the costs of cleaning, grounds maintenance, general repairs, heating, lighting, costs of any future alterations for expansion, and general maintenance such as painting and decorating.

Market position

Clients often require a building to be located somewhere that will bring them a market. For example, a fast food service is ideally situated next to a cinema where it will attract customers after a film. Market position is important to clients for the success of their business. Access via road networks is important along with ample car parking spaces.

The site

Finding the right site on which to construct the client's proposed building can be difficult. Often this results in purchasing a building and demolishing it to reuse the land it occupies. The price of land depends on several factors, including:

- geographical location – the price of land in and around London is higher due to greater demand
- the area – a prime location next to a motorway attracts value
- infrastructure – the services that are available on the site or next to it
- access to the site – how much work will have to be done on the roads and any junctions onto a main route
- contamination – the cost of the removal of any contamination from brownfield sites will have to be factored into the budget
- market availability – land in a central location in any town or city attracts a higher price because of its prime location and infrastructure connections
- planning permission – land that has **outline planning permission** will cost more to buy due to the opportunity this presents

- planning classification – land set aside for development in the **local plan** will cost more to buy because of the added value of planning permission
- access and services – a plot of land next to a motorway junction or a site with installed mains drainage will attract a higher price.

Local planning and building control requirements

The two main **statutory** building controls that any design has to satisfy are:

- the Town and Country Planning Act
- the Building Regulations.

The Building Regulations relate to the quality and safety of a new or refurbished building. They cover many different aspects of the construction, including structural safety, water supply and distribution, heating, levels of insulation, access and egress, and fire safety. The regulations are made up of 'Approved Documents' which are available on the planning portal website.

Key terms

Local plan – this is a legal document that every local authority in the UK uses to set out their local planning policies in the area under their authority. It defines where residential and industrial developments can be built, and any planning application is checked against the plan.

Statutory – something that has to be done by law.

Activity 2.7

You are working on a new and innovative hotel development project. It is in the centre of a large city and must have parking for 30 cars as part of the development, but this parking needs to be in a basement. The hotel's style must also fit in with the surrounding built environment. Your client is concerned about the number of constraints that have been identified.

1 What could be a site constraint on this project?
2 Would finance be a constraint?
3 What parts of the design might be subject to planning constraints?

Further legislation that must be obeyed may be classified under health and safety. For example, the Construction Design and Management Regulations cover the risk assessment of a building's design to ensure that it is safe to construct, operate and maintain.

The local plan is a record of a local authority's planning policies for their area. It also contains a set of maps indicating what types of development are allowed. Sustainable developments are very much favoured by planning authorities, as they have a reduced impact on the local environment.

The planning authority also has to approve many other aspects of a proposed design:

- local needs – the planning authority must consider whether the project will benefit the community. They must also consider whether a development could cause problems. For instance, a new shopping centre may cause problems such as traffic congestion, increased demand for parking or a lack of development on the traditional high street
- style – the style of a proposed building may need to be modified in order to fit in with the existing buildings around it

Why is it important for the planning authority to consider the impact of a new development's style or height?

- height – this is often an important aspect for planning authorities as a tall building can dominate the skyline and take light away from its neighbours. It can also affect TV reception and create a wind-tunnel effect at ground level
- materials – the colours and often the texture of the building materials have to be agreed so that the development fits in with its surroundings. This includes the choice of materials such as roof tiles, such as in the choice between slates or clay tiles. Their decisions can cover brickwork type, brick colour and mortar colour
- density – this is the number of houses that can be developed on the proposed site. If too many were built, the development would feel cramped
- community consultations – the community must be consulted on the proposed development. The local community is informed of a new development through notices posted on lampposts adjacent to the site and advertisements in the local press. The planning authority also writes to neighbours. Any objections should be sent to the planning authority
- planning objections – the authority will search for previous planning applications that were made on the site. Any objections that were either upheld or refused will be used to make an informed decision on the new proposal.

Activity 2.8

A ten-storey office building has been proposed for the plot of land next to your house. In groups, consider the following questions:

1 How would you feel about this?
2 Would you object to its height?
3 What might you ask to be altered?
4 How would it affect you?

Timescale

The project's timescale is an important constraint for clients. Often, clients need to get a building constructed to start earning income from rent or building leases.

The two timescale constraints usually agreed between a client and the main contractor are the completion date and the contract period.

The main contractor has a legal duty to meet the completion date or they may face financial penalties. The site manager's salary, **plant** hire and site accommodation all cost in terms of time as well. If a contractor runs over, it can be very expensive. Time really is money!

Key term

Plant – machinery used in the building process, such as diggers and bulldozers.

Activity 2.9

In pairs, discuss the importance of the following constraints. Which could be the most serious? Which is the least serious? Then rank them from most important to least important.

- Local opinion
- Site contamination
- Timescale
- Aesthetic style
- Local needs

Just checking

1 Name the two major building controls that designs have to comply with.

2 Why is it important to discuss the project constraints with the client?

3 Is the opinion of the local community a constraint?

TOPIC   B.3

Producing a client brief

Introduction

When producing a client brief, you will need to assess carefully the client's needs and weigh them against the constraints on the client's project. This will help you to produce a brief for a building that is possible to construct within the client's timescale and budget.

You will need to describe and analyse a **client's needs**. This means that you need to understand what the client wants from their project. This often involves questioning a client about what they want and using examples to give them choices. This information then needs to be written up and reviewed with the client to seek approval. Once this has been granted, you will proceed with the next stage of sketch proposals.

You will also need to describe and analyse the **constraints on a design**. This means discussing timescale and budget with the client, as well as examining the local plan and talking to the planners. You would also visit the proposed site to find out about any site constraints.

This process may involve several discussions with the client to ensure that your proposal matches what they are imagining.

Did you know?

Many of the processes and stages in developing a client's brief are listed within the RIBA (Royal Institute of British Architects) Plan of Work. Architects and designers follow this plan to ensure that all stages are completed and dealt with properly.

▶ Factors to consider

When developing the client brief, you should always consider:

- existing situation – this is the site of the proposed development. It may be empty land, or there may be existing buildings or structures on the site.
- project requirements – this is the exact specification of the client's needs and the requirements of the final building.
- budget – this is the financial plan for the client's design and construction of the project. It may need to change depending on the client's requirements. If it is fixed, the design may have to be changed so that the final building can be paid for.

Figure 2.1 Sketches and photographs can be combined like this to make it easier to visualise the proposed development. Remember, you don't have to be an artist to produce good sketch proposals.

- end users – these are the people who are going to use the final building once it has been constructed. It is important to find out their requirements at this stage to make sure that the final building meets their needs.

▶ Mood boards

A mood board is produced to help the client visualise their requirements. It demonstrates all the proposed materials and colours alongside the elevations to show and illustrate themed colour schemes. Mood boards can be created for both internal and external views to inform a client of what the proposal may look like. It illustrates the style or theme that the designer has intended for the project.

Assessment activity 2.2   *English*

A client comes to you with a concept for a sustainable housing estate. It contains 50 affordable low-rise homes with no access for cars or vehicles to the front of the properties. The design is very similar for all the houses and it is to be completed within 18 months.

1 Describe the needs that must be identified in order to develop the client brief.
2 Now describe the constraints that will affect the client's design.
3 Finally, analyse these needs and constraints to produce a client brief.

Tips

- In order to improve your response, you need to undertake some analysis. This means considering the advantages and disadvantages of a client's design, taking into account the project's constraints.
- How will you develop this analysis? How will you explain the advantages of site constraints? These are evaluative questions that you will need to answer in order to produce merit-level work.
- To work towards distinction level, you should examine the client's needs and constraints for a site, then prioritise them. Prioritising is often done from the point of view of a client, which can be in terms of money, aesthetics or the phases of a scheme. Brain-storming can help you to prioritise these factors before putting them in a list.

Take it further

Identify a new building in your local area and place yourself in the position of the client who had it built. What do you think were the top five needs on this project?

Generation of initial sketch ideas

Introduction
This part of the design process allows you to be most creative. It allows you to express freely the client's ideas in a series of developmental sketches that will grow into the final sketch design for the client to approve. Here, you can use your drawing and design skills in producing building concepts that are three-dimensional (3D) and colourful.

Initial sketch ideas

While this is the fun part, it also has a serious side. What you produce at this stage must meet a client's needs, as they may be investing millions of pounds in the project. The finished construction must therefore be exactly what they wanted.

This is the stage of the design process that turns a client's brief into a sketch proposal. These sketches are often three-dimensional to give a client a good idea of what the completed project will look like.

Several different sketch design proposals can be used to give a client a wider choice. It can also help the client to decide whether different aspects of each proposal could be used to create an improved final idea.

Figure 2.2 An artist's impression of a street scene. What does this show to the planning officers?

Activity 2.10

You are designing a living space made out of portable pod-like units that can be moved around the plot of land that you have available. They need to be made from natural materials, including the furnishings. You need a small living space, a toilet/shower room, a one-bed unit to sleep in and a small kitchen. Only one door is required to the front.

Prepare a mood board containing different materials, small sketches of what you might want one of these units to look like and the materials that will be used. Compare it against the written brief in the paragraph above and evaluate how the mood board that you have produced fits the client's brief. Think about what you could have done to improve it.

Link
This topic links to *Unit 5: Construction Drawing Techniques*.

▶ Presenting your ideas

During the sketch proposal stage, you may use some or all of the methods shown in Table 2.2 to help define the client's ideas.

Table 2.2 Methods of design process

Stage	Details
Initial sketches	These will be purely pencil outline sketches that give an impression of how a designer interprets the client's ideas into a shape and form.
	For example, John Utzon's initial sketches of the Sydney Opera House clearly show the concept of the shape of this iconic building that visitors from all over the world go to see and admire. From these sketches he had a mini model built to show his ideas in 3D, so the Australian client could see the concept in three dimensions.
Floorplans	Functional buildings will often start with a sketch design of the floor plans, showing the movement of people around the building. This is closely linked to the size of the rooms that are required for each function, e.g. classrooms, toilets, dining facilities.
	With low-level buildings, the position of the stairs must be considered both for access to the first floor and escape in case of a fire. Here the Building Regulations start to influence the floor plan sketch designs with the application of the fire regulations.
External elevations	These are drawings of the external appearance of the design from all angles. Colour can be introduced into the sketches to indicate the materials that are going to be used. Sample materials can also be brought together to show a client what they will look like.
	Using perspective within the elevation drawings and showing a person or car against the elevation gives a sense of the size of the building. This gives a realistic idea of what it would look like when built.
Concept ideas	These are the key ideas or the focus of the design. External concepts could include: curved or straight lines, vertical walls, sustainable materials, use of height, different textures and reflective surfaces.
	Internal concepts include: colours, contrasts, use of light, open plan, flexibility, textures, high ceilings and atriums.
Mood boards	These bring together elements such as proposed materials, possible colours and the external elevations to show and illustrate the designer's chosen style. Mood boards can be created for both internal and external views.

Figure 2.3 A design sketch for a swimming pool. What are the constraints on this design?

Activity 2.11

The design brief below has been obtained from a client. Use the following information from the brief to create two sketch proposals for the project that will meet the client's requirements:

Design Brief for Exandit.com offices

The function of the building is to provide a workspace for telephone customer services employees of a large internet service provider.

- Two-storey low-level building
- Large sections of glazed features
- Sloping roof
- L-shaped on plan
- External parking required for 100 cars
- Entrance canopy required for visitors
- Building exterior to blend into the surrounding hill at the rear of the site
- Green technology roof
- Internal light well

Client approval and responding to client feedback

Once the sketch designs have been completed, you will meet the client to discuss the sketches and ensure that they meet the client's original brief. A client may like elements from each of the sketches that you have produced, not just one of the sketches in full. In this case, you will have to take on this feedback and combine the design elements that the client likes into one design for approval.

Once a final design has been sketched out, it will be reviewed by the client before the final design stage can start. At this point, every element of the client's brief should be discussed and checked off against the sketched design. This will ensure that the brief has been met. Annotations can be made on the sketch drawings to ensure that the design discussions are recorded for future reference.

This meeting and agreement must be signed off by the client to ensure that no future design changes are made. Any changes after this point would have serious consequences for the client in terms of costs and delays.

 Discussion point

Why do you think it is so important to ensure that the proposed designs match the brief?

Assessment activity 2.3

A client has approached your design company and a design brief has been approved with the following initial outline for a restaurant offering a high-quality outdoor dining experience.

- Size of plot available: 300 m × 100 m
- Restaurant-style dining in the evening, offering café-style refreshments during the day
- Ground-level external mood lighting
- Fifty covered external dining areas for the evening (50 tables of 5 m² each)
- Natural materials to be used
- Internal kitchen 25 m × 25 m
- Internal restaurant 50 covers 5 m² each
- Internal bar area 30 m² with seats and a bar display
- Offices 15 m²
- Parking for 40 cars
- Landscaped grounds with drive-in and drive-out access.

First, produce two initial design concept sketches for this restaurant. Then review these sketches against the original design brief and comment on the suitability of your proposals.

Now produce two additional concept sketches for two aspects of the restaurant. When you have finished, ask your tutor for feedback on one of your four sketches. Once you have received this feedback, review it and refine the design further.

Take it further

Produce an additional concept sketch for a different aspect of the restaurant. Make sure that all five sketches fully comply with the client's requirements, and that each shows a different design style. Annotate your sketches with appropriate comments to help your client understand your thinking.

Tips

- To improve your response, make sure that you have produced four fully annotated sketch ideas. Remember that these sketches should contrast with each other and give a range of suitable ideas.
- To take it further, listen to your tutor's feedback on your sketches and take notes. Then read the comments back to them so you can reach an agreement on what needs to be refined.
- The best responses make sure that all sketches meet the client's brief by using a checklist to confirm every detail.

Just checking

1 What is an external elevation?
2 What would you use a floor plan to show?
3 Would you use colours in your sketches?

WorkSpace

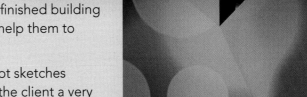

▶ Lizzie Liu

Assistant Designer

I am an assistant designer for an architectural practice in the south of England. Many of our clients work in London but are able to commute each day, so they want to live outside London. We produce unique houses that are individually designed and constructed to meet the client's design brief and also comply with statutory legislation and regulations.

Obtaining a brief from the client is the most difficult part of my job. We will interview a client several times to ensure the finished building meets their requirements, and on each occasion we help them to develop and refine the brief.

When the brief is approved we start the initial concept sketches using a 3D rendering computer program. This gives the client a very realistic model of what their final house will look like.

Often they will want to change aspects of the design when they see it in 3D. This is easily done as it is all electronic and it doesn't waste any paper materials. When the final design includes all of the client's revisions, we get them to sign it off. At that point we can start on the working drawings, which we will use for obtaining planning permission.

The best part of my job, definitely, is seeing a client moving into the new home that came out of our original brief and sketch proposals.

Think about it

1 Think about different ways of obtaining the client's brief. Which do you think will work best? Explain why.

2 Is it important to have experience of using Computer-Aided Design and Drafting (CADD)?

3 Why is it important for Lizzie to get her clients to sign off the design before starting the working drawings?

Introduction

Why are mathematics and science important in construction?

The modern construction industry is based on mathematics and science. To get a craft, technician or professional job in the industry, you should have enough knowledge of the necessary science and mathematics so that you can apply this knowledge to various construction activities. For example, you need knowledge of trigonometry while setting out a building and you need to know the strength of concrete when designing and constructing foundations.

The first part of this unit deals with the properties of a number of construction materials. This will help you to understand which materials are suitable to construct different parts of a building and why. You will have the opportunity to investigate the effect of physical forces and temperature change on these materials.

The second part of the unit is about construction-related mathematics. You will perform a wide range of mathematical calculations relating to, for example, dimensions, areas, volumes, material quantities and costs. You will learn the mathematical principles and apply these to solve a variety of construction problems.

Assessment: You will be assessed by a series of assignments set by your teacher/tutor.

Learning aims

In this unit you will:

A understand the effects of forces and temperature changes on materials used in construction

B use mathematical techniques to solve construction problems.

> I was surprised to find that the mathematics part of this unit was actually great fun. We learned it by doing practical construction activities like setting out and designing a staircase. The practical work meant the maths all made sense. The materials part of the unit was also really interesting and it got me thinking more about why we use what we use in construction – now I can calculate the load on a structure for different materials.
>
> Bahar, *16-year-old BTEC learner*

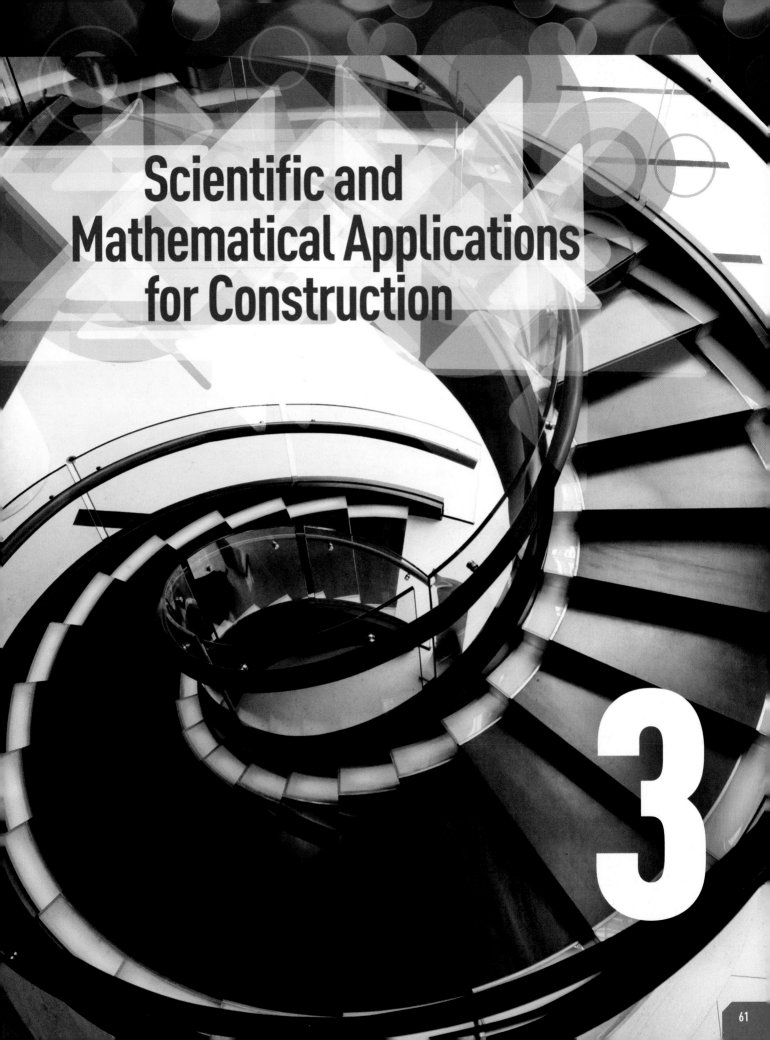

Scientific and Mathematical Applications for Construction

3

Assessment Zone

This table shows what you must do in order to achieve a **Pass**, **Merit** or **Distinction** grade, and where you can find activities in this book to help you.

Assessment and grading criteria			
Level 1	**Level 2 Pass**	**Level 2 Merit**	**Level 2 Distinction**
Learning aim A: Understand the effects of forces and temperature changes on construction materials			
1A.1 Identify the effects of forces on materials used in construction using scientific principles.	**2A.P1** Explain the action and effects of forces on three different construction materials applying scientific and mathematical principles. **See Assessment activity 3.1, page 75**	**2A.M1** Discuss how two different construction materials behave under load in practical construction contexts. **See Assessment activity 3.1, page 75**	**2A.D1** Evaluate two different construction materials in terms of their behaviour under load and their response to changes in temperature in practical construction contexts. **See Assessment activity 3.1, page 75**
1A.2 Identify the effects of temperature change on materials used in construction using scientific principles.	**2A.P2** Explain the effects of temperature change on three different materials used in construction applying scientific principles. **See Assessment activity 3.1, page 75**	**2A.M2** Discuss the action and effect of extremes of temperature change upon two different construction materials in practical construction contexts. **See Assessment activity 3.1, page 75**	
Learning aim B: Use mathematical techniques to solve construction problems			
1B.3 Maths Plot linear relationships and extract information in two construction contexts.	**2B.P3** Maths Apply algebraic and graphical methods to solve two different practical construction problems. **See Assessment activity 3.2, page 94**	**2B.M3** Maths Solve a practical construction problem using trigonometric, mensuration and algebraic methods. **See Assessment activity 3.2, page 94**	**2B.D2** Maths Justify the application of algebraic and graphical methods, mensuration and trigonometry to solve a practical construction problem. **See Assessment activity 3.2, page 94**
1B.4 Maths Find lengths, areas and volumes in three construction contexts.	**2B.P4** Maths Apply mensuration and trigonometry to solve two different practical construction problems. **See Assessment activity 3.2, page 94**		

Maths   Opportunity to practise mathematical skills

How you will be assessed

The unit will be assessed by a series of internally assessed tasks. You will be expected to show an understanding of the behaviour of construction materials due to forces and temperature changes. You will also show that you can apply mathematical principles in a variety of construction situations.

The tasks will be based on scenarios which will place you in a work-based position in the industry, such as a training manager, consultant, site engineer or a similar construction professional role.

Your actual assessment could be in the form of:

- a presentation to include text, diagrams, tables, graphs and test results
- a written report to include text, diagrams, tables, graphs, test results and calculations as appropriate, sometimes with explanations or discussions demonstrating your science and mathematics skills, or an evaluation or justification of a selected solution to a problem.

▶ Effect of forces

Introduction

You can see a variety of materials used in the buildings around you, including bricks, steel, concrete, wood and glass. All these materials are subject to various forces, such as **loads** from the structure and the weight of people, furniture and machinery, as well as natural agents including water, wind, sunlight and extremes of temperature. Different materials have different properties and should be used to suit different requirements.

Key terms

Load – the weight pressing down on one element of the building or structure, such as a load-bearing wall or a floor.

Mass – the amount of matter in a body, measured in kilograms (kg).

Volume – the amount of three-dimensional space an object occupies.

Did you know?

SI stands for Système International and is the international system of units of measurement. In this system, the length is measured in metres (m) and not feet (ft), mass is measured in kilograms (kg) and not pounds (lb) while time in measured in seconds.

▶ Forces and construction materials

Key properties of construction materials

Each construction material that you will work with has three key properties that you need to know about. These are:

- strength – this relates to how much load a material can take safely. The stronger a material is, the more suitable it is for supporting the structure
- ductility – this relates to how much a material can be deformed without losing its toughness. This means that a material with high ductility gives a 'warning' before it fails, either in the form of cracks or change in shape
- density – describes the **mass** per unit **volume**. The denser a material is, the less space it takes up and the more suitable it is for supporting a structure.

Activity 3.1

Select part of a house, school or college building which you have access to. Make a list of various materials and their location in the building. Think of a reason why these materials have been used in a particular location. Record your findings in a table like the one below. You may add more rows. An example has already been done for you.

Material	Location	Reasons
e.g. Bricks	e.g. External wall	e.g. To take the load from the structure above

Stresses caused by forces

When a force is applied to a construction material, there is likely to be a change in the material's shape. This change may result in the material becoming longer (tensioned), shorter (compressed) or twisted (torsioned). The material resists this change and is said to be in a state of stress.

Loads or forces can affect a structure in a number of ways. These different effects are known as stresses, and they include:

- compressive stress – the forces acting on the structure act towards each other, which often squashes the object, and so these forces have a **push** effect
- tensile stress – the forces acting on the structure act away from each other. This stretches the material and hence these forces have a **pull** effect
- shear stress – this is when a force makes the surfaces of a material slide away from each other, relative to one another
- bending stress – this is when forces acting on a beam result in **deflection**. This shows a combined effect of **push** and **pull** (tension and compression).

Knowing what you know now about these properties and behaviours of construction materials, go back to Activity 3.1 and add to the reasons you gave for each material you found. Remember to think about the stresses that might affect each one in their given location.

Key term

Deflection – the distance a structure moves or changes position under stress

▶ Nature of forces

Identifying forces

A force is what moves an object. If the object is heavy, more force is needed. How much force is needed also depends on how quickly the movement is needed.

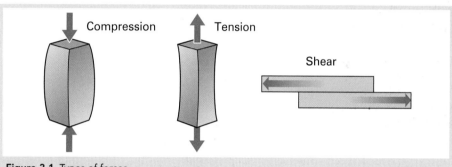

Figure 3.1 Types of forces.

An object's **mass** (m) is its heaviness while its acceleration (a) is the 'quickness' needed.

The forces affecting buildings are usually static (motionless or in equilibrium). They are opposed by equal and opposite forces (known as reactions) from within the material or structure.

For example, if a beam rests on a brick wall, the load from the beam produces a **downward force** on the wall. This is opposed by an **upward reaction** from the wall and the ground. If the reaction from the wall is less than the downward force, the weight from the beam would cause the structure to fail.

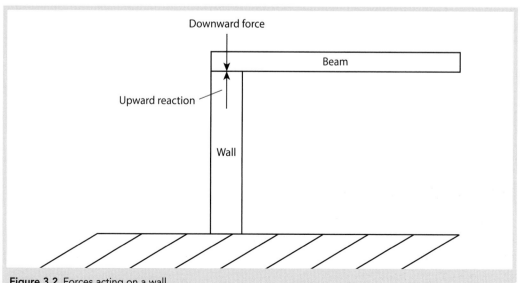

Figure 3.2 Forces acting on a wall.

Did you know?

A force is not visible, so it cannot be observed directly. It is usually measured by the deformation it causes.

Calculating force

Newton's second law of motion sets out that the amount of force (F) needed to cause movement can be worked out by multiplying the mass of the object to be moved (m) and the required acceleration (a). This is expressed as:

force = mass × acceleration

F   **= m**   **× a**

Force is measured in newtons (N) and may be calculated using the equation:

force (N) = mass (kg) × acceleration (m/s²)

All objects on the earth are held down with the force of gravity. We are all under the influence of this gravitational force. You can calculate the force of gravity by multiplying your mass in kilograms (kg) by gravitational acceleration, which is approximately 9.81 metres per second squared (m/s²).

▶ Determining the effect of forces

Calculating stress

Stress is measured as the force applied per unit area. It can be calculated by the formula:

$$\text{stress} = \frac{\text{force}}{\text{area}}$$

Stress is represented by the symbol σ (a Greek letter called sigma). It is measured in the units N/mm² or kN/m².

Weight is a force which can be obtained by multiplying the value of gravity (9.81 m/s²) with the mass of any material. This means if, for example, we know how many kilograms of tiles are on the roof of a house, we can find out how much force this will exert on the structure.

Worked example 3.1

A force of 60 kN is acting on a circular steel rod of diameter 20 mm. The rod is fixed at one end. Work out the tensile stress in the steel rod due to this force.

Step 1 Write down the data you know and look for the unknown:

Diameter, d = 20 mm; Force, F = 60 kN

Tensile stress, σ =?

Step 2 Use the appropriate formula:

$$\text{stress} = \frac{\text{force}}{\text{area}}$$

Step 3 Calculate the area of the steel rod:

$$A = \pi r^2$$

$$A = \pi \times 10^2 = 314.16 \text{ mm}^2$$

Step 4 Substitute values into the formula

$$\text{stress} = \frac{\text{force}}{\text{area}}$$

$$\text{stress} = \frac{60 \times 10^3 \text{ N}}{314.16 \text{ mm}^2}$$

$$\sigma = 191 \text{ N/mm}^2$$

Just checking

1 A load of 70 kN is acting on a steel rod of 25 mm diameter. Calculate the stress in the rod.

2 A steel rod is allowed a maximum stress of 150 N/mm². Calculate the required diameter for the rod if a load of 50 kN is acting upon it.

Calculating strain

Remember

Strain is the ratio of the change in a dimension to its original value (that is, a length divided by a length). Therefore strain has no units.

As stated previously, when a force is transmitted through a solid body the body is often deformed. The measure of this change in shape is called **strain**.

All materials alter slightly in their shape when they are stressed. If part of a structure is subjected to tensile stress, it increases in length and its cross-section becomes slightly smaller. Similarly, if it is subjected to compressive stress, it becomes shorter and slightly larger in cross-section.

The symbol used to represent strain is ε (a Greek letter called epsilon). Strain is expressed as follows:

$$\text{strain} = \frac{\text{change in length}}{\text{original length}}$$

$$\varepsilon = \frac{\Delta l}{l}$$

Worked example 3.2

Find the strain in a body of original length 1.2 m, when it is extended by 2.4 mm.

Step 1 Write down the given data and look for the unknown:

Length, l = 1.2 m; change in length, Δl = 2.4 mm

Strain = ?

Step 2 Use the appropriate formula:

$$\varepsilon = \frac{\Delta l}{l}$$

Step 3 Put the given values into the formula:

$$\varepsilon = \frac{2.4}{1200 \text{ mm}} \quad \text{[Change 1.2 m to millimetres by multiplying by 1000]}$$

$$\varepsilon = 0.002$$

Remember

In any formula, you should make sure that the units of measurement you use are the same. In step 3, you can see that you have 1.2 m and 2.4 mm in the same formula. This means that you need to change 1.2 m to millimetres, and you do this by multiplying it by 1000. This represents it as 1200 mm.

Just checking

Did you know?

1 What unit do you use to measure strain?

2 A concrete column is 3 m in height. Work out the compressive strain in the column if the recorded shortening in length is 15 mm.

3 What would be the new deformation (change in length) if an increase in loading conditions produced a compressive strain of 0.006?

Deformation is a result of one or a combination of:
- applied loads
- changes in moisture content
- changes in temperature.

Hooke's law

If a load is exerted upon a material, the material becomes either longer or shorter. As the load is increased, the length increases or decreases in the same ratio. If the load is removed, the material can return to its original length. This means that there is a relationship between load or stress and change in length or strain.

The relationship between strain and the stress causing it is found to be constant in **elastic** materials. According to Hooke's law, strain is proportional to the stress that causes it, as long as the **limit of proportionality** has not been exceeded.

This may be written:

stress α strain (α means 'proportional to')

stress = constant (E) × strain

$$\sigma = E \times \varepsilon$$

$$E = \frac{\text{stress}}{\text{strain}}$$

Since stress $= \frac{F}{A}$ and strain $= \frac{\Delta l}{l}$

Therefore:

$$E = \frac{(F \times l)}{(A \times \Delta l)}$$

Where:

Δl = the change in length

F = the applied force (N)

l = the original length (mm)

A = the area of cross-section (mm²)

E = Young's modulus of elasticity (N/mm²)

Calculating Young's modulus of elasticity

All materials deform when subjected to a force, but some materials return to their original shape and size. For instance, rubber bands and steel beams recover their shape, but putty and lead pipes do not.

Therefore a material or a body that recovers its original shape is said to be elastic. This property is measured by the elastic modulus or **Young's modulus of elasticity (E)**.

In a typical experiment to observe a material's elasticity, two wires made out of mild steel, A and B, are hung from the same support. Wire B is kept taut using a fixed weight, while wire A has a scale pan attached to the end. To test wire A, loads in newtons are progressively added to the scale pan. Wire A is then tested against the constant length of B and the extension is recorded each time. A micrometer is used to find the diameter of the wire so that the cross-sectional area after each addition can be calculated.

A graph of load against extension is then plotted.

Figure 3.3 gives useful information about the behaviour of steel under the action of tensile forces.

- Elastic range of stress – this is the straight line section of the graph, and it is the portion over which Hooke's law is obeyed.

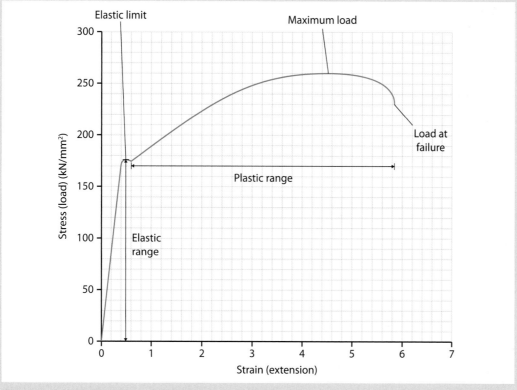

Figure 3.3 The stress-strain curve for mild steel.

- Elastic limit – this is the amount of stress up to which the steel recovers its shape and size when the force is removed.

- Limit of proportionality – this is the amount of stress up to which Hooke's law is obeyed. It usually occurs just below the elastic limit.

- Plastic range of stress – this is the curved portion of the graph between the elastic limit and the failure point. If the load is removed in this region, the material will not recover its original length. The lengthening which remains is called the permanent set.

- Maximum or ultimate load – this is the maximum amount of stress the steel can take. Rapid failure starts after this point.

Worked example 3.3

Work out the increase in length of a steel tie rod 3 m long and 30 mm diameter, when subjected to a tensile load of 120 kN. *E* for steel is 205 kN/mm².

Step 1 Write down the given data and look for the unknown:

Length, $l = 3$ m; diameter, $d = 30$ mm; force, $F = 120$ kN

Change in length, $\Delta l = ?$

Step 2 Use the appropriate formula:

$$E = \frac{(F \times l)}{(A \times \Delta l)}$$

$$\Delta l = \frac{(F \times l)}{(A \times E)} \text{ [rearranging for } \Delta l]$$

Step 3 Calculate the area of the tie rod:

$$A = \pi r^2$$

$$A = \pi \times 15^2 = 706.9 \text{ mm}^2$$

Step 4 Put the given data into the rearranged formula:

$$\Delta l = \frac{(120 \times 3000)}{(706.9 \times 205)} \text{ [remember to keep units to kN and mm, as given in the question]}$$

$$\Delta l = \textbf{2.48 mm}$$

Just checking

1 A pre-stressing wire of diameter 7 mm is loaded with 50 kN. If its modulus of elasticity is 210 kN/mm^2 and its extension is 150 mm, find its original length.

2 An aluminium rod with an area of 25 mm^2 is loaded with 10 kN. Its original length was 1 metre. After the load was applied, the length was 1.04 metres. What is its modulus of elasticity?

▶ Changes in temperature

Introduction

Construction materials are exposed to a variety of natural forces. Whether the weather is fine and sunny or cold and dark, these materials are designed to perform their function while resisting these weathering elements. Construction materials need to be able to resist the forces of extreme temperatures and water as much as possible.

▶ Typical construction materials

Key properties of construction materials

There are five key properties of typical construction materials that are affected by temperature changes. These are:

- thermal conductivity – this is a material's ability to conduct heat through itself. A material that has a high value of thermal conductivity means that it is a good conductor, or that it conducts heat through itself without much resistance
- thermal resistance – this is the amount that a material resists the transfer of heat through itself
- porosity – a measure of how much a material lets water through
- strength – this is the ability of a material to support its own weight and any applied loads without distortion. Strength generally relates to a material's resistance to tension, shear and compression stresses
- rate of hydration – the speed at which a material will absorb water.

You looked at the effect of forces on common construction materials in Topic A.1. Now you will learn about the way that differences in the environment, like heat or moisture, affect these construction materials.

▶ Scientific principles

Changes of state

There are three possible states of matter:

- solid – the molecules in a solid have fixed positions. This means that **volume** and shape are fixed
- liquid – the molecules in a liquid are held together, but they can move. This means that the volume is fixed but the shape is not
- gas – the molecules in a gas have complete freedom of movement. This means that the volume and shape are not fixed.

Matter can change state, and **latent heat** allows this to happen. The change of state depends upon whether heat is withdrawn or added. For example, adding heat to iron will change it from solid to liquid, while cooling moist air by withdrawing heat can cause condensation.

Evaporation

Evaporation is the change of a liquid or a solid substance to a **gas** or a **vapour**. Water boiling into steam is an example of evaporation.

Remember

There is no real difference between the words **gas** and **vapour**. The word gas usually describes a substance that appears as a gas under normal pressure and temperature, while vapour usually describes the gaseous state of a substance that is normally a liquid or a solid.

Expansion and contraction

When water freezes and becomes solid ice, the molecules of the water have arranged into an ordered rigid state. When heat is applied, the solid ice then turns back into water. Water expands when it freezes and contracts again when it thaws.

Water can enter a **porous** material either by **capillary action** from the ground or through the material's surface. If it then freezes and expands, the material surrounding it cannot fit this expansion and the material cracks. In the same way, if water gets into a crack in a surface and then freezes, it can cause fissures. Water then enters these fissures, freezes and expands, damaging the surface even further. This is known as the 'freeze-thaw cycle' and is a common cause of the deterioration of exposed building materials, particularly brick and stone.

Heat storage

Thermal energy can be stored in a material as **sensible heat** by raising the material's temperature.

The heat storage can be calculated as:

$Q = V \rho\, C \Delta T$

Key terms

Latent heat – the energy needed to change the state of the material.

Porous – a porous material has a lot of pores or air pockets. These allow air or liquid to pass through the material.

Capillary action – the absorption of liquid into the pores in a porous material.

Density – mass per unit volume, measured in kilograms per cubic metre (kg/m^3).

Did you know?

Most substances undergo changes of state in the order **solid – liquid – gas** as their temperature is raised. However, a few substances change directly from a solid to a gas. This is known as sublimation.

Did you know?

A material's porosity is closely linked to its **density**. High-density materials are unlikely to be porous. For example, steel does not absorb any moisture and so can be said to be waterproof, while lightweight low-density blocks used as insulators are very porous.

$Q = m\,C\,\Delta T$

Where:

Q = sensible heat stored in the material measured in joules (J)

V = volume of substance (m³)

ρ (the Greek letter rho) = density of substance (kg/m³)

m = mass of substance (kg)

C = **specific heat capacity** of the substance (J/kg°C)

ΔT = temperature change (°C)

Worked example 3.4

Calculate the heat stored in 2 m³ of a material heated from 20°C to 40°C. The material has a density of 2,400 kg/m³ and has a specific heat capacity of 790 J/kg°C.

Step 1 Write down the given data and look for the unknown:

Volume, V = 2m³; density, ρ = 2400kg/m³; specific heat capacity, C = 790 J / kg°C

Change of temperature, ΔT = 40°C − 20°C = 20°C

Heat stored, Q = ?

Step 2 Use the appropriate formula:

$Q = V\rho\,C\,\Delta T$

Step 3 Put the given data into the formula:

$Q = (2\text{ m}^3) \times (2{,}400\text{ kg/m}^3) \times (790\text{ J/kg°C}) \times (20°C)$

$Q = 75{,}840$ kJ

Specific heat capacity

The specific heat capacity of a material is the amount of heat taken in or given off when the material is heated or cooled by 1 **kelvin**, without a change of state like melting or evaporating taking place. It is represented by the formula:

$$C = \frac{\Delta Q}{(m\,\Delta T)}$$

Where:

C = specific heat capacity (J/kg°C)

ΔQ = amount of heat (J)

m = mass of the material (kg)

ΔT = difference of temperature (°C)

A high value of specific heat capacity indicates that more energy will be needed to heat it up. However, a material with high specific heat capacity will also cool down slowly.

Worked example 3.5

Water has a specific heat capacity of 4,187 J/kg°C. Work out the amount of heat stored in 8,000 kg of water if temperature is increased by 1°C.

Step 1 Write down the given data and look for the unknown:

$C = 4{,}187$ J/kg°C

$m = 8{,}000$ kg

$\Delta T = 1°C$

$\Delta Q = ?$

Step 2 Use the appropriate formula:

$$C = \frac{\Delta Q}{(m\,\Delta T)}$$

$$\Delta Q = \frac{(C \times m)}{\Delta T} \quad \text{[rearranging the formula]}$$

Step 3 Put the given data into the formula:

$$\Delta Q = \frac{(4{,}187 \times 8{,}000)}{1}$$

$$\Delta Q = 33{,}496{,}000 \text{ J}$$

> **Did you know?**
>
> The specific heat capacity of ceramic materials is higher than that of metals.

Thermal conductivity

Heat flows through solid materials by conduction. A material's ability to conduct heat is measured by its thermal conductivity. A material that has a high value of thermal conductivity means that it is a good conductor.

Thermal conductivity is worked out as the amount of heat loss in 1 second through 1 m² of material whose thickness is 1 metre, with a 1°C temperature difference between the faces.

The symbol used to represent thermal conductivity is k or λ (the Greek letter lambda). Conductivity is measured in W/mK (watts per metre kelvin).

Thermal resistivity (r) is the opposite or reciprocal of conductivity. It is measured in m K/W (metres kelvin per watt) and is represented by the formula:

$$\text{thermal resistivity} = \frac{1}{\text{thermal conductivity}}$$

$$r = \frac{1}{k}$$

> **Did you know?**
>
> Resistivity is sometimes easier to use than conductivity when calculating a material's thermal conductivity. The thermal resistivity (r) can often be worked out from the manufacturer's data sheet for a material.

Thermal resistance

The insulating properties of a material are related to the material's thickness. Thermal resistance takes the thickness into account and is expressed by the formula:

$$\text{thermal resistance} = \frac{\text{thickness}}{\text{thermal conductivity}}$$

The formula tells us that to increase thermal resistance, thicker material should be used. To achieve a higher value of thermal resistance, material should have the lowest possible thermal conductivity.

Worked example 3.6

Cathy is choosing insulation material for her house. She found out that the thermal conductivity of expanded polystyrene is 0.034 W/mK. She was advised by the seller that a thickness of 50 mm is required. She wants to know what the thermal resistance of it would be. Calculate this for Cathy.

$$\text{thermal resistance} = \frac{\text{thickness}}{\text{thermal conductivity}}$$

$$r = \frac{50}{0.034}$$

$$r = 1.47 \text{ m}^2\text{K/W}$$

Activity 3.2

Cathy is pouring a concrete floor. What thickness should the concrete be in order to get the same thermal resistance as in the above example?

The thermal conductivity of concrete is 1.44 W/mK.

Thermal expansion and contraction

Different materials expand and contract at different rates when heated and cooled. This expansion and contraction can cause movement known as thermal movement. If this is not controlled, it can cause problems such as the cracking of walls and glass in windows, as well as expansion of roofing felt.

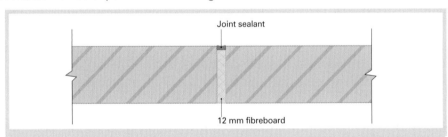

Joint sealant

12 mm fibreboard

Figure 3.4 An expansion joint between concrete slabs, filled with plywood and sealant.

Structures need to allow for expansion and contraction. Many do this using a feature known as an expansion joint. This is a gap between slabs of concrete, bricks or other materials that is designed to allow for this movement. This means that damage is avoided because the movement is taken in by the expansion joints rather than by the wall or floor materials.

The amount of expansion or contraction depends on the type of material used, and it is measured by the coefficient of linear expansion. This is the change in length per unit of length that occurs to a substance when the temperature is raised by 1 °C. It is represented by the Greek letter alpha (α) and is given at ordinary room temperature. It is measured in millimetres per metre degrees Celsius (mm/m °C) and is calculated using the formula:

$$\alpha = \frac{\Delta l}{(l \times \Delta T)}$$

Where:

Δl = change in length l = original length ΔT = change in temperature

Did you know?

Long pipes used for central heating have a bend called an expansion bend to avoid cracking due to thermal movement.

Worked example 3.7

Rajesh has been contracted to fix an aluminium gutter to the outside of a building. The total length of the gutter is 60 m. Work out the maximum thermal movement of the aluminium gutter assuming that no gaps were allowed for and the temperature can vary from −10°C to 35°C. The coefficient of linear expansion for this is 2.4×10^{-5} mm/m°C.

Step 1 Write down the given data and look for the unknown:

Length, $l = 60$ m;

$\alpha = 2.4 \times 10^{-5}$ mm/m°C;

$\Delta T = 35 - (-10) = 45$ °C; $\Delta l = ?$

Step 2 Rearrange the formula:

$$\alpha = \frac{\Delta l}{(l \times \Delta T)}$$

$$\Delta l = \alpha \times l \times \Delta T$$

Step 3 Substitute the given data into the formula:

$$\Delta l = 2.4 \times 10^{-5} \times 60 \times 45$$

$$\Delta l = 0.0648 \text{ m}$$

$$\Delta l = \mathbf{64.8 \text{ mm}}$$

Just checking

Rajesh is trying to decide whether he should use a PVC pipe instead of the aluminium pipe mentioned above. What would be the amount of thermal movement if a PVC pipe was used with an α value of 70×10^{-5} mm/m°C?

Activity 3.3

Using the same building as you used in Activity 3.1, look again at your list of materials and the reasons why you think these materials have been used in each location. Now suggest alternative materials and give reasons for your suggestions.

Assessment activity 3.1

You are the site manager on a new housing development. You have to assess two different materials to build the houses from. Choose two different construction materials, then answer the following questions:

1 How would these materials behave under a load?

2 How would extremes of temperature change affect these materials?

Now consider all of the information you have put together to answer these questions and decide which material you would choose for the purpose. Make sure that you offer evidence for your decision.

▶ Algebraic and graphical methods

Did you know?

There are four arithmetic operations: addition, subtraction, multiplication and division. In algebra, we only use two: addition and multiplication. Why do you think this might be?

Key terms

Inverse operation – doing something (e.g. an equation) the other way around.

Indices – these are numbers or symbols (often written as superscript). For example, the number 25 can be written as 5^2, where the ^{2} (or the 'square') is the index. This means that 5 is multiplied by itself in order to make 25. An index is also called the power or exponent. All numbers without specified indices are referred to as being 'to the power of 1'.

▶ Introduction

Algebraic and graphical methods are frequently used to understand and solve problems in construction. For instance, these methods help us to understand the relationship between stress and strain or between a material's thickness and its thermal resistance. These methods can also be used to calculate the quantities and costs of materials needed for a construction activity.

▶ Rearranging simple formulae

During any calculations, it may be necessary to rearrange formulae in order to get a certain value. This is made much easier by following these basic rules:

1 In any equation, whatever you do on one side of the equals sign you should also do on the other side. Remember that it is an equation and is already equal – so keep it equal!

2 If you move a term from one side to the other, you are doing an **inverse operation** or balance. For example, you can subtract similar terms from both sides to move a positive term or divide the same term on both sides to move a term being multiplied. See Worked Example 3.8 to see this in action.

3 The inverse of addition is subtraction and vice versa.
  For example, the inverse of +2 is −2

4 The inverse of multiplication is division and vice versa.
  For example, the inverse of 2 is ½

5 The inverse of a square is a square root and vice versa.
  For example, the inverse of 5^2 is $5^{1/2}$ or $\sqrt{5}$

Look at the formula:

$v = u + (a \times t)$

To work out u, u needs to be the subject of the formula. This means that the equation must be rearranged so that u is on one side of the equals sign and all other terms are on the other side. To move $+(a \times t)$, add $-(a \times t)$ to both sides as an inverse. This means that if you take a term to the other side of the equals sign, you should change its sign.

$v - (a \times t) = u + (a \times t) - (a \times t)$

$v - (a \times t) = u$

$u = v - (a \times t)$

Worked example 3.8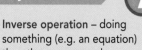

Rearrange the formula below to make t the subject.

$v = u + (a \times t)$

Move u by taking its inverse:

$v - u = u - u + (a \times t)$

$v - u = a \times t$

Move a by taking its inverse:

$\dfrac{(v - u)}{a} = \dfrac{(a \times t)}{a}$

$\dfrac{(v - u)}{a} = t$

$t = \dfrac{(v - u)}{a}$

Activity 3.4

Rearrange the formula $F = ma$ to make m the subject.

Rearranging formulae that have **indices** and square roots may look more complicated. However, it works in exactly the same way as the example above. The worked example below has indices.

Worked example 3.9

Rearrange the formula to make x the subject:

$y = (2x^3)^4$

Step 1

$y^{1/4} = (2x^3)^{4 \times 1/4}$ [taking inverse]

$y^{1/4} = 2x^3$

Step 2

$\dfrac{(y^{1/4})}{2} = \dfrac{2x^3}{2}$ [divide both sides by 2]

$\dfrac{(y^{1/4})}{2} = x^3$

Step 3

$\dfrac{(y^{1/4})^{1/3}}{2} = (x^3)^{1/3}$ [taking inverse]

$x = (y^{1/12})$ or $(y^{1/4})^{1/3}$

Activity 3.5

1 Rearrange the formula to make cos A the subject: $a^2 = b^2 + c^2 - 2\,b\,c\cos A$

2 Rearrange to make v the subject of the formula: $E_k = \frac{1}{2}mv^2$

Evaluating formulae

To evaluate a formula, you need to substitute the letters in the formula with given values. More simply, evaluating a formula means to 'work it out'. For example: work out V, if you are given the values for I and R.

Make sure you take into account any exponents. For example, Ohm's law relates the voltage, V, across a resistor with resistance value, R, to the current, I, through it. The formula states $V = IR$.

If $I = 13A$ and $R = 5\Omega$, we can use this formula to calculate V as below:

$V = IR$

$V = 13 \times 5$

$V = 65$ volts

Worked example 3.10

Kinetic energy is given by the formula $E_k = \frac{1}{2}mv^2$. If a cyclist has a mass of 100 kg and is moving at a velocity of 10 m/s, calculate his kinetic energy.

Step 1 Write down the data you have been given:

Mass, $m = 100$ kg; velocity, $v = 10$ m/s

Step 2 Substitute the given values into the formula:

$E_k = \frac{1}{2}mv^2$

$E_k = \frac{1}{2}\,100 \times 10^2$

$E_k = \frac{1}{2}\,100 \times 100$

$E_k = 5{,}000$ kg m²/s²

Activity 3.6

Michael is a site engineer. He is working on installing an electric hoist to be attached to the side of the scaffold for a multi-storey building in progress. The hoist will raise bricks as far as the 12th floor, 36 metres above ground level. The safe working load of the hoist is 500 kg, and the manufacturer's data states that the hoist is designed to work at a speed of 1.75 m/s. Michael needs to work out the kinetic energy used by the hoist, so that he can attach it to the correct power source.

Using the equation $E_k = \frac{1}{2}mv^2$, find the energy required to run the lift at maximum load and height.

Solving equations

An algebraic equation is a sentence or a statement written with the use of mathematical symbols. It consists of some constants (e.g. 2, 5, 6.5) and some variables whose values have to be worked out. The variables are often written as x, y or z, although any letter can be used. Often, as we have seen before, Greek letters are used.

Every equation has two sides separated by an equals sign. Whatever is on the left-hand side should always equal whatever is on the right-hand side. Similarly any operation (e.g. addition, multiplication) carried out on one side should also be done to the other side.

To solve an equation, you need to find the values of the variables.

Solving equations with one unknown

Solving an equation with one unknown value involves some basic operations. For example, look at the following equation:

$x + 3 = 2$

To solve this, move $+3$ to the right-hand side of the equation by subtracting 3 from both sides of the equation. This gives the value of the unknown 'x'. Remember, moving $+3$ means applying its inverse to both sides of the equation:

$x + 3 - 3 = 2 - 3$

$x = -1$

Worked example 3.11

Solve the equation: $3x = 7(8 - 2x)$

Step 1 Remove the brackets:

$3x = 7(8 - 2x)$

This means that you need to multiply both 8 and $-2x$ by 7 to remove the brackets:

$3x = 56 - 14x$

Step 2 Add the inverse of $-14x$ to both sides:

$3x + 14x = 56 - 14x + 14x$

$17x = 56$

Step 3 Divide both sides by 17 to get the value of x:

$\frac{17x}{17} = \frac{56}{17}$

$x = \frac{56}{17}$

Activity 3.7

Solve the following equations:

1 $6m + 11 = 25 - m$
2 $2(x + 1) = 8$

Linear equations

The variables in the equations you have just solved above have a maximum power of 1. These equations are examples of linear equations. Equations without any squares (powers of two), cubes (powers of 3) or other powers over 1 are called linear equations. For example, in the equation $x + 3 = 8$, x has a power of 1. This means that the equation is a linear equation. Linear equations are used in a number of construction and engineering contexts.

The solved example below shows the application of linear equations.

Worked example 3.12

Earthworks are to be carried out at a construction site. Plant A can complete the work in 5 hours, while Plant B needs 3 hours. Your manager has asked you to use both Plants A and B. Calculate the time it will take.

Step 1 Plan and write out the problem:

It will take time, t, for both plants to do the earthwork.

Work by Plant A + work by Plant B = total work

The total work can be considered as equal to 1

Work by Plant A + work by Plant B = 1

(work rate of Plant A × t) + (work rate of Plant B × t) = 1

Step 2 Solve for Plants A and B:

Part of the work will be done by Plant A as shown below:

work by Plant A = work rate × time

Assume that work is like one job or equal to 1.

Use the values given in the question: 1 = work rate × 5 hours

Rearrange the equation: work rate = $\dfrac{1}{5}$

Similarly:

work by Plant B = work rate × time

Assume that work is like one job or equal to 1.

Use the values given in the question: 1 = work rate × 3 hours

Rearrange the equation: work rate = $\dfrac{1}{3}$

continued

Worked example 3.12 continued

Step 3 Put the given values into the equation:

(work rate of Plant A × t) + (work rate of Plant B × t) = 1

$$(\frac{1}{5} \times t) + (\frac{1}{3} \times t) = 1$$

Taking 15 as LCM (lowest common multiple):

$$\frac{(3t + 5t)}{15} = 1$$

$$(3t + 5t) = 15$$

$$8t = 15$$

$$t = \frac{15}{8}$$

$$t = 1.875 \text{ hours}$$

It will take **1.875 hours** or 1 hour 53 minutes to do the earthworks if both plants are used.

Activity 3.8

Your site office is cleaned by two cleaners. Mark comes on a Monday and takes three hours to complete the job. Manjit does the cleaning on Tuesdays and takes two hours. Both work together on Wednesdays. How long would it take when both of them do the work on Wednesdays?

Did you know?

Satellite navigation systems, such as a sat nav in a car, are used in surveying equipment. In a car, satellite navigation helps you reach an unknown place, while in surveying equipment it helps set out a building as accurately as possible. The system does this by plotting the location on the map as if it were on a graph.

Use of graphs

Graphs are used in newspapers and on television to help people to understand issues more clearly, particularly when comparing quantities or values.

Graphs are used extensively in the construction industry. They can show the effects of loading on a material or the increase in thermal insulation when a material's thickness is increased. This helps to calculate the correct loading in the first case and the appropriate thickness of insulation in the second.

Graphs are drawn between several points. For any graph, locating the points is the first step.

Location of a point

A point can be located on a graph if its position is known. For this, two values or coordinates are needed. The most commonly used system is called the Cartesian coordinate system. You can see an example of this in Figure 3.5.

On this plane, there are two lines at right angles to each other. These are called axes. Generally, the horizontal is called the x-axis and the vertical is called the y-axis. The point where both axes meet is called the origin. Moving to the right and upwards from the origin increases the values – almost like a number line.

Locating points by coordinates

Points can be located on the graph by specifying their x and y coordinates. For example, the x coordinate of Point Q is 1, and its y coordinate is 4. This means that it can be located by moving one unit from the origin along the x-axis to the right and four units upwards from the origin along the y-axis. It is written as Q (1,4).

Graphs of linear equations

Earlier we looked at linear equations. A linear equation can be used to produce a straight-line graph. Linear equations have the standard form:

$y = mx + c$

In this equation, m is the **gradient** and c is the **intercept** with the y-axis.

So in the equation $y = 3x + 2$, the slope is 3 and the intercept is 2.

$$y = 3x + 2$$
$$y = mx + c$$

This equation can be used to construct a straight-line graph.

This has two properties: the gradient of the line (m) and the intercept (c).

The gradient of a line shows the relationship between the distance travelled on the x-axis and the distance travelled on the y-axis.

Look at Figure 3.6, where a line joins two points: P (5,6) and Q (2,3).

$$\text{gradient } (m) = \frac{\text{distance travelled in } y}{\text{distance travelled in } x}$$

$$m = \frac{(7 - 4)}{(6 - 1)}$$

$$m = \frac{3}{5}$$

The gradient of this line is $\frac{3}{5}$.

The second property of a straight-line graph is the intercept. This is the point where the line passes through the y-axis. This is written as c. In Figure 3.6, the intercept is equal to 3.5.

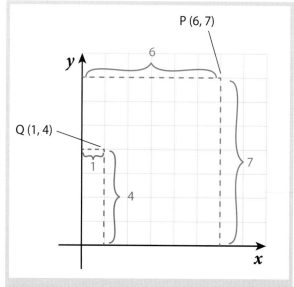

Figure 3.5 Locating Cartesian coordinates.

Key terms

Gradient – the slope.

Intercept – where one thing interrupts or cuts off something else. In the equation for a straight-line graph, it is where the line cuts the y-axis.

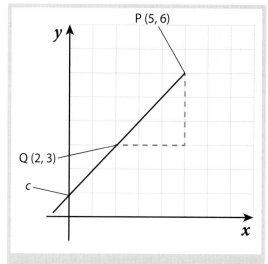

Figure 3.6 A straight-line graph.

Activity 3.9

Locate the following points on a coordinate plane and calculate the gradient of the line joining the two points:

1 A (−4, −2) and B (−3, 2)

2 P (0, 0) and Q (3, 6)

Plotting a linear equation

To plot a linear equation, certain values can be taken as an input. These values are then put into the equation to get the output. Each set of input and output values are then plotted choosing an appropriate scale.

Worked example 3.13

Plot the linear equation $6x + 8y = 16$

Step 1 Rearrange the equation for y:

$y = (16 - 6x) / 8$

Step 2 Construct the table of values:

First split the equation into individual terms. In this example, the left-hand column of the table below shows how the equation can be split – for example, into $(-6x)$, $(16-6x)$ $\frac{(16-6x)}{8}$. The values of x are assumed. You can take some negative and some positive values. In this example, the values are taken from –5 to +5.

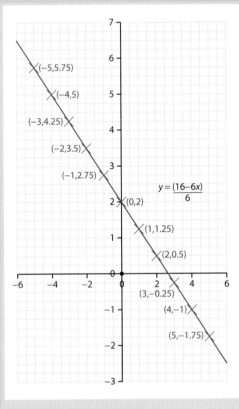

x	–5	–4	–3	–2	–1	0	1	2	3	4	5
-6x	30	24	18	12	6	0	–6	–12	–18	–24	–30
16 – 6x	46	40	34	28	22	16	10	4	–2	–8	–14
$y = \dfrac{(16-6x)}{8}$	5.75	5	4.25	3.5	2.75	2	1.25	0.5	–0.25	–1	–1.75

Step 3 Plot the results:

The values of x on the x-axis and the values of Y on the y-axis. Choose an appropriate scale so that your graph will fit on the paper.

Figure 3.7 Plotting a linear equation.

Step 4 Check your work:

You can check the slope and intercept of the graph and compare it with the equation to verify the results.

Activity 3.10

Draw the graph of following equations and check your work:

1 $5x + 12y = 17$
2 $7x + 4y = 500$

Interpolation and extrapolation

A graph is plotted using only a few given values. Interpolation is the process of finding those values on the straight line graph that were not given originally. Sometimes, the values required are not on the graph. Extrapolation is the process of finding probable values by extending the graph following the same trend line.

Worked example 3.14

Figure 3.8 represents the relationship between resistance, R, and temperature, t. Work out the approximate value of R when $t = 60\ °C$.

Step 1 Identify the point where $t = 60\ °C$.

Step 2 Draw a vertical line up from the x-axis to intersect the graph.

Step 3 From the point where the vertical line intersects the graph, draw a horizontal line to meet the y-axis.

Step 4 Find out the value of R, where the horizontal line you have just drawn meets the y-axis.

$R = 132\ \Omega$

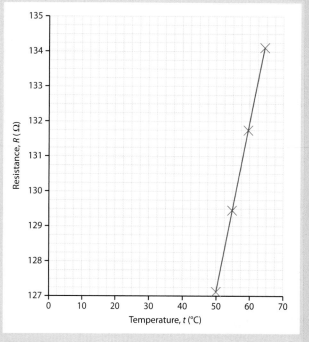

Figure 3.8

Activity 3.11

Using Figure 3.8, work out the temperature when the resistance is 135 Ω.

Worked example 3.15

Figure 3.9 represents the relationship between the crushing strength of mortar and the percentage of water used to prepare it.

Work out the intercept of the graph.

As the graph does not intersect the y-axis, extrapolation is needed to find the intercept. The dotted line is the extrapolation.

To extrapolate, extend the trend line far enough so that it cuts through the y-axis, then read the intercept from the graph.

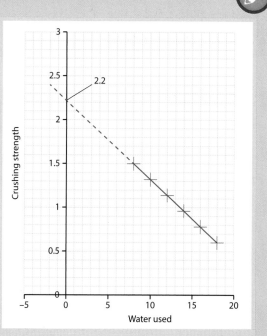

Figure 3.9

Rounding numbers

If area of a plot of land is 309.69 m², it is normal practice to round it to 310 m². However, if you are cutting a piece of wood to fit in a shelf, you will have to be more accurate. You might end up having measurements like 1.35 m. This means that rounding numbers depend upon the type of task you are doing.

If the digit to the right of where you want to round off is 5 or more than 5, round off 'upwards' otherwise round off 'downwards.

Take the example of a number 5.8396 which you have to round off to two decimal places. For this number, you could see there are four places (or digits) to the right of the decimal point. Count from left to right after the decimal point. The second digit is **3**. This is what is to be rounded off. To the right of this digit is **9**. As this is more than 5, 3 will be rounded up to 4. Hence the answer will be 5.84 which is correct to two decimal places.

Accuracy of calculations

It is important that your calculations are as accurate as possible. This may not be easy when the numbers you are working with are not certain. This means that when you plot data onto a graph, the points are not all exactly on a straight line. This is because of observational and practical errors. The relationship may still be linear.

In such cases, instead of joining all the points, a line of best fit is drawn. As the name describes, it is what fits best. The line of best fit may pass through some points or may not pass through any point at all. However, it must be as close to all the points as possible.

Worked example 3.16

Hooke's law states that stress is directly proportional to strain and is expressed as $\sigma = E \times \varepsilon$. Find the value of E using the results of an experiment. Work out the gradient of this graph. What does the slope indicate in this case?

Stress σ (MN/m²)	120	104	88	75	59	48	35
Strain $\varepsilon \times 10^{-4}$	5.5	5.13	4.59	3.75	3.6	2.61	1.58

Step 1 Plot the graph:

Choose an appropriate scale so that the graph fits on the paper:

Plot strain along the x-axis and stress along the Y-axis.

As strain has very small values, it has been multiplied by 10^{-4}.

As the values are based on experimental data, draw a line of best fit.

Step 2 Choose two points on the graph:

The points chosen in this case are A (5, 100) and B (2.2, 40), as shown in Figure 3.10.

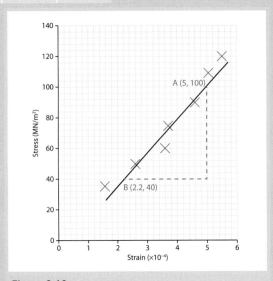

Figure 3.10

Worked example 3.16 continued

Step 3 Find the gradient:

$$gradient = \frac{\text{change in } y}{\text{change in } x}$$

$$gradient = \frac{(100 - 40)}{(5 - 2.2)}$$

$$gradient = 21.4286$$

Step 4 Interpret the result:

$$gradient = \frac{\text{change in stress}}{\text{change in strain}}$$

This is also known as Young's modulus of elasticity (*E*). Hence by finding the slope, we have worked out a value of *E* for the material used in the experiment.

$$gradient = E = \frac{21.4286}{10^{-4}}$$

$$E = 214,286 \text{ MN/m}^2$$

Activity 3.12

Figure 3.11 shows a result of a test on a wire specimen. Work out:

- the slope of the graph
- the intercept.

Now interpret the results.

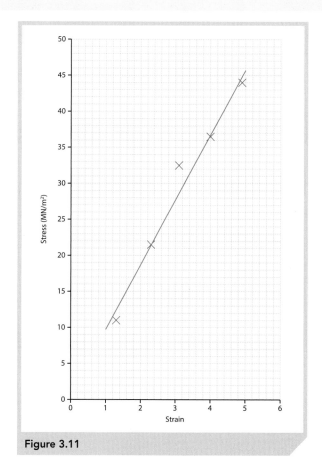

Figure 3.11

▶ Mensuration

Introduction

Mensuration means measurement. Mensuration techniques are applied in construction to calculate lengths, areas and volumes. These techniques help when calculating quantities of materials needed and their costs. It also helps to estimate other resource requirements (such as labour and plant requirements) to carry out construction activities.

▶ Areas

Simple shapes include squares, rectangles, triangles and circles. The area of a shape is the size of its surface. All construction professionals need to be able to work out areas – for instance, a painter and decorator needs to know the area of a wall before buying the wallpaper to cover it.

Squares

The area of a square is calculated by multiplying two sides, like A and B in Figure 3.12. If the square's sides are measured in metres, the area is expressed in square metres (m^2).

If A = 5 m and B = 5 m, the area is 25 m^2.

Rectangles

The area of a rectangle is calculated in exactly the same way by multiplying two sides. Again, if the rectangle's sides are measured in metres, the area is expressed in square metres (m^2). So if one side is 5 m long and the other is 10 m, the area of the rectangle is 50 m^2.

Worked example 3.17 shows how you can use these simple calculations to help calculate the area of shapes that look more complicated.

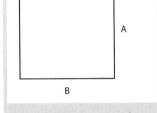

Figure 3.12 A square with sides A and B

Did you know?

An I-beam is also called a Universal Beam or UB, and is considered to be very good at resisting the loads discussed in the first part of the unit. The top and bottom rectangles are called flanges while the middle rectangle is called a web.

Activity 3.13

You want to paint your bedroom. You will have to calculate the wall areas and ceiling area of the room so that you buy the correct quantity of paint needed. Your room measurements are as follows:

- Overall size = 4 m × 5 m
- Height = 2.9 m

There is a window in one of the walls having a size of 1.2 m × 1.2 m. There is a door in another wall measuring 1.1 m × 2.0 m.

Calculate the total area of the room that you need to cover with paint.

Worked example 3.17

Figure 3.13 shows the cross-section of a steel I-beam. Calculate its area in square millimetres (mm^2).

Step 1 Examine the shape and split into simple shapes:

The beam can be split into three rectangles.

The area of each rectangle is calculated.

Total area is worked out by adding all individual areas.

Step 2 Calculate individual areas:

The top and bottom rectangles are similar having a width of 75 mm and height of 7 mm.

Hence their area is:

= 75 × 7 = 525 mm^2 [area of one rectangle]

= 2 × 525 = 1,050 mm^2 [area of both rectangles]

Area of middle rectangle = 130 × 4 = 520 mm^2

Step 3 Calculate the total area by adding all individual areas together:

Total area = 1,050 mm^2 + 520 mm^2

Total area = 1,570 mm^2

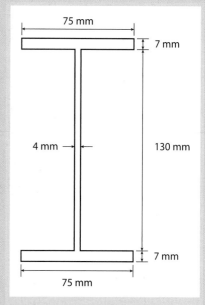

Figure 3.13 A steel I-beam.

Triangles

There are several different types of triangle. You need to know about right-angled triangles, equilateral triangles and irregular or scalene triangles.

Figure 3.14 shows a right-angled triangle. Two of the sides have been measured: A = 5 m and B = 4 m. The dotted lines show how this sort of triangle is half of an imaginary rectangle. To calculate the area of right-angled triangles, multiply the lengths of both sides either side of the right angle and divide by 2 as below:

$$\text{Area} = \frac{(5 \text{ m} \times 4 \text{ m})}{2}$$

$$\text{Area} = \frac{(20 \text{ m}^2)}{2}$$

$$\text{Area} = 10 \text{ m}^2$$

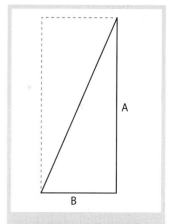

Figure 3.14 A right-angled triangle is half of a rectangle.

To calculate the area of an equilateral triangle, we need to divide it in a way that it forms two right-angled triangles, as shown in Figure 3.15.

To calculate the area of such a triangle, multiply both sides and divide by 2.

$$\text{Area} = \frac{(A \times B)}{2}$$

An irregular or scalene triangle is shown in Figure 3.16. To calculate its area, divide the triangle in a way that it forms two right-angled triangles as shown below. You then use the same formula as given earlier.

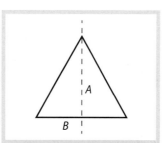

Figure 3.15 An equilateral triangle can be split into two right angled triangles.

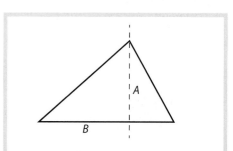

Figure 3.16 An irregular triangle can be split into two right-angled triangles.

Pythagoras' theorem

If you know the length of any two sides of a right-angled triangle, you can calculate the third side by using this theorem.

Consider a right-angled triangle with three sides *a*, *b* and the longest side *c* as shown in Figure 3.17.

According to Pythagoras' theorem:

$$c^2 = a^2 + b^2$$

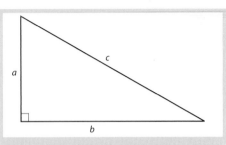

Figure 3.17 A right-angled triangle.

Worked example 3.18

Figure 3.18 shows the gable end of a roof. Calculate the area of the roof so that an estimate of the number of roofing tiles can be made.

Step 1 Examine the diagram and record the data:

We need to find out the length of the sloping side so that we can calculate the area of the roof.

Height = 3.2 m; width = 4.8 m

Step 2 Consider the diagram as two right-angled triangles with three sides. This means that the base of each right-angled triangle is half the width of the original triangle:

$a = 3.2$ m, $b = \dfrac{4.8}{2} = 2.4$, $c = ?$

Step 3 Apply Pythagoras' theorem

$c^2 = 3.2^2 + 2.4^2$

$c^2 = 10.24 + 5.76$

$c^2 = 16$

$c = 4$ m [taking square root of both sides]

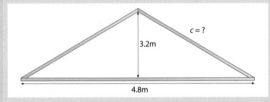

Figure 3.18 The gable end of a roof.

Just checking

1   If the roof is 6 m long, what will be the area of the roof? (Tip: a pitched roof has two sides.)

2   If 1 m² of the roof needs 10 tiles, how many tiles will be needed in total?

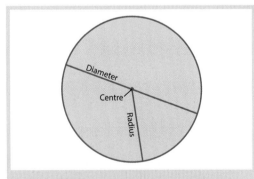

Figure 3.19 Circle showing radius and diameter.

Circles

The width of the circle across its widest point is called its diameter. The radius is half of the diameter and runs from one edge of the circle to its centre, as shown in Figure 3.19.

The area (A) of a circle can be calculated by using the following formula:

$$A = \pi \times r^2$$

Worked example 3.19

Find the cross-sectional area of a drainage pipe, in square millimetres (mm²), having a diameter of 150 mm.

Step 1 Record the data and look for the unknown:

Diameter, d = 150 mm

Area, A = ?

Step 2 Use an appropriate formula:

$A = \pi \times r^2$

Step 3 Work out value of radius, r:

Radius, $r = \dfrac{\text{diameter}}{2}$

$r = \dfrac{150}{2} = 75$ mm

Step 4 Substitute values into the formula:

$A = \pi \times 75^2$

$A = 17671.46$ mm²

✓ **Just checking**

1 Find the cross-sectional area of a drainage pipe, in mm², having a diameter of 380 mm.

2 If the cross-sectional area of a circle is 200 cm², can you find its radius?

Trapezium

Figure 3.20 shows a shape called a trapezium.

The area of a trapezium can be calculated by splitting the shape into a rectangle and two right-angled triangles as shown by the red dashed lines. Combine the red triangles to make one larger triangle with a base ($a - b$). You can then calculate the area of each shape and add these together to find the area of the trapezium.

You can also work out the area of a trapezium using the formula:

$\frac{1}{2} \times h \times (a + b)$

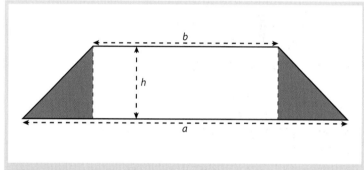

Figure 3.20 Calculating the area of a trapezium.

Worked example 3.20

A piece of land is in the shape of a trapezium. John is constructing a house on this land and has to clear the area before he can start. To find out the cost and time required, John needs to calculate the land area. John has taken some measurements as shown below and is doing calculations.

What answer should John get?

Step 1 Record the data:

a = 20 m, b = 14 m, h = 12 m

Step 2 Split the area into a rectangle and two triangles. Combine the triangles into one larger triangle.

Step 3 Calculate the areas of the triangle and the rectangle.

For the triangle:

$a - b$ = 20 – 14 = 6 m

Area = ½ base × height

Area = ½ ($a - b$) × h

Area = ½ (6 × 12) = 36 m²

For the rectangle:

Area = $b \times h$

Area = 14 × 12 = 168 m²

Step 4 Calculate the total area by adding both areas together.

Area = 36 + 168

Area = 204 m²

Cylinder

A cylinder is like two circles with a vertical height between them. If you know the circle's diameter or radius and its height, as shown in Figure 3.21, you can calculate its surface area.

surface area = area of the top + area of the bottom + area of the side

$A = \pi \times \text{radius}^2 + \pi \times \text{radius}^2 + 2\pi \times \text{radius} \times \text{height}$

$A = \pi \times r^2 + \pi \times r^2 + 2\pi \times r \times h$

$A = 2\pi \times r^2 + 2\pi \times r \times h$

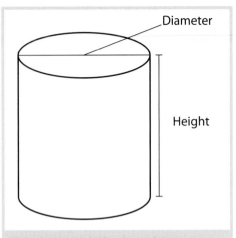

Figure 3.21 A cylinder shape showing diameter and height.

Worked example 3.21

Mark is going to paint a cylinder having a diameter of 450 mm and height of 1.1 m. He wishes to calculate the surface area of the cylinder to estimate the quantity of paint required.

Step 1 Record the data and look for the unknown:

diameter, $d = 450$ mm

height, $h = 1.1$ m

Area, $A = ?$

Step 2 Use an appropriate formula:

$A = 2\pi \times r^2 + 2\pi \times r \times h$

Step 3 Work out value of radius, r:

Radius, $r = $ diameter / 2

$= 450 / 2 = 225$ mm

$= 225$ mm / 1,000 $= 0.225$ m [convert mm to m by dividing 225 mm by 1000]

Step 4 Substitute values into the formula:

$A = 2\pi \times 0.225^2 + 2\pi \times 0.225 \times 1.1$

$A = 1.87$ m²

▶ Volume

Volume is calculated by multiplying three dimensions: length, width and height. If these dimensions are measured in metres, volume is expressed in cubic metres (m³). Figure 3.22 shows a cube with all dimensions measuring 1 m. This means that its volume will be:

volume, $V = 1$ m × 1 m × 1 m

$V = 1$ m³

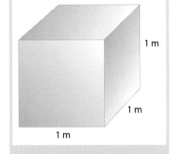

Figure 3.22 A cube with a volume of 1 m³ (1 m × 1 m × 1 m).

Cylinder

To calculate the volume of a cylinder, you need to know its diameter and its height.

Volume = π × radius² × height

$V = \pi \times r2 \times h$

Worked example 3.22

Find the volume of a cylinder having a diameter of 450 mm and height of 1.1 m.

Step 1 Record the data and look for the unknown:

Diameter, $d = 450$ mm; height, $h = 1.1$ m; volume; $V = ?$

Step 2 Use an appropriate formula:

$V = \pi \times r^2 \times h$

Step 3 Work out value of radius, r:

Radius, $r = \dfrac{\text{diameter}}{2}$

$r = \dfrac{450}{2} = 225$ mm

$r = \dfrac{225 \text{ mm}}{1{,}000} = 0.225$ m **[convert mm to m by dividing 225 mm by 1000]**

Step 4 Substitute values into the formula:

$V = \pi \times 0.225^2 \times 1.1$

$V = 0.175$ m³

Cone

A cone is a three-dimensional solid shape. Its base is a circle with a radius (r) while its sides are slanted lines (s) that connects to the top point of the cone, which is called a vertex. The height (h) of a cone is its perpendicular distance from the vertex to the base as shown in Figure 3.23.

As the base is circular, the area of the base is $\pi \times r^2$, while the area of the side is $\pi \times r \times s$. Hence total surface area of a cone is:

Surface area $= (\pi \times r^2) + (\pi \times r \times s)$

Volume of a cone, $V = \frac{1}{3}\pi \times r^2 \times h$

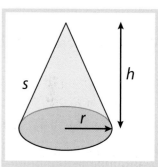

Figure 3.23 A typical cone.

Worked example 3.23

A cone is to be constructed using concrete. It will have a height of 5 m and a base of radius 2 m. Calculate the volume of concrete needed. If the cone is to be painted after construction, what will be its surface area?

Step 1 Record the data and look for the unknown:

Height, $h = 5$ m, radius, $r = 2$ m

Volume, $V = ?$, surface area, $A = ?$

Step 2 Use an appropriate formula:

Volume, $V = \frac{1}{3}\pi \times r^2 \times h$

Surface area, $A = (\pi \times r^2) + (\pi \times r \times s)$

Step 3 Using Pythagoras' theorem, work out the value of s:

$s^2 = 5^2 + 2^2 = 2^5 + 4 = 29$

$s = \sqrt{29}$

$s = 5.39$ m

Step 4 Substitute values into the formula:

$V = \frac{1}{3} \times \pi \times 2^2 \times 5$

$V = 20.94$ m³

$A = (\pi \times r^2) + (\pi \times r \times s)$

$A = (\pi \times 2^2) + (\pi \times 2 \times 5.39)$

$A = 46.4$ m²

Prism

A prism is a solid shape that has a constant cross-section all the way through. For instance, a cylinder is a circular prism. A common prism used in construction calculations is the shape of a pitched roof. The volume of any prism can be calculated by multiplying the cross-sectional area with the length.

Worked example 3.24

Figure 3.24 shows the measurements for a building. Calculate the volume of the loft space.

Step 1 Examine the shape:

The shape of the roof is like a prism with a triangular section.

Step 2 Calculate the area of the cross-section:

Area, $A = ½ (8 × 4)$

$A = 16$ m²

Step 3 Calculate the volume:

Volume = area of cross section × length

Volume = $16 × 10$

Volume = 160 m³

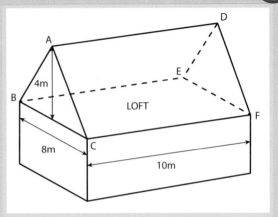

Figure 3.24 The measurements for a building.

Just checking

1 What will be the surface area and volume of the cone in Worked example 3.23 if the height of the cone is increased to 7 m?

2 Calculate the volume of loft space in Worked example 3.24 if the height is reduced from 4 m to 3 m.

▶ Trigonometry

Introduction

Trigonometry is the branch of mathematics that deals with the relationship between the sides and angles of triangles. It is used in construction for many things, including staircase design and when working out the angles of a pitched roof.

Trigonometric functions

Trigonometric functions describe the relationship between angles and length of sides in a triangle.

Consider the right-angled triangle in Figure 3.25. The two sides making a right angle are called the **opposite**

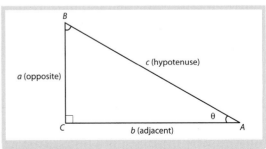

Figure 3.25 A right-angled triangle.

and the **adjacent**. The third side is the **hypotenuse**. The angle at point A is expressed as θ (a Greek letter called theta).

A relationship between the opposite and hypotenuse is called the sine of the angle, or sin θ, and is written as:

$$\sin \theta = \frac{\text{opposite}}{\text{hypotenuse}}$$

A relationship between the adjacent and hypotenuse is called the cosine of the angle, or cos θ, and written as:

$$\cos \theta = \frac{\text{adjacent}}{\text{hypotenuse}}$$

The tangent function relates to slope or gradient: opposite side divided by adjacent side. It is expressed as tan θ and is written as:

$$\tan \theta = \frac{\text{opposite}}{\text{adjacent}}$$

Did you know?

The tangent of an angle can also be worked out when you divide sin θ by cos θ:

$$\tan \theta = \frac{\sin \theta}{\cos \theta}$$

Worked example 3.25

A brick pathway is planned to cross a square garden diagonally, as shown in Figure 3.26. The path will be 20 m long. Using trigonometric functions, calculate the length of each side of the garden.

Step 1 Examine the work area and record the data in the form of a sketch:

Diagonal = 20 m

Length of side = ?

Step 2 Apply appropriate trigonometric function:

Consider that the square is split into two right-angled triangles. You need to solve only one of the two, as they are exactly the same.

Hence the diagonal is the hypotenuse of the triangle. The angle θ is 45°.

You know that:

$$\cos \theta = \frac{\text{adjacent}}{\text{hypotenuse}}$$

You know the hypotenuse is 20 m.

Step 3 Substitute the values:

$$\cos 45° = \frac{\text{adjacent}}{20}$$

$$0.707 = \frac{\text{adjacent}}{20} \ [\cos 45° = 0.707]$$

adjacent = 0.707 × 20 [rearranging formula]

adjacent = 14.14 m

Hence each side of the square is **14.14 m**

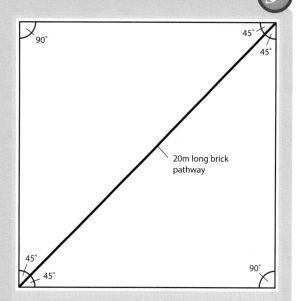

Figure 3.26 A brick pathway crossing a garden.

Just checking

Could you solve Worked example 3.25 using another trigonometric function? Which one(s) could you use?

Did you know?

In a triangle with angles 45°, 45° and 90°, if the sides making the right angle are each of length S, the area can be calculated as $\frac{S^2}{2}$. Look at Worked example 3.24 again – two such triangles make a square.

Worked example 3.26

A building is 60 m away from you. From this distance, you measure the angle to the top of the building which is 30°. What is the height of the building?

Step 1 Record the data in the form of a sketch like Figure 3.27.

Step 2 Apply appropriate trigonometric function:

You know that:

$$\tan \theta = \frac{\text{opposite}}{\text{adjacent}}$$

Step 3 Substitute the values:

$$\tan 30° = \frac{\text{opposite}}{60}$$

$$0.577 = \frac{\text{opposite}}{60} \quad [\tan 30° = 0.577]$$

opposite = 0.577 × 60 [rearranging formula]

opposite = 34.62 m

Hence the building is **34.62 m** high.

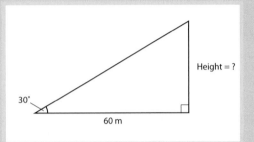

Figure 3.27

Worked example 3.27

A staircase has risers of 180 mm each and goings of 230 mm each, as shown in Figure 3.28. The staircase is made up of 16 risers and 15 goings or treads. Calculate the pitch of the staircase.

Step 1 Calculate the height and length of the staircase:

Height = 16 risers × 180 mm = 2,880 mm

Length = 15 goings × 230 mm = 3,450 mm

Step 2 Calculate the pitch:

Identify the appropriate trigonometric identity.

The angle or pitch can be calculated by using:

$$\tan \theta = \frac{\text{opposite}}{\text{adjacent}}$$

$$\tan \theta = \frac{2,880}{3,450}$$

$$\tan \theta = 0.8348$$

θ = **39.85** [round up to 40°]

θ = **40°**

Hence the pitch of the staircase is 40°.

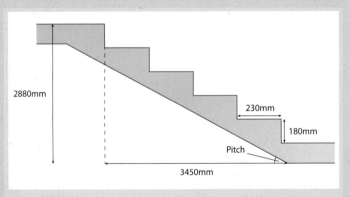

Figure 3.28

Assessment activity 3.2

Maths

What will be the pitch of the staircase in Worked example 3.27 if the height of a riser is 190 mm and the width of a going is 220 mm? Is this acceptable according to the Building Regulations?

WorkSpace

▶ Ellie Wise

Junior design engineer

I'm a junior design engineer working for a local consultant firm. My job involves designing structural elements of buildings such as beams, columns and roofs. I get to work on lots of different projects and I also meet lots of different people. It is an interesting job as every project is different and challenging. I am involved in all stages of designing from client meetings to designing a whole project. In time, I hope to become a design engineer and take responsibility for a project of my own.

Having a good knowledge of mathematics and science is really valuable in my job. Mathematics helps me to do all the calculations such as areas and volumes as well as applying trigonometry, especially for roof structures. Without a good knowledge of science and construction materials as well, I wouldn't know what materials to choose for various parts of the structure as all materials have different properties.

All this knowledge has helped me to talk confidently to our clients and to explain technical details. It gives them confidence in me too!

Think about it

1 Why do you think it is important for everyone who works in the construction industry to know about mensuration?

2 How do you think the information about the properties of materials could benefit Ellie in her job?

3 What sorts of characteristics do you think a design engineer needs to have?

4 Is this a job you would be interested in? If so, why?

Introduction

Planning is vital in construction. Having a plan in place means construction tasks will be done in a sensible order. It also allows work to start and finish on time, to budget and to the necessary quality. Part of this quality is managed through using the right types of materials. Materials can be natural, processed or manufactured.

Once planned, construction work starts. Buildings are constructed using traditional as well as modern methods of construction. These modern methods are becoming more and more popular, as they are quicker than traditional methods.

Understanding and applying the knowledge of sequencing, materials and construction processes is really important as it is used in almost all job roles in construction, including plumbing, site managing and planning.

Assessment: You will be assessed by a series of assignments set by your teacher/tutor.

Learning aims

In this unit you will:

A understand planning and sequencing of construction work

B know about traditional and modern construction processes and operations used in low-rise construction

C understand the properties and uses of construction materials.

> This unit was great. It was really interesting to learn how a project is planned – I never knew how complicated it was. I also enjoyed learning about the different materials that buildings were made of and how they work, which is one of the reasons I decided to take this course in the first place.
>
> Luke, *16-year-old BTEC student*

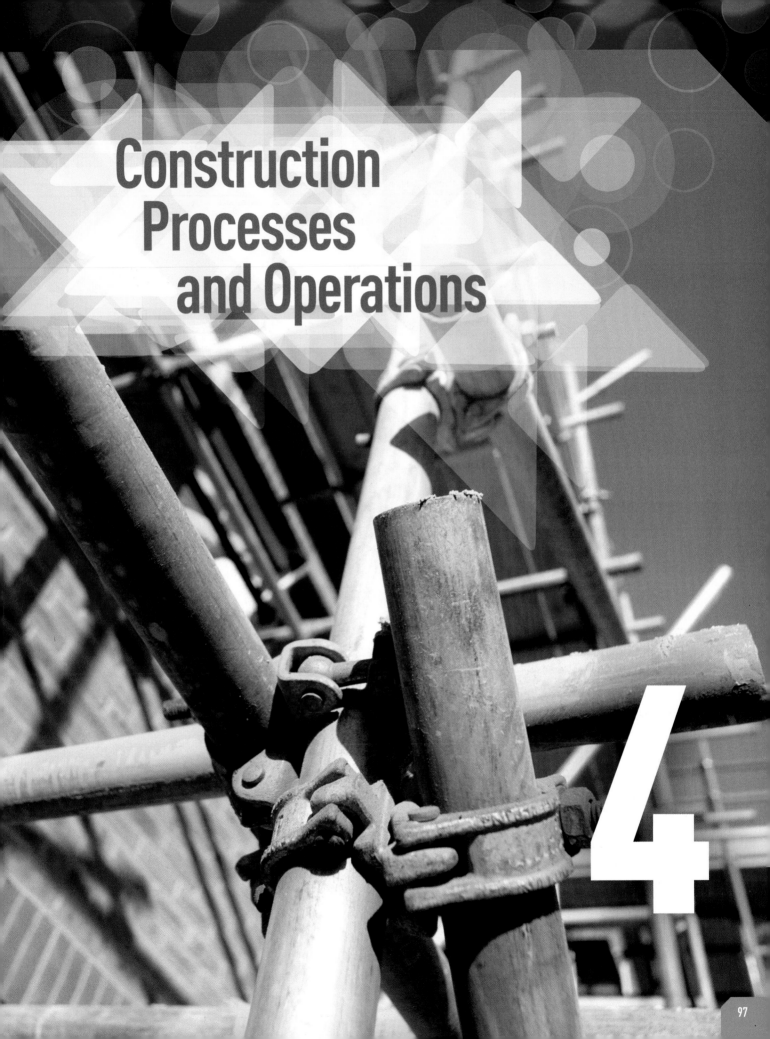

Construction Processes and Operations

Assessment Zone

This table shows what you must do in order to achieve a **Pass**, **Merit** or **Distinction** grade, and where you can find activities in this book to help you.

Assessment criteria			
Level 1	Level 2 **Pass**	Level 2 **Merit**	Level 2 **Distinction**
Learning aim A: Understand planning and sequencing of construction work			
1A.1 Outline the construction stages for a low-rise building.	**2A.P1** Describe the construction stages for a low-rise building. **See Assessment activity 4.1, page 108**	**2A.M1** Explain the construction stages and operations for a low-rise building. **See Assessment activity 4.1, page 108**	
1A.2 Outline the construction operations for a low-rise building.	**2A.P2** Describe the construction operations for a low-rise building. **See Assessment activity 4.1, page 108**		
1A.3 List the sequence of construction operations for a low-rise building.	**2A.P3** Explain the importance of sequencing construction operations for a low-rise building. **See Assessment activity 4.1, page 108**	**2A.M2** Analyse the sequence of construction operations in relation to the problems caused by inappropriate planning and sequencing of construction operations. **See Assessment activity 4.1, page 108**	**2A.D1** Evaluate the sequence of construction operations in relation to the effects of production problems and unforeseen events on productivity and cost for a low-rise building. **See Assessment activity 4.1, page 108**
Learning aim B: Know about traditional and modern construction processes and operations used in low-rise construction			
1B.4 Identify key elements of a low-rise building.	**2B.P4** Describe functional requirements of key elements in low-rise buildings. **See Assessment activity 4.2, page 118**		
1B.5 Outline the processes and operations used in traditional methods of construction.	**2B.P5** Explain the processes and operations used in traditional methods of construction. **See Assessment activity 4.2, page 118**	**2B.M3** Compare traditional and modern construction operations and processes. **See Assessment activity 4.2, page 118**	**2B.D2** Evaluate traditional and modern construction operations and processes. **See Assessment activity 4.2, page 118**
1B.6 Outline the processes and operations used in modern methods of construction.	**2B.P6** Explain the processes and operations used in modern methods of construction. **See Assessment activity 4.2, page 118**		

Level 1	Level 2 **Pass**	Level 2 **Merit**	Level 2 **Distinction**
Learning aim C: Understand the properties and uses of construction materials			
1C.7 Classify construction materials as natural, processed or manufactured	**2C.P7** Describe the construction materials as natural, processed or manufactured. **See Assessment activity 4.3, page 124**	**2C.M4** Explain how the properties of a natural, a processed and a manufactured construction material determine their performance in use. **See Assessment activity 4.3, page 124**	**2C.D3** Justify the specification of two different construction materials and their performance for use in two different situations. **See Assessment activity 4.3, page 124**
1C.8 Identify the properties of common construction materials.	**2C.P8** Describe the properties of common construction materials. **See Assessment activity 4.3, page 124**		

How you will be assessed

The unit will be assessed by a series of internally assessed tasks. You will be expected to show an understanding of planning and sequencing of construction work, as well as properties of common construction materials. You will compare the construction methods of traditional and modern buildings.

Your actual assessment could be in the form of:

- a written report to include text, diagrams, tables, and graphs as appropriate, as well as oral questioning
- group presentations on material properties and their uses, as well as sequencing and planning of construction activities.

▶ Construction operations

Introduction

In this topic you will learn about the different stages of a construction project. Most construction operations, such as brickwork and blockwork or carpentry, usually happen at the same stage of construction, even on very different projects. After all, it would be very unusual to install a staircase before the walls had been constructed on any project! Understanding these stages and the sequence in which they occur is important when planning a project, estimating costs and carrying out the actual construction.

▶ Stages of low-rise construction

Setting up a site

First of all, a site has to be set up before construction can start. This involves making the site safe and creating welfare facilities for workers like kitchen and toilet facilities. A well-planned site means that work can progress smoothly and safely.

When you are planning, you should consider:

- accommodation – such as offices, welfare facilities and plant rooms
- storage of materials – in open areas or in sheds? How much material will you have on site at one time and does it need to be covered?
- car parking – how many people will be working on site every day? Could you get visitors like planning officers who will need to park?
- security of the site – what sort of lighting, CCTV, fencing and signs will you need?
- temporary services – such as water, electricity and communication links. Will you need a generator?
- disposal of waste – how much waste do you think you might have and how will you remove it?

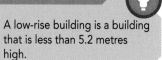

Remember

A low-rise building is a building that is less than 5.2 metres high.

Discussion

What sort of effect could poor planning have on the later stages of a construction project?

Activity 4.1

You are planning the construction of a new housing development in your town. As part of your setting up, you need to think about where you are going to store your materials, which will include:

- bricks and blocks
- wooden floorboards
- steel I-beams
- plastic guttering.
- cement

Now decide what you will need to store in sheds or under cover.

Groundwork

This involves clearing the site, removing topsoil and digging up the bushes and trees so that work can start, including demolishing existing buildings on the site. The topsoil is then removed so that construction work starts on firm, level ground.

Site clearance in progress.

Sub-structure

The sub-structure is the underlying structure of a building. It includes all the works below floor level like foundations and drains. A very important operation at this stage of the project is the **excavation** and construction of the foundations.

Superstructure

The superstructure is all the parts of a building above ground level, including walls, floors and roof. Internal services such as gas, electricity, telecommunication, drainage and hot and cold water are added during this stage.

External works

This is the additional work done around the building. It includes the construction of paved areas and driveways as well as garden landscaping. It also includes routing in utilities such as gas, electricity, drainage, telecommunications and water.

Finishes

These finishes are the final works that finish the building. This includes the installation of suspended ceilings and the flooring, as well as painting, decorating and tiling.

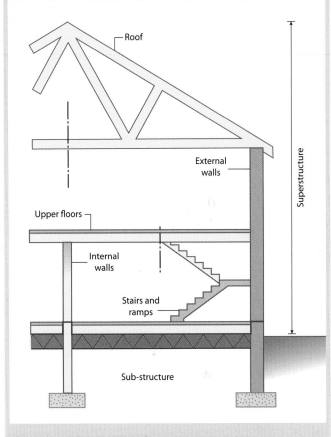

Figure 4.1 Sub-structure and superstructure.

Link

For more about the sub-structure and the superstructure, see *Unit 1: Construction Technology*.

Activity 4.2

Look at Figure 4.1. Now cover the diagram and list three parts of the building that are included in the superstructure.

Link

To learn more about brickwork and blockwork, see *Unit 7: Exploring Brickwork and Blockwork Principles and Techniques.*

Key terms

Mortar – a mixture of cement, sand, lime and water. It is used to join bricks and blocks together.

Bond – an arrangement of bricks and blocks. The term is also used to describe how various courses of brick or block work are joined together.

Did you know?

- A brick is usually 215 mm long, 102.5 mm wide and 65 mm deep.
- A block is normally 440 mm long, 215 mm high and 100 mm wide.
- Mortar is normally laid 10 mm deep.

▶ Construction operations

Before you can start planning a construction project, you also have to know about the operations that are part of each stage of construction. These involve different skills and specialist trades people, so you will have to think about them when thinking about the timing of project tasks.

The three key activities in most construction projects are:

- brickwork and blockwork
- carpentry and joinery
- roofing.

Brickwork and blockwork

This involves the construction of walls. Traditionally, the external walls are constructed in two halves or skins. The outer half or skin is constructed in brickwork while the inner half or skin is constructed in blockwork. The two layers give good insulation.

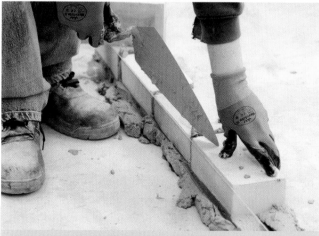

'Laying to line' is a method of making sure your brickwork is straight. The line is the yellow string in this photograph.

Bricks and blocks are laid in layers called courses using cement sand **mortar** (this is how ratios are referred to in construction). The mortar gives an even surface for the courses and joins the bricks or blocks together.

The **bond** is the pattern of bricks, which gives the wall its strength and stability. Bonds commonly used in brickwork and blockwork include:

- the stretcher bond, which has only stretchers
- the English bond, which has alternate stretcher and header courses
- the Flemish bond, which has both headers and stretchers in the same course.

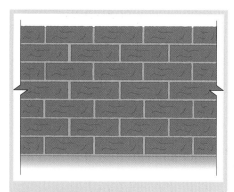

Figure 4.2 Stretcher bond.

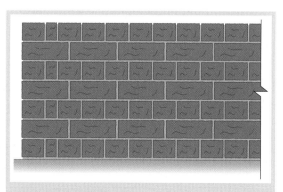

Figure 4.3 English bond.

Figure 4.4 Flemish bond.

Carpentry and joinery

This is another very common operation and involves working with timber on tasks such as installing window and door frames and staircases, and fixing and assembling floors and roofs. It also includes wooden finishes such as laminate flooring. Usually, a joiner makes an item in the workshop and a carpenter installs it on site.

Roofing

Roofers install **roofing battens**, attach the **roofing felt** and tile the roof. Roofing work starts quite early in the construction stage so that the building is weatherproof before work begins inside.

Roofs can be flat or sloping (pitched) depending upon the building's needs and local climate.

The roof is finished by fixing roof tiles to the wooden battens. There is a wide variety of tile types such as single and double lap. Finally, the roof space is insulated to keep the house warm.

Painting and decorating

Living in an undecorated house would not be very nice. Paints are applied to interior and exterior surfaces including walls, doors, ceilings and skirtings. Painting surfaces, such as walls, makes them more attractive. It can also be done for special reasons, such as making surfaces resistant to water or mould. Painting involves applying wet paint to a surface with rollers or brushes, which then dries to form a perfect coating.

Decorating is the application of wall coverings using wallpapers. Wallpapers come in a range of finishes, including raised patterns, soft textures and washable coatings.

Concrete work

Concrete is a mixture of cement, sand, **aggregates** and water. These materials are mixed in varying proportions. The strength of concrete depends on the ratio used to make concrete.

Concrete can be used to construct foundations, beams and columns, as well as under the floors to give a firm base for their construction. It can be mixed on site or can be ordered ready-mixed.

Painting and decorating.

Link

To learn more about carpentry and joinery, look at *Unit 6: Exploring Carpentry and Joinery Principles and Techniques*.

Key terms

Roofing battens – strips of wood fixed to rafters, used to attach roof tiles to a roof.

Roofing felt – a protective layer between the actual roof structure and the building. It is made up of waterproof materials.

Aggregates – an aggregate is a mixture of pieces of crushed stone and gravel. They are used in making concrete as well as more generally in construction activities.

Did you know?

Tiles are usually fixed to a roof in an overlapping pattern. This allows water to run off the roof without letting the water in through the joins between the tiles. This overlap can be single or double depending on the type of tiles. Natural slates are normally fixed as double lap tiles.

Link

If you want to know more about painting and decorating, see *Unit 8: Exploring Painting and Decorating Principles and Techniques*.

Stonemasonry

Stonemasonry is a highly skilled craft. It involves working with stone in construction activities, such as creating stone walls and columns as well as interior features such as fireplaces. From construction of walls to producing various architectural features and patterns, stonemasons have to be very precise to produce a good-quality product.

Floor, wall and ceiling finishes

Like painting and decorating, this makes the interior of a building pleasing to look at and comfortable to live in. Floor finishes range from carpets to wooden and vinyl flooring. Walls and ceilings can be either painted or decorated in a range of finishes.

Plumbing and heating

This includes laying and installing pipes, fittings, fixtures and equipment to supply hot and cold water, drainage and heating in a building.

Electrical installation

This includes wiring buildings to give light and warmth, as well as connecting power appliances such as televisions and refrigerators.

Activity 4.3

1 Research the construction of a new house on a greenfield site.
2 Create a presentation to give to the rest of the group, covering various stages of construction as well as the operations carried out during each stage.

Just checking

1 List three operations that are carried out during brickwork and blockwork.
2 Make a list of the ceiling, floor and wall finishes in your classroom.

▶ Sequencing and planning

Introduction

Good planning is essential for the success of any building project. Planning involves a systematic way of working through what needs to be done, how it would be done and when it should be completed. In this section, you will learn about the order in which construction activities are carried out and how these are planned.

▶ What is a plan?

Most of us make plans all the time in our lives. You almost certainly planned to take this course. You want to work in the construction industry, so you planned to take this BTEC.

So what exactly is a plan in construction?

In construction, planning is vital. From simple tasks such as carrying materials from the factory to the site to complex operations like building the Olympic village, all construction activities need a plan. Without planning, success is almost impossible.

Activity 4.4

Make a list of all the plans you have made over the past five days and then answer the following questions:

1 Did you do everything that you planned to do?
2 Who else was involved in the planning?
3 Did you have to make any changes to your plans to allow for unforeseen circumstances?
4 How did you communicate your plans to other people involved?

▶ How to plan

Project planning should start as soon as the client has the initial idea for the project. It continues until the final handover of the building, as well as during a set period of time after construction, where the builder is responsible for any defects. This is called the defects liability period.

To plan, the project is divided into small parts or tasks. Each task is planned first and then added to the overall plan.

Construction projects need tools to plan and control them, to ensure they run to time and budget. They also need methods for taking action if things do not work out.

? Did you know?

Project planning is a specialist area of construction. Professionals called construction planners use computer software to make sure everybody knows their job and that their work is communicated to everyone involved.

Gantt charts

A Gantt chart shows the time allocated to each task or activity in the construction process (see Figure 4.5). The time can be given in hours, days or weeks.

Gantt charts give the order of activities so it is obvious which tasks need to be done before the next task can be started. Gantt charts also show which activities can be done at the same time. This means that they can be used as the schedule and the order of work.

Interpreting Gantt charts is an important skill for anyone working on a project. You need to know the sequence of activities as well as time allocated.

Figure 4.5 shows part of the Gantt chart for the construction of a bungalow. The time is given in weeks and the time taken to complete each activity is shown as a bar. The longer the bar is, the more time will be needed to complete the activity.

For instance, in Figure 4.5, the bar against site set-up is only one week long. In comparison, the construction of the concrete foundations starts in week 6 and the bar is five weeks long so the activity will be complete by the end of week 10.

Project: Factory extension

Contract Activity	Duration Week Nr
Site set up	1
Excavation	3
Concrete fnds	5
Hardcore flr slb	4
Erect steelwork	2
Clad roof	2
Concrete flr slab	2
Clad walls	3
Brickwork walls	8
Doors and frames	1
Drainage	4/5
Painting	4
Electrical Instn	5
Heating Instn	2
External Landscaping	7
Clean & handover	3

Figure 4.5 What do you think are the benefits of Gantt charts? Can you see any drawbacks?

▶ Sequencing activities

Sequencing is when you arrange activities in the most logical way. A Gantt chart sequences activities in the order that they are started, so each activity relates to the activities around them.

Some activities cannot start until the time the previous one is completed. In Figure 4.5, the cladding of the roof cannot start until the steelwork is in place.

Some activities can be done at the same time. For example, Figure 4.5 shows that although the brickwork walls will take five weeks to complete, wall cladding, drainage installation and other tasks can happen while the brickwork walls are being built. This means that the schedule is as efficient as possible.

Figure 4.5 shows part of a Gantt chart for the construction of a bungalow. Look at it and then answer the following questions:

1 When will painting start?

2 How long will electrical installation take to complete?

3 When will drainage be complete?

4 What other activities will happen at the same time as heating installation?

5 Why do you think drainage starts so early and happens in two phases?

6 How many weeks will it take before painting is complete?

Advantages and disadvantages

Gantt charts are very popular with construction professionals. This is because they:

- are easy to use
- give a visual understanding of the project activities
- show the sequence of activities
- are helpful when planning to arrange labour, **plant** and materials
- help monitor progress.

However, for larger projects, Gantt charts can be confusing as all the activities cannot fit on one page.

▶ Production problems and unforeseen events

You may have to deal with a number of problems during a project. These include problems such as bad weather, a shortage of materials or **industrial action** by lorry drivers or other construction workers. Things might go wrong with the construction, such as the collapse of foundation trenches or a plumbing leak. The site might also be flooded, robbed or vandalised.

Because there are many possible problems, careful planning helps you to:

- foresee these potential problems
- make these problems less likely to happen – for instance, by fitting good locks to the site gates
- make alternative plans in case these problems do happen – for example, finding several suppliers of a needed material.

This means that, even if something does go wrong, the project will probably still complete on time. Planning also helps you keep an eye on the progress of work so that action can be taken if things are held up. This will help to make sure the project does not finish late.

Key terms

Plant – machinery used in the construction process, such as bulldozers and excavators.

Industrial action – protest action taken by the employees of a company or organisation, such as striking.

Just checking

1 Why is planning so important when preparing for a construction project?

2 How does a Gantt chart represent time against particular activities?

3 When do you think a Gantt chart would not be suitable?

Remember

'If you fail to plan, then you plan to fail.'

You are a trainee planner with a local construction firm that is planning to construct a house. Your manager has listed a number of activities for the project. Now put them in the correct sequence.

Code	Activity	Days
A	2nd fix carpentry	3
B	Decorating	5
C	Install timber first floor	3
D	Excavate and lay foundations	5
E	Erect timber truss roof	3
F	Final clean	1
G	Fit uPVC fascia and soffit	3
H	Tile roof	4
J	Install external windows and doors	3
K	Construct sub-structure masonry	4
L	Construct metal studwork internal walls	3
M	Install staircase	1

Code	Activity	Days
N	2nd fix electrics	2
O	Conduct 2nd lift superstructure masonry	8
P	1st fix plumbing	2
Q	1st fix electrics	2
R	Construct suspended ground floor	6
S	2nd fix plumbing	2
T	Connect services	2
U	Install bathrooms	4
V	Construct 1st lift superstructure masonry	8
W	Install kitchen	3
X	Dry-lining	5

Now that the project is under way, there have been some problems on site. Read the problems listed below and answer the questions, before evaluating each problem's effect on sequencing and your schedule.

1 The plumbers started installing bathrooms last week but the services still have not been connected. Will this delay the completion of the project? What could you do to avoid any delay?

2 While installing roof tiles, a worker fell and was injured. There was no emergency plan and nobody on the site knew what to do, so there was a delay in taking the worker to hospital. This delay added an extra few days to his recovery. The lack of a plan also took up valuable time, as several members of staff had to work out what to do. The result is compensation payments and delay in work. What could you do to avoid this sort of thing happening again?

3 What is the earliest point that Activities E and H could happen? What will happen if you leave these activities until Activity X is complete?

4 Three weeks after the project started, the site was hit by heavy snow. This was followed by heavy rain, which caused flooding on site. How can you remedy this situation?

Tips

- Remember to explain why it is important to organise the project so that the activities are in the right order.
- Think about the importance of each activity in comparison to the importance of other activities.
- Think about what might go wrong in each activity. The best answers will keep in mind the impact of possible unforeseen events on their project's budget and schedule.

▶ Key elements of low-rise buildings and their functions

Introduction

A building is made up of number of parts or elements. Each element has its own specific function. Some elements give support to the structure of the building, while others make the building comfortable to live or work in.

▶ Key elements and their functions

Foundations

The foundations of a building are the lowest level of the building and are usually below the ground. They support the **load** of the building above by spreading the pressure over a large area. The soil on which a building is constructed can take some of this load. Spreading the load through the foundations uses the soil strength and means you do not have to spend extra money on more materials.

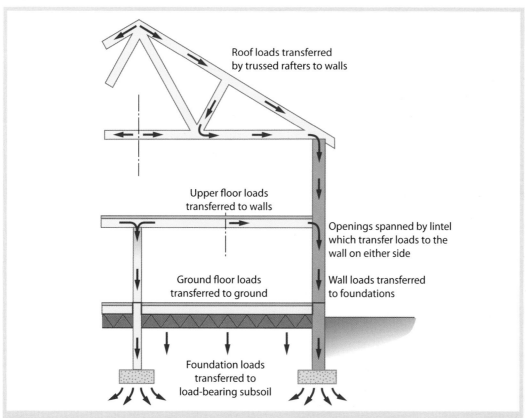

Roof loads transferred by trussed rafters to walls

Upper floor loads transferred to walls

Openings spanned by lintel which transfer loads to the wall on either side

Ground floor loads transferred to ground

Wall loads transferred to foundations

Foundation loads transferred to load-bearing subsoil

Figure 4.6 Loads from walls and floors are supported and spread out by the foundations.

Link

For more about these key elements of buildings and their functions, see *Unit 1: Construction Technology*.

Key term

Load – this is the weight that an element of a building has to bear.

Link

For more about loads, see *Unit 3: Scientific and Mathematical Applications for Construction*.

Activity 4.6

In pairs, look at Figure 4.6. Now describe to your partner how loads are transferred to the ground.

There are four types of foundations:

- strip foundations – these are shaped like a strip. These are the most common types used in low-rise construction like the construction of a house. These are designed to support the loads of continuous walls and transmit it to the ground.
- pad foundations – these support loads from columns and piers and transmit these loads to the ground. This sort of foundation is like a concrete pad or slab supporting a column, normally in the middle of the pad.
- raft foundations – these take the load from the whole building and transfer it to the ground. These are more expensive than strip or pad foundations. These are used when soil conditions are poor or variable.
- pile foundations – these are constructed when soil is very weak to support the load. Through piles, load is transferred deeper into the ground to a stronger base.

Link

To see what these foundations look like, see page 22 of *Unit 1: Construction Technology*.

Research

Using the internet, find out what sort of buildings might use each of these four types of foundation.

Floors

Floors make a building functional, allowing people to move around inside it. They also make it **habitable**, supporting any interior features and furniture. They are usually level, horizontal surfaces designed to:

- support both live loads (moving pressures like people, furniture and movable equipment) and dead loads (unmoving pressures like the weight of the floor itself or the building)
- safely transfer these loads to either beams, columns or directly to the ground
- stop moisture from coming into the building from the ground
- fit in runs of mechanical and electrical lines
- give sound and thermal insulation
- be safe against fire.

A **solid floor** is a solid concrete slab resting directly on the ground.

Suspended floors do not rest directly on the ground, but are supported by beams or joists. These can be constructed using a variety of materials, including concrete and timber.

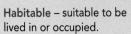

Key term

Habitable – suitable to be lived in or occupied.

Link

Floors are discussed in more detail in *Unit 1: Construction Technology*.

Activity 4.7

In groups, discuss the following questions.

1 Why do floors have to give sound insulation?
2 What kind of building would need this insulation most?

Walls

Walls enclose our living spaces to provide comfort and protect us from the weather. They also allow us to build structures with more than one floor or storey, by supporting the loads from the upper storeys. Walls can be:

- load-bearing walls – these are designed to take the load from other parts of the building. Usually, the external walls and some of the internal walls are load-bearing walls

- non-load-bearing walls – these are only designed to enclose a space and are not capable of taking any load from other parts of the building

- cavity walls – these are made up of two halves called leaves or skins, with a gap or cavity in between. External walls are generally constructed as cavity walls. The cavity stops moisture from travelling into the building and is usually filled with insulating materials to keep the building warm.

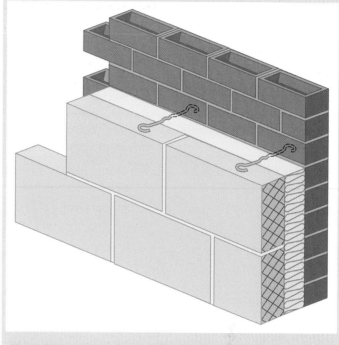

Figure 4.7 A cavity wall filled with insulation.

Roofs

Like walls, roofs make buildings comfortable and weatherproof. Roofs need a system of drains, gutters and downpipes to drain rainwater and melting snow. Roofs can either be constructed as flat or sloping (pitched).

Roofs are designed to:

- cover the internal space of a building, making it weatherproof
- look attractive
- resist the force of wind and other weather
- take both dead loads, such as its own weight, and live loads, such as people moving over it
- protect against heat and cold.

Doors

Doors give access to a building from the outside. They also allow movement between rooms in a building. A door gives privacy, weather resistance (for exterior doors), sound reduction and fire resistance. Doors can be made from a variety of materials such as timber and glass. They can be made to open, swing, slide or fold.

Windows

Windows allow natural light into a building and let fresh air circulate. Like doors, they can open in a variety of ways: swinging, hanging or sliding. Windows are installed in window frames, which are made from a variety of materials such as timber and plastic.

Links

Cavity walls are discussed in more detail in *Unit 1: Construction Technology* and *Unit 7: Exploring Brickwork and Blockwork Principles and Techniques*.

Flat and pitched roofs are covered in more detail in *Unit 1: Construction Technology*.

Discussion

Do you think that roofs should look attractive?

Stairs

A staircase gives safe access from one level of a building to another. Stairs can be constructed using a variety of materials, including timber and concrete. Each step is made up of a riser (the vertical part) and a going (the horizontal part). A staircase is designed so that all risers (the vertical part of a step) and goings (the horizontal part of a step) are the same size.

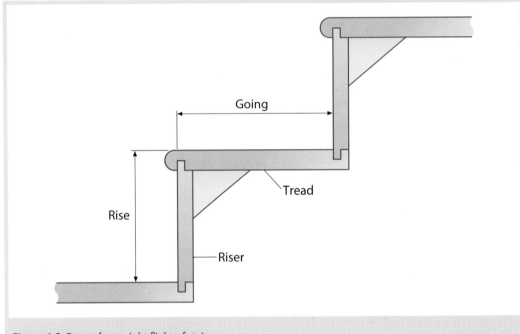

Figure 4.8 Parts of a straight flight of stairs.

Services

Various services are provided in a building. These include:

- clean water for drinking, washing and cleaning purposes
- drainage for **foul water** and **surface water**
- electricity and gas.

Activity 4.8

Think about the key elements of your house, school or college. Identify and describe the functional requirements of two of these elements. Remember that the functional requirements are what an element needs before it can work properly.

Create a presentation using your findings.

▶ Traditional construction of low-rise buildings

Introduction

In this topic, you will learn about the processes and activities that are part of traditional construction. In a traditional project, materials are brought to site and either mixed and put in place to create the building. Some components are made in a factory, such as windows and doors, and installed on site. This section discusses processes to construct traditional buildings.

▶ Processes and operations

Setting up a site

In a project using traditional construction methods, setting up a site will include the following considerations:

- the size and position of the site will help in deciding the entrance and exit points – these should be kept to a minimum to keep control over what comes in and goes out
- try to avoid access points on roads that are narrow, fast or busy
- the size of the entrance is decided by the size of the largest item that will need to fit through it.

The size and layout of the site will usually decide the route of your roadway. Having a one-way system helps to control the site traffic. You will need to leave space for turning and unloading of site vehicles, as well as adequate parking space. If an entrance or exit will cross a public footpath, you must have permission from the local authority.

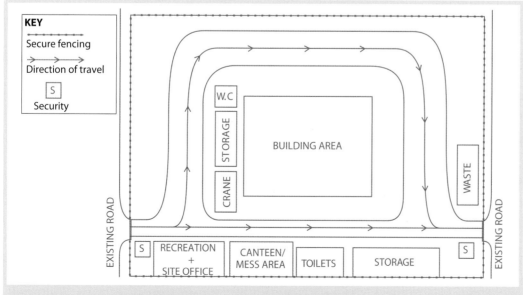

Figure 4.9 Creating a site plan can help you foresee any possible problems.

Look at Figure 4.9. This is a site plan for an apartment block. There is a primary school to the south-west of the site. There is also a busy road to the east of the site, running roughly north–south. In groups, discuss where you would put the site entrance and exit. Remember to explain why you made your choices.

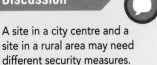

Discussion

A site in a city centre and a site in a rural area may need different security measures. What differences can you think of?

Activity 4.10

Look again at Figure 4.9.

1 Suggest space to store materials.

2 Identify the security arrangements.

3 Suggest a location for welfare facilities.

The site should have a suitable security fence, plenty of lighting and CCTV cameras. Further security arrangements will depend on factors such as the type of project and the location of the site.

Safety notices should be visible to anyone working, visiting or passing the site. Clear signposting is also needed to make sure that people entering and leaving the site know exactly where they are going.

Materials storage

How you store your materials on site depends on what kind of materials you are using and the quantity. This will also affect where you store the materials.

Figure 4.10 Why is it important that passers-by can see site safety notices?

Setting out a building

Setting out is where you mark out the shape of a building on the ground. It transfers the sizes from the drawings to the site. Setting out is an essential process for any building.

First, a baseline is set out. From this line, the measurements can be taken. The main building lines are then marked out using stakes and twine. These should be checked using a steel tape.

On-site craft operations

Traditional buildings projects usually involve a lot of on-site craft operations. These on-site activities normally include:

- the use of in-situ concrete – either mixed on site or bought ready-mixed, to be used in foundations or under floors
- brickwork and blockwork – to construct the walls of the building
- roofing works – this includes tiling and insulating the roof
- carpentry and joinery – to produce elements such as the door frames
- finishes, such as painting, decorating and tiling
- service installations, including for gas, electricity and water.

Activity 4.11

You need to explain processes and operations in traditional construction. To help you do this, use the table below to list some of the activities carried out on buildings made using traditional methods. Fill in the craft operatives and materials used in columns 2 and 3. In the last column, list the sequence of the activities.

Activity	Craft operative	Materials needed	Sequence of work
Excavate and lay foundations			
Construct suspended ground floor			
Construct superstructure masonry			
Erect timber truss roof			
Install staircase			

Understanding the impact of traditional production

Traditional construction methods primarily rely on a large number of labourers attending site every day until the project is finished. Some components are made in a factory, brought to site and installed at a suitable stage. However, most of the work is done by the labour on site with the help of suitable plant and materials.

Activity 4.12

1 A housing estate with 50 houses is being built in your local area. The builder is using traditional methods of construction. What problems can you foresee for people living in the area?

2 You wish to reduce the waste and noise on this project. Which activities would you change to do this?

Traditional production needs lots of space for site accommodation and material storage facilities. As all operations are carried out on site, the work can be delayed due to a number of factors – for example, bad weather affecting productivity on site. Due to the longer time taken and the quantity of labour needed, on-site operations are more expensive. Quality control is another issue on such projects.

▶ Modern construction of low-rise buildings

Introduction

Modern construction relies heavily on making the components of a building in advance and ordering these in good time. The aim is to improve quality while reducing the environmental impact and time spent on a project.

Did you know?

The person who sets out a building using modern equipment is called a site engineer.

▶ Site set-up and setting out

Site set-up for modern construction projects is not as extensive as for traditional ones. All the site facilities mentioned in the previous section are provided, though material storage is kept to a minimum.

The key difference between traditional and modern construction is the degree of accuracy needed when setting out a building. As components in a modern build are made off-site, there is hardly any room for error: whatever you have ordered should fit in precisely. Computer programs and even satellite technology can be used to set out a building correctly.

Did you know?

If all new houses built in the UK since 1945 had been timber-framed houses, it is thought that more than 300 million tonnes of carbon dioxide would have been saved.

▶ Frame construction

Frame construction is a method of building that relies on a frame as a basic means of structural support, and framed buildings are often referred to as lightweight construction. Frames can be made using timber, concrete or steel. Some of the features of frame construction are that they:

- are made with the highest level of accuracy and quality
- simplify on-site construction
- give greater control to the construction process
- improve construction health and safety
- have fewer defects and high customer satisfaction
- are easy to build.

Key term

Fabrication – another word for manufacturing.

▶ Off-site fabrication and modular construction

Think about dividing a building into a number of parts. These are made at various place and assembled on site. The parts are called modules (an example of a modular building is shown opposite).

These modules and other components are made off site. They are then brought to the site and are erected and fixed in place using lifting equipment. This means that far less time and labour is needed on site to finish a project.

A modular building. Can you see how this technique might be beneficial?

Some buildings may be constructed completely off site, with all the services installed, and just be assembled on site. In other cases, most elements such as structural frames are made off site. Even the roof can be constructed in parts or sections.

Non-load-bearing curtain walling

Curtain walls are made of glass and are designed to enclose the space and to give protection only. These walls do not take any load. As they are non-structural, they are lightweight. Curtain walls allow natural light into the building and are therefore pleasing to look at.

Cladding

Cladding is enclosing a building using prefabricated panels. The cladding panels can give the traditional look to a brick-faced building.

A modern building with wood cladding.

Lightweight demountable internal partitions

These are made of lightweight materials and can be taken down and moved to a new location. They usually have a permanent finish, which needs no decoration. These partitions divide the internal space quickly and can be fixed or sliding.

Integrated services

Modern buildings fit in a wide range of increasingly complex services in addition to water, gas, drainage and electricity, such as broadband and high-speed data cables. These services are **integrated** in to components such as raised access floors.

Just-in-time delivery

If the project is well planned, a manufacturer can be asked to deliver the components on site on the day and even at the exact time when they are going to be installed. This is known as just-in-time delivery. This approach needs precise planning and coordination between the project staff and the manufacturer. When just-in-time delivery is managed well, it means that the site does not need to waste space or labour to store materials.

Key term

Integrated – to become a part of something.

Benefits and downsides of off-site production

Before a decision is made whether a building is to be constructed using off-site construction, an **evaluation** needs to be carried out. This means that the benefits and downsides of this type of construction have to be looked at and considered.

Benefits of off-site production

- No storage is needed as components are brought to site just-in-time.
- Off-site manufacture reduces the need to work at height, making accidents on site less likely.
- Less time is needed to complete the project as components can be ordered to be made according to the timescale of the plan.
- Local environmental conditions are improved, as less site work means less noise and dust.
- Off-site manufacture is under factory conditions, where there will be minimum waste produced.
- Due to factory-controlled conditions, the quality of the finished product is much higher.
- Less skilled on-site labour is needed. On-site productivity is also improved because pre-made items are quicker to build.

Possible downsides of off-site construction

- It can take a long time to make and deliver the components.
- Excellent management skills are needed to coordinate the project activities.
- Reliability of the products is an issue in terms of how well they perform when used.
- The cost of the components can be very high.

Assessment activity 4.2

1 Make a list of activities carried out during construction of a building using modern methods. Explain each activity.
2 Using the table below, complete the following tasks.
  - Identify which components of the building you can make off site.
- Which activities will not be needed as a result of this?
- How much time could you save on the project, with these changes?
- Would you have to face any challenges?
- Discuss in your group and present your findings.

Activity	Craft operative	Materials needed	Sequence of work
Excavate and lay foundations			
Construct suspended ground floor			
Construct superstructure masonry			
Erect timber truss roof			
Install staircase			

▶ Common construction materials

Introduction

The construction of buildings needs people to use and deal with a large variety of materials. These materials can be naturally occurring and can be used as they are, while other materials have to be made.

▶ Natural materials

Natural materials can be used in their natural form. These include:

- timber – this is taken from trees and can be grouped into softwoods and hardwoods.
- stone – this is quarried from rock beds. There are various varieties of rock, including granite, sandstone and limestone.

Research

Lots of different insects damage timber. Carry out research about some of them and find out how this damage can be avoided.

▶ Processed materials

Processed materials are made from natural materials and then processed to make them more suitable for their intended purpose.

Key term

Bitumen – a black sticky by-product from oil refining.

Table 4.1 Some common processed materials

Material	Characteristics
Aggregates	Aggregates are processed rock mixtures. Rock is taken out of the ground and can then be crushed to produce different sizes of crushed or uncrushed aggregate.
Concrete	Concrete is produced by mixing: • water – this must be free from contamination • fine aggregates – these are the sands and fine gravels that fill the small holes in concrete • coarse aggregates – these larger-sized aggregates give strength • cement dust – this binds all the materials together.
Bricks	Bricks are usually made from clay. The bricks are shaped out of clay and dried in air, then fired in a kiln to harden them up.
Metals and alloys	Metals such as iron and aluminium are made from ores that are extracted from the ground. A metal alloy, such as steel, is made by mixing two or more metals. Steel is a combination of iron and other elements such as carbon.
Timber products	These are products made from timber. Glued Laminated Timber or Glulam is made by bonding thin layers of timber under pressure. This makes a product that is stronger than the original timber. Other common timber products include plywood, mouldings and laminated timber.
Bituminous materials	Bituminous materials are made from **bitumen**. They are black or dark-coloured materials which have cementing properties. They are also often used in waterproofing materials.

Research

What are the stages in the production of cement? Use the internet and textbooks to find out.

▶ Manufactured materials

Materials are also made through extensive manufacturing processes, for example plastics and paints. Table 4.2 lists some of the manufactured materieals used in construction.

Table 4.2 Manufactured materials

Material	Characteristics
Cement	Cement is a fine powder made by mixing limestone or chalk with clays and fine sands. It is used to make mortars and concrete because it acts as a binding agent.
Limes	Lime is an additive that is added to mortars and plasters to make them more workable and easier to spread.
Plastics	Plastics belong to a family of materials called polymers. Polymers are like chains of chemical materials. They are a by-product of refining oil and natural gas. Different combinations produce plastic resins. These are then moulded to make different plastic products. There are two kinds of plastic. • **Thermoplastics** can be heated and shaped several times. They become mouldable after reheating as they do not undergo lots of chemical changes when they are made. They are easily recycled. One example of a thermoplastic is polythene (PE). • **Thermosetting plastics** cannot be reheated to be reshaped once they have set. The molecules of these plastics are linked in three dimensions and this is why they cannot be reshaped or recycled. The bond between the molecules is very strong, which means that thermosetting plastics are very long-lasting and strong. Glass-reinforced polyester (GRP) is lightweight and used in cladding and roofing panels.
Paints	Paints are used to protect bare surfaces such as wood and make them more attractive. They are made up of: • thinner – the liquid part of the paint, which is either water or white spirit, which evaporates when paint dries • pigment – the solid colour of the paint which comes from organic, inorganic and synthetic sources • binder – combines pigment and other additives in the paint. It decides how well paint sticks to the surface being painted.

Take it further

Using the internet and this book or other textbooks, look up the following types of paint:

• glosses   • limewashes

• primers   • emulsions.

Name one suitable application for each type of paint. For each one, explain why this paint is suitable for this job.

Activity 4.13

Choose one of the materials listed in this topic. Use the internet or go to your local builders merchants and find out as much as you can about this material, then answer the following questions:

1 What are the possible uses for this material?

2 What is it about this material that makes it suitable for these uses?

Material uses and properties

Introduction

It is important to know about the properties of common construction materials, as these properties affect the finished structure.

Link

The properties of construction materials are covered in more detail in *Unit 3: Scientific and Mathematical Applications for Construction*.

Physical properties

If you look around, you will see that buildings are constructed using lots of different construction materials. This is because these materials all have different physical properties which make them good for certain purposes. Bricks might be used for strength in some cases instead of timber or metal, for example.

Table 4.3 lists the different properties that you need to think about when looking at construction materials.

Table 4.3 Physical properties

Property	Description	Examples
Density	A measure of how dense or compact a material is. Usually, the denser a material is, the stronger and heavier it is.	One example of a dense material is steel.
Tensile strength	A material has high tensile strength if it resists pulling or stretching forces. This means it does not stretch out of shape when put under pressure.	High tensile strength is useful in bridges and building. Materials with low tensile strength include natural stone and concrete. If these materials are put under tensile pressure, they will eventually break or crack.
Compressive strength	A material's ability to resist pushing or shortening forces. This means that the material does not get squashed or cracked under pressure.	Materials with high compressive strength include natural stone and concrete.
Elasticity	The ability of a material to return to its original shape once the load is removed.	Steel is an elastic material. This means that it can be used for structural purposes.
Ductility	Able to be deformed without losing its strength. Ductile materials often change shape or crack before failing. A 'warning' could be in the form of cracks or change of shape.	Steel is quite ductile and this means it can be used for structural purposes. Glass is not ductile. This means that it is brittle and breaks easily.
Porosity	A material's ability to allow moisture to pass through it. A porous material lets a lot of moisture through.	Foam insulation is porous and lets water through. Polythene is not porous, and so is good for damp-proof courses.

continued

Table 4.3 continued

Property	Description	Examples
Durability (or resistance to **degradation**)	A material's ability to resist wear and tear. A durable material is suitable for use on the outside of a building.	Concrete is durable because it does not get worn down by wind and rain. Steel, though durable, can degrade quickly if exposed to water and salts.
Workability	How easy a material is to work or handle – for instance, if it does not need a lot of energy to shape or cut. Modelling clay is very workable.	This term is often used to describe how easily concrete can be poured. The workability of a concrete mix depends upon the water : cement ratio.
Thermal conductivity	A material's ability to conduct heat through itself. Materials with high conductivity include copper and aluminium.	Expanded polystyrene and sheep's wool are examples of materials with low thermal conductivity. These are therefore used for thermal insulation.
Thermal resistance	A material's ability to stop heat passing through it. Materials with high thermal resistance are good insulators, because they do not allow heat to escape through them.	Sheep's wool has high thermal resistance, so it is an excellent insulating material. Glass has low thermal resistance, which is why single-glazed windows lose a lot of heat.

Key term

Degradation – when a material is exposed to sunlight, water and wind, it starts losing its strength, shape or appearance.

Did you know?

Just because a material has high tensile strength, it does not necessarily also have compressive strength. This is also true the other way around.

You can tell that this house is well insulated because the snow on its roof does not melt. This is because the insulation materials in the loft have high thermal resistance and don't let heat escape.

Just checking

1 What is compressive strength?
2 What are the elastic properties of timber?
3 Name two suitable applications for a material with high tensile strength.
4 Name three materials that are dense.
5 Why might ductility be an advantage?

Activity 4.14

1   Select part of your house, school or college that you can easily access. Make a list of the materials you can see around you and think of a reason why each of these materials has been used in this particular place. Record your findings in a table like the one below, adding more rows as needed. An example has been done for you.

Material	Location	Reasons
e.g. Bricks	e.g. External wall	e.g. To take the load from the structure above

2   Choose one natural, one processed and one manufactured construction material that could be used to fulfil the same function. For instance, you could choose timber, timber products and plastics as these could all be used to construct doors. Create a presentation about this subject, keeping in mind their resistance to degradation.

Common construction materials and their properties

Now you know about the different properties of construction materials, you can apply this knowledge to the most common construction materials.

Bricks

Bricks need to have good compressive strength to support structural loads. This means that bricks can be used for walls, columns and even larger structures such as bridges.

Concrete

Concrete has high compressive strength, but low tensile strength. The strength and workability of concrete depends on the quality of the materials in it, and the amount of water used. It has low ductility, porosity and elasticity, but it is dense.

Concrete is **non-combustible**, which means that it is fire-safe and able to withstand high temperatures. It is durable as it can resist wind, water and insects.

Timber

Timber has very good tensile and compressive strength. It is easily damaged by weather, **fungi**, insects and fire, and external timbers gradually lose their natural colours and turn grey. Timber is a natural material, so its properties vary according to its origin and **seasoning**.

Because of its properties, timber is used structurally in timber frames, joists, rafters and trusses. It is also used inside buildings, in staircases, doors and window frames.

 Key terms

Non-combustible – does not burn.

Fungi – (singular: fungus), these are micro-organisms such as moulds.

Seasoning – treating natural timber so it is not affected by changes in moisture.

Did you know?

Cement has 'set' when it has become solid. Cement has only 'hardened' when it has developed strength.

Discussion

Cement shrinks as it dries and has low ductility once this has happened. What do you think might happen if cement was allowed to set too quickly?

Cement

Cement is used to bind the materials together. It is used in concrete to bind sand and aggregates. Cement requires water to start a chemical reaction resulting in a bond.

Metals

Different metals have different properties, but you are most likely to work with steel. Steel is the most common metal used in structural building work. It does not react well to extreme temperatures and also rusts easily if not protected, meaning that its durability is limited. Because of these properties, steel is used for reinforcing bars, wall ties, structural steel frames and lintels.

Bituminous materials

Bituminous materials like asphalt and tar are highly adhesive and are water resistant. They are also strong and durable, which makes them ideal for use in road surfaces.

Paints

Some paints are more durable than others. These paints are often used in areas that are used a lot, for example hallways and stairwells, or in areas with high humidity such as kitchens and bathrooms.

Assessment activity 4.3

You are working in an architectural practice, and have been asked for advice by a client. She is renovating her house and wants to know what her options are. For each of the following locations, produce a report specifying the materials that could be used. Remember to include more than one option for each location and give reasons for your choice:

- bathroom and kitchen
- external walls
- lounge and bedroom.

Tips

- The best answers justify their choice of materials. This means that you should give reasons or evidence for any decisions that you make. This demonstrates how you made your decision.
- For each location, try to choose a construction material from each of the three main categories: natural, processed and manufactured.

WorkSpace

▶ Immanuel Mjojo

Junior planner

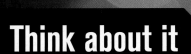

I work at a local planning firm. Planning is a great job: I get to work on lots of different projects and I also meet lots of different people. I am involved in all stages of project planning, from client meetings to planning a whole project. I hope to become an assistant planner and take responsibility for a project of my own.

Having a good knowledge of construction processes and materials is really valuable in my job. Without this, I wouldn't know how much time to allocate to different tasks when I'm preparing Gantt charts. It would be really hard to plan a schedule of work if I didn't know how long it would take to excavate foundations or construct a roof frame.

An understanding of how buildings are constructed and what materials are used also helps me to talk confidently to our clients and to explain technical details. It gives them confidence in me too!

Think about it

1 Why do you think it is important for everyone who works in the construction industry to know about general construction processes and operations?

2 How do you think knowledge of the properties of materials could benefit Immanuel in his job as a planner?

3 What sorts of characteristics do you think a planner needs to have?

4 Is this a job you would be interested in? Explain why.

Introduction

At some point in your construction career, you will need to be able to interpret a drawing. Drawing is the main language of the construction industry as it is a clear, accurate and convenient way of communicating information. This unit gives you opportunities to interpret the information in various types of drawings.

The first part of this unit looks at different kinds of drawings used in the construction industry. You will be learn about the resources you need to produce these drawings. You will become familiar with the drawing equipment and materials in common use. You will also be introduced to computer-aided drafting (CAD).

You will then build on this knowledge and understanding to explore drawing standards and conventions in common use. This will include scales, hatchings, lines, dimensions, annotations and projection methods used in construction drawing. It is often best to learn construction drawing by practising, and that is what you will do. You will develop skills in producing construction sketches and drawings using relevant techniques, conventions and standards. In this unit you can draw by hand, use CAD or use a mix of the two.

Assessment: You will be assessed by a series of assignments set by your teacher/tutor.

Learning aims

In this unit you will:

A understand the requirements to produce construction drawings

B explore the production of construction drawings.

"This unit is really hands-on and we learned by producing a number of drawings. We drew them by hand as well as doing some CAD work. This helped me to understand layouts and details, and also why we use certain types of drawing for different purposes. It all made so much sense once I got to grips with it!

Laura, *16-year-old aspiring architect*

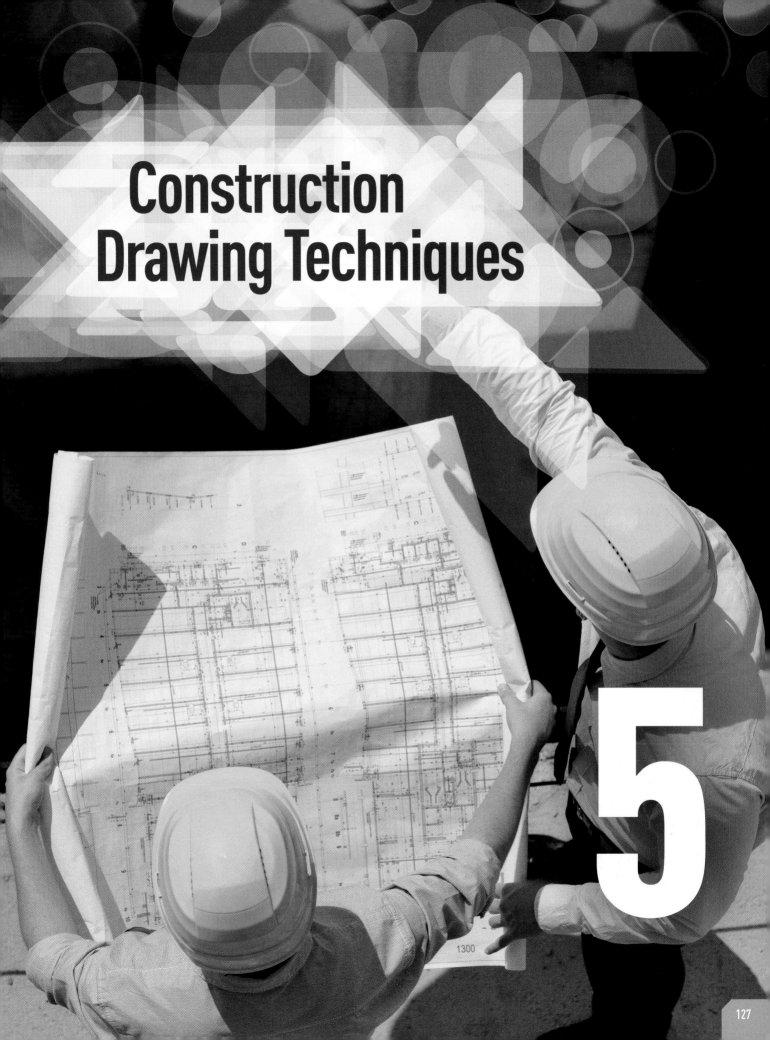

Construction Drawing Techniques

5

Assessment Zone

This table shows what you must do in order to achieve a **Pass**, **Merit** or **Distinction** grade, and where you can find activities in this book to help you.

Assessment criteria

Level 1	Level 2 **Pass**	Level 2 **Merit**	Level 2 **Distinction**
Learning aim A: Understand the requirements to produce construction drawings			
1A.1 Identify different types of drawings used at various stages of the construction process.	**2A.P1** Describe the purpose of different types of drawings required at various stages of the construction process. **See Assessment activity 5.1, page 138**	**2A.M1** Explain the production of drawings and the equipment/media used to produce them. **See Assessment activity 5.1, page 138**	**2A.D1** Evaluate the production of drawings using computer aided design and traditional drafting techniques. **See Assessment activity 5.1, page 138**
1A.2 Interpret information communicated through different types of drawings, with guidance.	**2A.P2** Interpret information communicated through different types of drawings. **See Assessment activity 5.1, page 138**		
1A.3 Identify equipment and materials used to manually produce construction drawings.	**2A.P3** Describe the appropriate selection and use of equipment and materials needed to produce construction drawings manually. **See Assessment activity 5.1, page 138**		
1A.4 Identify the features of a computer-aided-design system.	**2A.P4** Describe the features of a computer-aided-design system. **See Assessment activity 5.1, page 138**		
Learning aim B: Explore the production of construction drawings			
1B.5 Outline standard convention requirements for production of construction drawings	**2B.P5** Describe drawing conventions and standards used in the construction industry. **See Assessment activity 5.2, page 144**	**2B.M2** **Maths** Produce construction drawings to meet a given brief that are: • precise • technically accurate • drawn to appropriate scales. **See Assessment activity 5.2, page 144**	**2B.D2** **Maths** Evaluate construction drawings produced to meet a given brief in terms of compliance with current British Standards. **See Assessment activity 5.2, page 144**
1B.6 **Maths** Produce construction drawings to meet a given brief drawn to an appropriate scale	**2B.P6** **Maths** Apply drawing standards and conventions to produce construction drawings to meet a given brief, drawn to appropriate scales. **See Assessment activity 5.2, page 144**		

Maths   Opportunity to practise mathematical skills

How you will be assessed

The unit will be assessed by a series of internally assessed tasks. You will be expected to show an understanding of types of drawings, their purpose, drawing equipment and materials, together with an introduction to CAD techniques. You will produce a number of construction drawings for a given building project.

Your actual assessment could be in the form of:

- a written report to include text, images, tables, and charts as appropriate, as well as oral questioning and direct observation
- a portfolio with two floor plans, one front and one rear elevation, one section showing staircase details, one foundation detail and one roof detail.

▶ Purpose of drawings

Introduction

The clear communication of information is essential in any construction project. This is achieved by using drawings. In this section you will learn about the different types of drawings used in the construction industry.

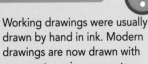
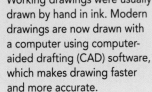

Did you know?

Working drawings were usually drawn by hand in ink. Modern drawings are now drawn with a computer using computer-aided drafting (CAD) software, which makes drawing faster and more accurate.

▶ Different purposes

Different purposes require different drawings. For example, a bricklayer and a local planning officer will need different kinds of drawing in order to do their jobs. Drawings may be used to:

- convey constructional information to the building contractor and other members of the building team
- get approval from the client
- get approvals from others such as planning authorities
- win a project
- estimate the materials needed
- estimate the cost of a project.

Location drawings

These show information related to the location of the building to be constructed. This could be in the form of a block plan, like Figure 5.1.

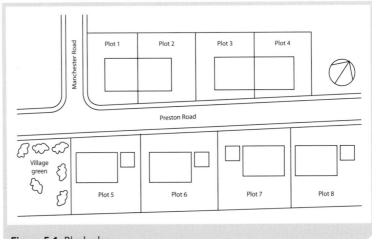

Figure 5.1 Block plan.

Activity 5.1

1 What can you see in the block plan in Figure 5.1? Describe the information it shows.

2 Who would create a block plan? Who would use the block plans they produce?

3 Produce a block plan of a building. This could be a building at your school or the house where you live.

Location drawings are also drawn as site plans showing the position of the buildings on the site. They include information about roads, drainage and services as well as other site information. Figure 5.2 shows a typical site plan.

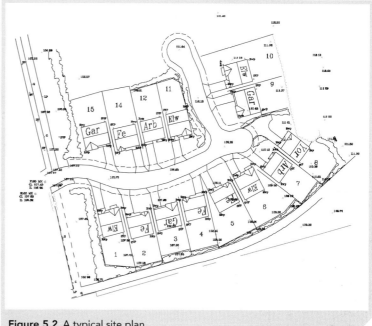

Figure 5.2 A typical site plan.

Plans

Plans or floor plans are drawn to show sizes and positions of spaces in a building, such as bedrooms and bathrooms. These drawings also show the location of various components and elements. Figure 5.3 is an example of the floor plans for a two-storey house.

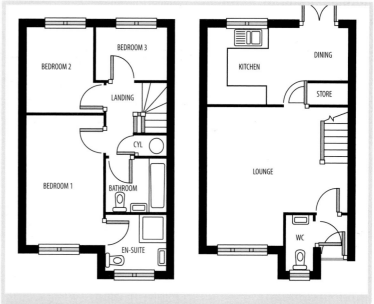

Figure 5.3 Typical floor plans show different storeys side by side.

Elevations

These are series of two-dimensional views of a building showing the finished building from all directions. These include front elevation, rear elevation and side elevations. An example is given in Figure 5.4.

Figure 5.4 Typical elevations.

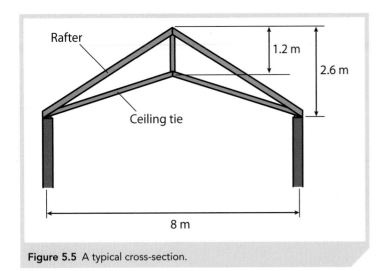
Figure 5.5 A typical cross-section.

Sections

Sections or cross-sections are drawn by 'cutting' a building either along its length or width. If you cut along the length, the section is called a longitudinal section. If you cut across the width, it is a transverse section or cross-section.

Sections give a view of a building showing details which otherwise would not be seen on the plans and elevations.

Component drawings

Component drawings show details of different components in a building. These include windows, doors and roof trusses. These can be obtained from any manufacturer to work out the necessary size of wall openings. This information is needed during the design stage.

Just checking

1 At what stage in the construction process do you think elevation drawings are produced?

2 How do you think a component drawing would be used by an architect and a site manager?

Assembly drawings

Assembly drawings show details of how various components and elements in a building will join together. These contain detailed information about connections, materials and sizes.

Presentation drawings

Presentation drawings are used to show a client the key features of a project. These do not contain construction details, and are of very high quality. Presentation drawings are normally finished in colour, showing the finished product as accurately as possible.

Did you know?

With Virtual Reality (VR) applications, it is possible to 'walk through' a proposed building design. These walk-throughs can be used to show the local community what a new development in their area will actually look like.

Activity 5.2

You have been asked to give a talk to other BTEC learners about some of the different types of drawing used in construction. Describe where and when you would use:

- a site plan
- a section
- an assembly drawing.

Manual materials and equipment

Introduction

It is important that your drawings are clear and easy to read. You can do this by using the correct materials and equipment. Producing drawings **manually** requires a wide range of materials, and it can be easy to choose the wrong pen or pencil for the job.

 Key term

Manually – by hand.

Manual drawing equipment

Pair of compasses

A pair of compasses is used to draw circles and angles. They can also be used as a divider.

Set squares

These are used to draw vertical lines or lines at an angle. Two set squares are needed: a 45° set square and a combination 30° / 60° set square. You can get adjustable set squares that combine both set squares.

Erasers

Erasers are used to erase both pencil and ink. A combination eraser can erase both. Coloured erasers will leave a stain on the paper, so good-quality erasers are grey or white. Overusing the eraser will spoil the surface of the paper and can even make a hole in it.

Scale rules

These are used to measure and draw according to an appropriate scale. These are available for various scales such as 1:100 and 1:50.

Protractor

Protractors are used to set out angles other than 30°, 45° and 60°.

French curves and flexible curves

These are used to draw various types of curves required in drawings.

French curves

Lettering and number stencils

Lettering has to be readable, as if it cannot be read, the information is worthless. You can letter freehand, but use a stencil to produce the best effect. The height of the lettering should be between 4 mm and 7 mm, and should be 0.5 mm thick. The spacing, angle and shading of the lettering need to be consistent throughout.

Drawing boards

These are available in various sizes. Some boards can be used on a desktop, while others are mounted on frames (that is, free-standing). An A2 drawing board is generally big enough, though professional architects and draughtspersons will need larger sizes. Drawing boards come with or without a sliding rule attached.

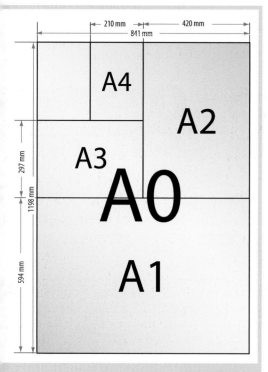

Figure 5.6 Different paper sizes.

▶ Materials

Paper

Cartridge papers are machine-made papers. These are available either as rolls or in A-size sheets. There are three types based on their thickness: thin, medium and stout. Medium is ideal for pencil drawing while stout is suitable for ink.

Handmade/moulded papers usually have three finishes:

- HP (Hot Pressed) – smooth
- NOT – medium
- R – rough.

HP is most commonly used for pencil, ink and wash drawings. Tracing papers, or detail papers, are used to trace from the original drawing. These are transparent enough to see through and are available as thin, medium and stout.

Papers come in different sizes, from A0 (the biggest) to A4. Figure 5.6 shows the relationship between the various sizes of paper.

Pencils

Drawing pencils are not normal writing pencils. They come in different grades or hardnesses. They are graded from the hardest (9H) to the softest (9B). H pencils make light marks and are used mainly for line work (simply drawing lines). B pencils make darker marks and are usually used for sketching and annotations.

Pencils softer than B and harder than 3H are generally not suitable for technical drawing.

Clutch pencils are also called mechanical pencils or propeller pencils. These use leads of various grades and thickness such as 0.3 mm, 0.5 mm, 0.7 mm and 0.9 mm. A number of leads can be kept in the pencil casing. These pencils do not need any sharpening and give lines of uniform thickness.

Pens

These are used to produce drawings in ink and are available in a variety of sizes. Drawings are produced in ink once they are finalised, so that clear copies can be made. Drawings in ink are also longer-lasting, so they can be stored safely for future use. All working drawings can be drawn in ink. Pens should be refilled using good quality ink.

Computer-aided drafting (CAD)

Introduction

People working in the construction industry have gradually moved to computer-aided drafting, because it is faster and it is also easier to amend and update drawings. This topic gives a general introduction to computer-aided drafting. The processes and commands described here may not be exactly the same as the processes and commands you will use with your CAD system, but they will be similar.

In this unit, AutoCAD® 2012 is used as an example. Remember: AutoCAD® 2012 is only one program. You may use other programs.

Starting AutoCAD 2012

1 When you start the program, you will usually see a startup window.

2 You will usually have the options to:

- open a previous drawing
- start a new drawing
- use a template
- use a setup tool.

3 Select the option to work in decimal units.

Discussion

In groups, discuss the benefits of CAD systems in the construction industry. Can you think of any drawbacks?

Remember

- Make sure that all scales are set to zero before starting your drawing.
- On the Area page, the two values in the Width and Length boxes specify the limits of your grid and working area.

Case study

Philippa is an architectural technologist. Her work involves producing various types of drawings. Her company has recently changed to using a CAD system. Philippa has found the CAD system really useful, as it is easy to make changes without starting a drawing all over again. The drawings can also be uploaded online and are easy to save. She does not print drawings as often as she used to, which is more environmentally friendly.

1 Could you list three advantages of using CAD?

2 Are there any disadvantages of using CAD?

Drawing

The CAD program that you use is likely to contain a number of features such as:

- standard Windows® drop-down menus
- a standard toolbar below the menus, including Open, Save, Plot, etc.
- additional toolbars (for instance, AutoCAD® 2012 has four: Properties, Layer Control, Draw and Modify)

- the drawing area – where you draw
- the command area – where you type commands
- the status area – this includes the current cursor position.

Command entry

Typically there are three ways of giving a command:

1 Type the command in 'Command Area' using the keyboard. The command will show in the command area. For example, 'circle' command can be given by entering:

- 'c⏎' at the command line
- 'line' by l⏎
- 'copy' by co⏎
- 'rotate' by ro⏎.

2 Select the command from a menu.

3 Select the command's icon from a toolbar.

Drawing a line

Worked example 5.1

Draw a rectangle 400 mm x 300 mm.

Drawing a rectangle will help you practise using commands, specifying coordinates and using the zoom command.

In AutoCAD® 2012, the process of drawing a rectangle is as follows:

Step 1 Select **Rectangle** (or type **rectang** ⏎), then type the coordinates of:

100, 100 ⏎

500, 400 ⏎

Step 2 Command: **RECTANG**⏎

Specify first corner point or [Chamfer/Elevation/Fillet/Thickness/Width]: 100,100⏎

Specify other corner point or [Area/Dimensions/Rotation]: 500,400⏎

Output AutoCAD® 2012 will draw a rectangle.

If you cannot see the shape you have drawn, try zooming out.

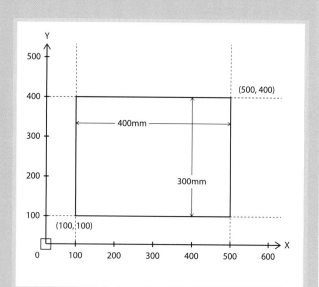

Worked example 5.2

You will now draw the same rectangle as in worked example 5.1 using the line tool.

This will help you to practise deleting unwanted drawings, drawing lines, using commands and using the zoom command.

Step 1 Delete the previously drawn rectangle (select and delete).

Click on the **Ortho** button in the **Status Area** to turn it on.

Step 2 Select the line command from the Draw Toolbar.

Type the coordinates of: **100, 100** ↵

Step 3 Move the cross hairs towards the right of the drawing area and type the length of the rectangle: **400** ↵

Shift the cross hairs towards the top of the drawing area and type the width of the rectangle: **300** ↵

Place the cross hairs towards the left and type the length of the rectangle: **400** ↵

Finally type c to close the rectangle: **c** ↵

Saving a drawing

Select the Save icon from the standard toolbar. If the drawing has not been saved before, AutoCAD® 2012 will display the SAVE AS dialog box. Select the appropriate location, type the drawing name and then select OK. You may choose file type as .dwg for storing all types of drawings, or .dwf for web applications.

Drawing circles

To draw a circle you can either pick the CIRCLE option from the menu and then pick 'centre, radius', or enter the command 'CIRCLE' or 'C' on the keyboard. You will then need to specify the coordinates of the centre and the length of its radius.

Zoom and pan

You can make your drawing larger or smaller on the screen. This is called zooming. You can zoom in (using the magnifying glass with a + symbol) to make the whole or part of the drawing larger or zoom out (using the one with the – symbol) to make it smaller.

Pan is a command that helps you to move around the drawing. Once you have used the zoom command and wish to move around the drawing, using pan is very helpful.

?   **Did you know?**

If you make a mistake, you can usually press the escape key (Esc), located at the top left of the keyboard. Then type u ↵. There is also usually a 'back' or 'undo' button.

Activity 5.4

In the drawing that you used to practise drawing lines and circles, add:

- a title block
- the projection
- the material
- your name
- your tutor's name.

Now ask your tutor to approve the drawing.

The benefits of using CAD

- CAD systems can free designers from unproductive activities, such as producing revision drawings.
- Designers can test and evaluate design alternatives faster than if they had to draw them all by hand.
- Clients can see how the building will look when it is finished.
- Building images can be placed in existing images of the site. This helps planners to make decisions on planning applications.
- CAD files can usually be emailed instantly, unlike manual drawings.
- More than one designer can work on the same project at the same time.
- Graphical CAD output can be used for estimating quantities of materials and their costs.
- Accurate and consistent information is given for the contract documents, as revisions to drawings can be securely recorded.
- CAD drawings can improve trust between various construction teams, as they can see exactly what is intended.

Health and safety in CAD

Anybody using CAD will be in front of a screen for several hours. It is important that the screen is at a height that is comfortable for the user. It is also important to adjust the height of the chair and to keep it as upright as possible. This will help you to avoid developing any back problems.

Using CAD also involves repetitive tasks using a mouse. This can cause repetitive strain injury (RSI). To avoid RSI, you can use the keyboard more, take regular breaks or use software where clicking a mouse is not required.

Just checking

1 What does CAD stand for?
2 What written details should you include on any drawing?
3 Are there any health and safety issues related to use of CAD?

Assessment activity 5.1

Your employer has asked you to produce a leaflet explaining the different methods of producing a construction drawing. It will be given to all new employees. You should include hand-drawn and computer-aided techniques.

The leaflet should also evaluate hand-drawn and computer-aided drawing methods. This means that you should review all the information you have given about these methods and then come to a conclusion about their use.

Tip

You should always support your conclusions with some evidence.

Drawing conventions

Introduction

Because construction drawings communicate very important information about the structure of buildings, it is important that conventions are followed. This means that everyone looking at the drawing will understand what it means so mistakes will not be made when constructing the building.

Conventions

Scales

Buildings are drawn on paper and have to be to a certain scale. A scale is like a ratio. It is like creating a 'scaled-down' version of the actual building or part of a building.

These scales or ratios depend on the type of drawing as well as the amount of detail needed. For example, a 1:100 scale would mean that every 1 mm on the drawing represents 100 mm or 0.1 m on the ground. If you draw the actual dimensions, it is a scale of 1:1.

Table 5.1 Scales used for drawings

Type of drawing	Scale used
Block plan	1:2500
Site plan	1:500
Floor plans	1:100
Elevations	1:100
Sections	1:50
Component drawings	1:20
Assembly drawings	1:10

Scale rules make these conversions easy to measure when drawing, as they are marked with the relevant scales.

Activity 5.5

Using appropriate drawing paper, draw lengths of 6 m, 3.5 m and 1 m on a scale of 1:100.

Did you know?

Construction drawings are produced in accordance with the standard BS 1192. This is the British Standard that regulates how construction information is communicated. It covers everything from details about hatching drawings for a range of materials and finishes to line types and their thicknesses.

Discussion

Why is it important to use standard scales in drawings?

Hatchings

Hatching is when you use standardised symbols or images to represent a variety of building materials and components used.

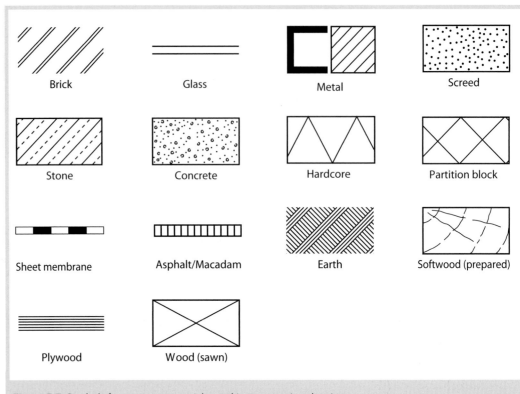

Figure 5.7 Symbols for common materials used in construction drawings.

Lines

Lines must always be clean cut, firmly drawn and of a consistent quality throughout the drawing. The style, type and weight of line used adds extra information to the drawing.

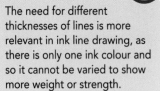
Table 5.2 Types of line and what they indicate

Type	Use
————————	Continuous line for dimensions and hatching
——— ——— ——— ⌐⌐ ———	Lines with a zigzag to show interrupted views or sections
— — — — — — —	Dashed lines to show hidden details
· —— · —— · —— · ——	Centre lines

Lines can be of three thicknesses:

- **thick** – these are 0.75–1 mm thick and are used for borders and drawing outlines
- **medium** – these are 0.35–0.5 mm thick and are used for hatching
- **fine** – these are 0.2–0.25 mm thick and are used for dimension lines.

Dimensions

Dimension lines are the lines used on a drawing to show the measurements or dimensions of the structure in the drawing. Rules for drawing dimension lines are given in the relevant British Standard and you can see an example in Figure 5.8.

In modular dimensions, the overall length, for example the length of a wall, is broken down into 'modules' of length, while running dimensions keep a running total of these modules of length. Dimensions are used to provide sizes of various parts of a building and to show how various components or modules are coordinated. For example, there is coordination between the size of a door and the size of the corresponding door frame.

Annotation

Drawings are annotated using either appropriate lettering and numbering stencils or writing in freehand. Both upper and lower case are permitted. Annotations should be legible. The height and thickness of the lettering depends on the size of paper used.

Projection methods

When you project or map the shape of an object on to a plane, this is called an orthographic projection or view.

There are two types of projections: first angle projections and third angle projections.

- A first angle projection is made up of at least two images with the elevation or front view always set out directly above the plan view.

- A third angle projection is also made up of at least two images, but in this instance the plan is always set out directly above the elevation/front view.

Figure 5.8 The top drawing uses dimension lines with closed arrowheads, while the bottom drawing uses dimension lines with oblique strike lines.

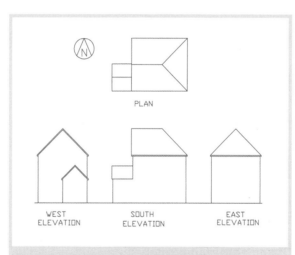

Figure 5.9 Orthographic projection in third angle.

Remember

The spacing, angle and shading of the lettering need to be consistent throughout.

Did you know?

Construction lines or projection lines are continuous thin faint lines that are used to work out the layout of each individual drawing and their connection to other drawings on the sheet. They should not be immediately visible and should only become apparent when you look closely at the drawing.

Standards

Standards are an official way of making or keeping something all the same. Information used in the construction industry should follow standards so that everyone understands the design and the information given in the drawings. Standards of design are often taken from the British Standards Institute (BSI):

- BS 1192:2007 is the code of practice for construction drawing. It also gives guidelines for structuring and exchanging CAD data.

- BS8541-2:2011 gives guidance for symbols used in drawings for the construction industry.

Just checking

1 What is an orthographic projection?

2 What is the name of the standard that your drawings need to meet?

▶ Drawings

Introduction

In this topic you will produce your own drawings, including floor plans, front and rear elevations, a section drawing, a roof detail and a foundation detail.

▶ Representing parts of a building

Everything that may be fitted into a building can be shown using a symbol from British Standards. This means that no matter who reads your drawings, they will understand exactly where they need to install every door, window, toilet or sink.

Doors

Doors can be of various types, including single **leaf** and double leaf. These are drawn in a specific way so that the carpenter hanging the doors knows where and how they should hang and open.

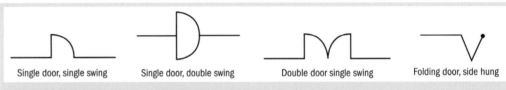

| Single door, single swing | Single door, double swing | Double door single swing | Folding door, side hung |

Figure 5.10 Ways to represent different doors in plan view.

Windows

When drawing windows, the symbol used indicates how they are hung and how they will open. For instance, Figure 5.11 shows windows hinged at two different points: the side and the top.

Staircases

Arrows show the upward direction of the steps. The steps are also numbered, with the bottom step being numbered 1, as shown in Figure 5.12.

Other common symbols

Table 5.3 shows some commonly used symbols along with their description. Using these symbols adds information to a drawing quickly.

Table 5.3 Other commonly used symbols

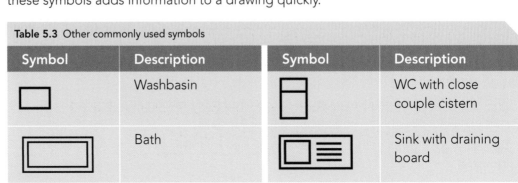

Symbol	Description	Symbol	Description
	Washbasin		WC with close couple cistern
	Bath		Sink with draining board

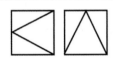

Figure 5.11 Windows in elevation hinged at the side (left) and top (right).

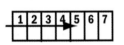

Figure 5.12 A straight flight of stairs with seven steps.

Activity 5.6

Consider the examples of bathroom and kitchen fittings in your house and produce an A3 sheet showing commonly used symbols for all the fittings and fixtures, in accordance with British Standards.

Take it further

Make a 'cheat sheet' showing the most common symbols from BS 1192:2007.

Abbreviations

Abbreviations are used to simplify the writing or annotations. For example, instead of **rain water pipe**, you can write **RWP** to convey the same information.

These abbreviations are standardised, so you do not need to make your own. Some commonly used abbreviations are given in Table 5.4.

Table 5.4 Commonly used abbreviations

Item	Abbreviation	Item	Abbreviation
Brickwork	bwk	Joist	jst
Cast iron	CI	Polyvinyl chloride	PVC
Concrete	conc	Unplasticised polyvinyl chloride	uPVC

North sign

The direction of true north is marked using a north sign. This is a useful detail on drawings such as site plans and block plans, to show the **orientation** of a building.

Figure 5.13 A typical north sign.

Key term

Orientation – the direction that a building faces.

Just checking

1. How do you show the upward direction of a staircase?
2. Why is it important to include a north sign on your drawings?

Producing drawings

Plan, section and elevation are vital to understanding what you are drawing. You need to see them as a series of related views. They are actually sections or cuts.

- The plan is cut horizontally.
- The section is cut vertically.

When creating a floor plan, the major outline and those lines that set out the position of structural elements and walls are drawn first.

The major walls and structural elements such as posts and columns are then given proper thickness.

Next, major built-in elements such as windows, doorways and stairways are drawn.

Finally, details such as fixtures, doors and stair treads are shown.

Did you know?

The horizontal section is generally cut through all major vertical elements and all door and window openings, and is about one metre above the floor.

General layout

The space on a drawing sheet is divided into:

- a space for drawing
- a space for text
- a title block.

Space for drawing

The main figure should be placed at the top left of the drawing. Think of it as though your drawing sheet is divided into a number of A4 sheets. Try placing figures into these A4-size sections.

Space for text

This has all the information needed to understand the contents of the drawing. The space for text is normally at the right-hand edge of the drawing sheet. Its width is equal to that of the title block, that is a maximum of 170 mm, or of at least 100 mm.

Information to be placed in space for text includes:

- explanations, using special symbols, abbreviations and units of dimensions
- instructions such as material, surface treatment and assembly
- references to other documents
- a revision table showing the date of revision and the signature of the person responsible for the revision.

Title block

A title block should contain:

- job title and number
- name and address of the firm
- description of the drawing
- scale
- date
- author
- person checking the drawing
- drawing number.

Assessment activity 5.2   *Maths*

You are applying to become an apprentice architect. The employer wants to check your drawing skills and has asked you to produce a set of drawings of your college.

Produce the following drawings of your college in accordance with British Standards:

- floor plans
- front and rear elevations
- one section
- one foundation and one roof detail.

Once you have produced your drawings, evaluate them. Make sure that you include:

- title block
- annotations
- consistency of lines
- correct use of symbols
- correct dimensioning.

WorkSpace

▷ Rob Hartnett

Senior technician

I'm a senior technician at an architectural practice. I work with a team of three technologists. At first I just had to produce working drawings. Now I get involved in everything from layout design and technical details to giving technical advice on site. Drawings are very important in communicating information to everybody involved, including the client, site managers, structural engineers, services engineers, planners, buyers and estimators. My clients trust me to do a good job, so I have to stay up to date with changes in drawing standards and Building Regulations.

I worked hard to learn the drawing skills when I was a student. I learned manual drawing, though I now use CAD at work because it's quick and easy to edit and save. Now I know that if you cannot read, interpret or produce a drawing, moving on to better jobs will be so much harder.

I enjoy my job and after just a few years of working, I oversee architectural jobs covering over 20 sites. I am looking forward to becoming a technical or design coordinator. This would mean I would also manage external consultants and other companies, as well as my team of technologists.

The company I work for gives me lots of training and development opportunities so I can strengthen my existing skills and learn new ones.

Think about it

1 Why is drawing so important for communicating information in Rob's job?
2 Which sort of jobs in the construction industry need you to be able to interpret and produce drawings?
3 What are the advantages of using CAD?

Introduction

This unit will introduce you to the tools, materials and personal protective equipment (PPE) used by carpenters and joiners. You will learn about the potential health and safety hazards in a carpentry and joinery work area, how to carry out a risk assessment, and what is safe working practice in the use of common tools and equipment.

The knowledge and skills you will develop in this unit are still relevant in today's construction industry. Both carpenters and joiners will at some time have to make a timber frame. For example, carpenters would assemble a door frame on site to fit into a brick wall, while a joiner would make a window frame in a workshop for an external wall. You will also have to make a frame in this unit.

Assessment: You will be assessed by a series of assignments set by your teacher/tutor.

Learning aims

In this unit you will:

A understand tools, materials and equipment used in carpentry and joinery

B develop practical skills using safe techniques to produce a timber frame.

When I went on two weeks' work experience last year, I worked at a joinery shop making windows. The experience was brilliant and it inspired me to take this unit.

Jianguo, *16-year-old aspiring carpenter*

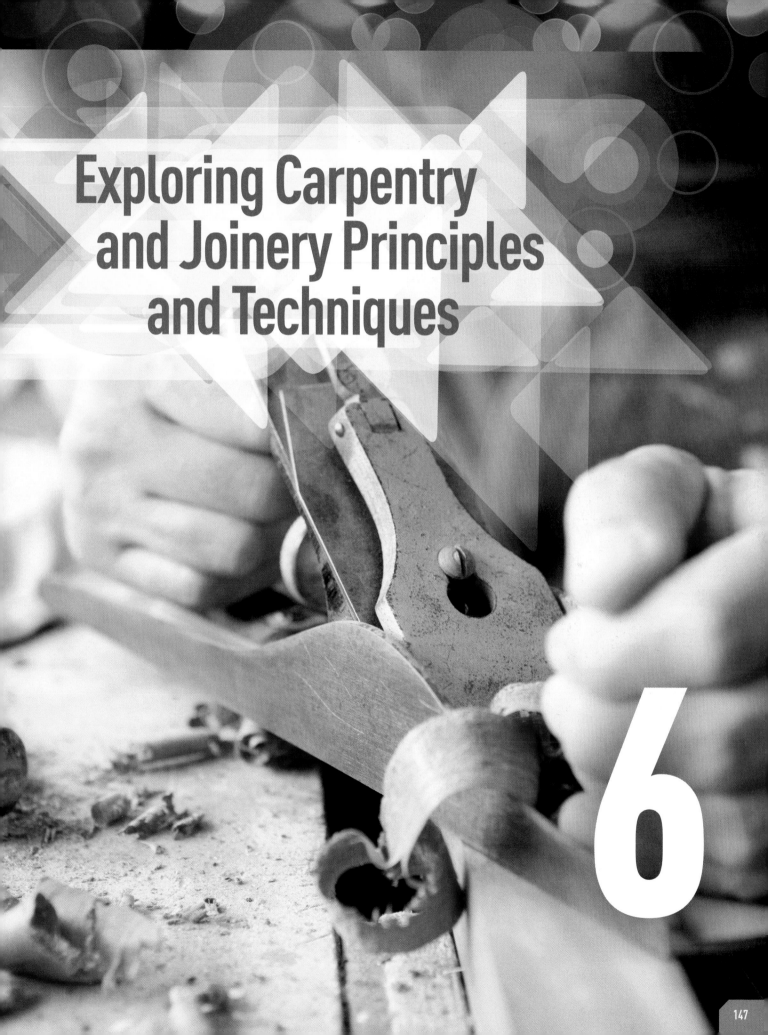

Exploring Carpentry and Joinery Principles and Techniques

6

BTEC
Assessment Zone

This table shows what you must do in order to achieve a **Pass**, **Merit** or **Distinction** grade, and where you can find activities in this book to help you.

Assessment criteria			
Level 1	**Level 2 Pass**	**Level 2 Merit**	**Level 2 Distinction**
Learning aim A: Understand tools, materials and equipment used in carpentry and joinery			
1A.1 Identify the purpose of tools and equipment, and the use of materials in carpentry and joinery.	**2A.P1** Explain the selection and use of appropriate tools, materials and equipment for carpentry and joinery. **See Assessment activity 6.1, page 159**	**2A.M1** Justify the selection of tools, materials and equipment for a specified carpentry and joinery task.	**2A.D1** Evaluate the use of alternative materials for a specified carpentry and joinery task.
1A.2 Outline the safe use and storage of carpentry and joinery tools, materials and equipment.	**2A.P2** Explain the safe use and storage of carpentry and joinery tools, materials and equipment. **See Assessment activity 6.1, page 159**		
Learning aim B: Develop practical skills using safe techniques to produce a timber frame			
1B.3 Identify hazards and control measures prior to commencing the construction of a timber frame.	**2B.P3** English Carry out a risk assessment prior to commencing the construction of a timber frame. **See Assessment activity 6.2, page 164**		
1B.4 Work safely using personal protection equipment with guidance.	**2B.P4** Comply with safe working practices including using appropriate personal protection equipment. **See Assessment activity 6.2, page 164**		
1B.5 Maths Measure and mark out four different types of joints for a 300 × 300 mm timber frame to a given specification with guidance.	**2B.P5** Maths Measure and mark out four different types of joints for a 300 × 300 mm timber frame to a given specification. Dimensionally square to 3 mm. **See Assessment activity 6.2, page 164**	**2B.M2** Maths Measure and mark out four different types of joints for a 300 × 300 mm timber frame to a given specification. Dimensionally square to 2 mm. **See Assessment activity 6.2, page 164**	**2B.D2** Maths Measure and mark out four different types of joints for a 300 × 300 mm timber frame to a given specification. Dimensionally square to 1 mm. **See Assessment activity 6.2, page 164**
1B.6 Maths Produce a timber 300 × 300 mm frame using four different types of joints to a given spec, with guidance: • ±3 mm joint gap tolerance.	**2B.P6** Maths Produce a 300 × 300 mm timber frame using four different types of joints to a given spec: • ±3 mm joint gap tolerance. **See Assessment activity 6.2, page 164**	**2B.M3** Maths Produce a 300 × 300 mm timber frame using four different types of joints to a given spec: • ±2 mm joint gap tolerance • not twisted. **See Assessment activity 6.2, page 164**	**2B.D3** Maths Produce a 300 × 300 mm timber frame using four different types of joints to a given spec: • ±1 mm joint gap tolerance • not twisted. **See Assessment activity 6.2, page 164**

Maths Opportunity to practise mathematical skills   English Opportunity to practise English skills

How you will be assessed

The unit will be assessed by a series of internally assessed tasks. You will be expected to show an understanding of the safe use and storage of tools, materials and equipment. This could be part of the induction session you need to produce for new trainees in the joinery workshop.

The practical assessment task will be based on a scenario where you produce, in a joinery workshop, a sample of a frame to go in the shop window to advertise its high quality of craft work.

Evidence for your assessment could be in the form of:

- training materials, such as leaflets and a PowerPoint® presentation
- a practical product such as a frame.

Tools and materials for carpentry and joinery

Discussion

Think about the various tools used in carpentry and joinery. In pairs, discuss how the different types of tools can be divided up into categories according to how they are used – marking and measuring tools, cutting tools, drilling tools and fixing tools.

Introduction

In this topic you will learn about the tools, materials and equipment used in carpentry and joinery. Carpenters and joiners have one of the largest and most varied toolkits in the construction trade.

Setting-out tools

Setting out is the first step in your practical work. It involves marking out and measuring the timber, which is done before you can start cutting.

Key terms

Mortise – a square or rectangular hole in timber.

Parallel – parallel lines run alongside each other and are always the same distance apart. They will never cross.

Did you know?

The mortise gauge is usually set to the size of the mortise chisel you are using. The mortise chisel is roughly one-third of the thickness of the timber you are cutting a mortise in. So if the timber was 19 mm thick, you would select a 6 mm chisel to cut the mortise.

Steel rule
This is either 30 cm or 1 metre (100 cm) long. It is used for measuring short lengths.

Marking gauge
This is used to draw a single line parallel to the edge of the timber. It has a single metal pin which is used to scratch a straight line on timber when marking out a joint.

Mortise gauge
This has two pins, one of which is adjustable. It is used to mark out a **mortise** and tenon.

Combination gauge
A combination gauge is similar but has three metal pins. The single pin can be used as a marking gauge, whereas the two together can be used to scratch **parallel** lines on timber when marking out a joint.

Combination square
This is a very useful tool as it can measure angles of 90° and 45°. The rule can also be used to measure small distances and depths.

Tri-square
This can be used to set out lines accurately at 90° to the edge of the timber. You can also use it to check that the corners of pieces of timber or timber frames are square.

Sliding bevel
A sliding bevel can be used to set out angled lines on timber.

Carpenter's pencil
A carpenter's pencil is a flat pencil with a soft lead, which makes it easy to see the marks it makes on sawn timber.

Tape measure

This is used to produce accurate measurements when measuring longer lengths of timber.

Spirit level

This is used to check that your timber is horizontally level, or vertically upright.

▶ Cutting tools

Using the correct tools when cutting will help improve the quality of your practical work. Some examples are pictured here.

Bevelled chisels

These are bevelled on the steel front edge of the blade, so they can easily get into small corners when cutting a joint. Typical sizes are 6, 12, 18 and 25 mm. They are used to cut joints.

Mortise chisels

Mortise chisel blades are made from thicker steel. Typical sizes are 6, 12 and 18 mm. They are used to cut mortises.

Mallet

This is usually made of wood and is used to strike a chisel to cut into timber.

Tenon saw

This is named after the **tenon** part of the joint in a mortise and tenon joint. It is used for cutting small pieces of timber.

Universal saw

This is a general purpose saw for cutting timber.

Smoothing plane

This is used to shave thin wood shavings from the surface of the timber. The plane levels the timber surfaces on a frame.

Block plane

This plane is used to remove **end grain** and small amounts of timber.

Nail pincers

These are used to remove nails from timber. They should be used by rolling the pincers over to one side, not pulling directly upwards.

Marking knife

This is used to scratch or score the surface of the timber before cutting it.

🔑 **Key terms**

Tenon – a rectangular shaped part of timber that fits exactly into a mortise.

End grain – this is the grain at the end of a piece of timber when the timber has been cut.

Drilling tools

These are the tools that you will use for drilling.

Twist drill bits These are steel drill bits that are used to drill circular holes for woodscrews. The drills range in diameter sizes from 0.5 mm up to 12 mm. The drill diameters increase by 0.5 mm at a time.	
Auger bits These are made of steel. The auger bits have a wide spiral for improved waste removal from the hole. The length of the auger bit is about 200 mm.	
Bradawl This is a small hand tool for making small holes in timber. You would use this tool to start a hole for a woodscrew.	
Cordless drill This is an electrical power tool and it uses a battery instead of plugging into the mains. It is used to make holes in timber, as well as drive in or take out screws.	

Fixing tools

These are the tools that you will use for fixing together pieces of wood using nails and screws.

Slotted screwdriver This is used for screwing in or removing slotted woodscrews.	
Phillips screwdriver This is used for screwing in or removing Phillips woodscrews.	
Pozidriv® screwdriver This is used for screwing in or removing Pozidriv® woodscrews.	
Nail punch This is used to punch nails so that they sit below the surface of the timber. The steel punch is hit with a hammer to force the nail into the timber. The nail punch avoids the hammer hitting the timber and leaving marks on it.	
Claw hammer This is used to hammer nails into timber. The claw part is used to extract nails by leverage.	

Discussion

The striking face of the hammer should be clean. If it is dirty, the hammer will not strike the nail properly and it will slip off the top of the nail. How do you think you could clean the striking face of a dirty hammer?

1 Find a block plane and a smoothing plane in your workshop. Compare the two, looking particularly at the blades. What differences do you see?

2 You have been asked to give a short talk to other learners on your course about when you would use each type of plane. Write a brief explanation that you could use to deliver this information.

3 Produce a poster for your workshop about the efficient use of a plane. Remember to cover the sharpness of the blade and the importance of setting the depth of the blade correctly.

Take it further

Practise adjusting the depth of the blades in your planes. A plane should only produce a **very** thin wood shaving. Do not worry if it seems difficult at first – this is a skill that takes time to master.

Research

Using books and the internet, find out why a mortise should be roughly one-third the thickness of the timber. How could the size of the mortise or tenon affect the strength of the joint?

▷ Equipment

These pieces of equipment will help you to keep your timber still and secure when you are working on it.

Bench hook This equipment is used to hold timber securely when cutting with a saw. It is designed for both left- and right-handed persons and should be held in a vice.	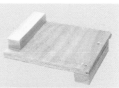
G clamps These are used to clamp pieces of timber while the glue is setting.	
Sash cramps These are used to clamp a timber frame together while the glue is setting.	
Woodworking vice This is attached to a bench and is used to hold the material that you are working on so that you can work with both hands.	

▶ Information

In carpentry and joinery, most of the information you will be working with will come in the form of drawings and symbols.

Purpose of drawings

Drawings are an easy way of exchanging information about an object such as a timber frame. In a drawing, you can show all the important details, including size, shape and design.

Imagine having to write an essay to explain how to make something without using a drawing. It would be very difficult and you probably would not get what you wanted!

How to read drawings

When you read a construction drawing, you are interpreting the drawn information and using this information to make something.

When the scale is 1:1, this means that the drawing is the same size as the final product. This means that you can lay the timber on top of the drawing and mark off the lengths as drawn.

Units of measurement

Usually, carpentry drawings are measured in millimetres. It is very important to pay careful attention to the unit of measurement used in the drawing. Imagine if you were making window frames and misread millimetres as metres!

Title box

The title box is where any additional information is put. This helps to identify the drawing.

▶ Materials

Wood and wood composites

Softwood timber comes in a variety of sizes to suit all different construction situations. It is used in building timber structures such as roofs and walls. It is also used for making windows and doors. Softwood timber is a very versatile material, and is tough and long lasting. It is easy to cut and fix. It is also lightweight in relation to its strength. Softwoods can include pine and cedar.

Wood grain is the lines you see on the planed surface of softwood. The grain gives timber its unique appearance which people find very appealing to look at. Knots on the planed surface of the timber also give the surface a unique character.

Discussion

Why do you think information is communicated through drawings and symbols rather than through written instructions and descriptions?

Link

For more on reading drawings, look at *Unit 5: Construction Drawing Techniques*.

Did you know?

Cedar has natural properties that make it resistant to moisture and insect damage.

Table 6.1 Some types of softwood timber

Name	Timber sizes	Drawn information
Rough sawn or carcass sawn	• 25 mm × 50 mm • 50 mm × 50 mm • 75 mm × 50 mm	
Planed all round (PAR)	• 19 mm × 44 mm • 44 mm × 44 mm • 69 mm × 44 mm	
Regularised	• 21 mm × 47 mm • 47 mm × 47 mm • 72mm × 47 mm	

A **wood composite** is a manufactured wood product. Wood composites can be produced in large sheets, unlike natural timber which is limited by the size of the tree. Two examples of this are medium density fibreboard (MDF) and plywood.

- **MDF** – this is made up of very small wood chips and wood fibres glued together. It is not suitable for outdoor use and is often used for kitchen units or bedroom furniture.
- **plywood** – this is made by overlapping thin layers of timber and gluing them together. The direction of the grain of each layer is at right angles to the layers either side of it. This increases the strength of the finished plywood.

These wood composites come in different thicknesses, including 4 mm, 6 mm, 9mm, 18 mm and 25 mm. The standard size of a sheet of wood composite is 1200 mm by 2440 mm.

It is very important for the environment that we use renewable wood sources. This means that we plant and replace trees as we use them for construction and building. This makes sure they will always be available to future generations. This work is done by the Forest Stewardship Council (FSC). Sustainable timber is clearly labelled, often with the FSC's logo.

Did you know?

The global forest area certified to FSC Principles and Criteria is growing worldwide. As of July 2013, 180.884 million hectares had been certified.

Just checking

1 Name three different types of prepared softwood timber sold.
2 What two features give planed timber its unique appearance?
3 What does FSC stand for?

Research

What is the FSC's logo?

Types of glue

Glues or adhesives are substances that bond two surfaces together. When timber is glued, the small timber fibres from the two surfaces are bonded together. The larger the surface area of the joint that is glued together, the stronger the bond is between the two components. Adhesives are made from either natural or synthetic materials.

Natural glues include casein and animal glue.

- **Casein glue** is made from a protein contained in milk. It is used in general joinery assembly work. It is not resistant to water, and is used for interior work only.
- **Animal glue** is also called scotch glue. It is made from animal tissue. It is used for restoration work for antique furniture, and also in musical instruments. It is for internal use only, and is not resistant to water.

Synthetic glues are man-made. They include PVA and polyurethane glue.

- **Polyvinyl acetate** (PVA) is a white water-based liquid glue. It is not resistant to water. It is used mainly for internal joinery work, for example on furniture which is not exposed to moisture.
- **Polyurethane glue** is a moisture-resistant adhesive. When used, the glue foams up and this is removed. The glue is strong and fast setting.

Types of fixings

Nails		Use	Common sizes
Oval nails		These are used for general joinery for fixing two pieces of timber together. Oval nails are less likely to split the timber. They are often used in skirting boards.	From 25 mm to 100 mm
Panel pins		These are used for attaching small mouldings and small sectioned timber.	From 20 mm to 40 mm
Round wire nails		These are used in general carpentry, often with carcass sawn timber.	From 25 mm to 15 mm

Other fixings		Use	Common sizes
Pozidriv® wood screws		These have a variety of uses, from fixing door hinges to fixing shelves to a wall.	Length – from 12 mm to 150 mm **Gauge** – from 2 mm to 6.5 mm
Wall plugs (red, brown)	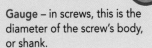	Wall plugs fit snugly in pre-drilled holes in brick walls. The plug holds the woodscrew in the wall by expanding when the screw is driven in. Different sizes are represented by different colours.	Brown – 7 mm diameter Red – 5 mm diameter

Activity 6.2

1 Use a woodscrew catalogue to research the different sizes of Pozidriv® woodscrew. Draw a table to show your findings.

2 Find out what the different parts of a screw are called. Now draw a screw and label the parts.

3 Why are there red and brown wall plugs?

Finishing materials

Abrasive papers are available in various **grades**. The lower the grade number on the back of the paper, the rougher it is. Coarse abrasive paper has a low grade number. The higher the grade number, the smoother it is. Fine abrasive paper has a high grade number.

Typical grade numbers found on abrasive paper are 40, 60, 80, 120 and 240. It is advisable to use a sanding block when sanding as this helps to keep the surface even.

More specialist abrasive papers include:

- garnet paper – this is made from natural crushed garnet stones. You can use it for hand sanding of timber. The garnet paper produces a smooth surface on the timber
- aluminium oxide paper – this is made from aluminium oxide particles. This paper produces a smooth finish and will not clog up with dust particles when used.

Key term

Grades – the grade depends on the size and quantity of abrasive particles on the abrasive paper.

TOPIC **A.2**

▶ Safe use and storage of carpentry and joinery tools, materials and equipment

Introduction

The quality of your carpentry and joinery depends on the safe use of the hand tools and equipment you use. Tools are not cheap, so you should look after them carefully. It is also very important to behave appropriately when using your tools because carpentry and joinery tools can be sharp or hazardous. Careless behaviour on a construction site can be very dangerous and you could be suspended from working on site because of this.

▶ Selecting and using PPE

Personal protective equipment or PPE is clothing and equipment that can be used to reduce the risk of injury. Use your PPE when safety signs show it is needed or you are instructed to do so.

PPE should always be the last resort when reducing risk in a workshop or on site. Do not use PPE until you have taken all other possible measures to remove or reduce hazards. This could be as simple as moving stored timber to a place out of the way.

Remember

Health and safety may sound dull but it is very important when working in a workshop or on site. You should always have a positive attitude towards health and safety – in construction, people's lives might depend on it.

Discussion

Why is it important to use the appropriate PPE?

Maintaining a tidy work area

Whether you are working in a workshop or on a construction site, it is always important to tidy as you go. Put tools back in the right place out of the way, as this means that they will not get damaged. It also means that people will not injure themselves on your tools.

Another way of maintaining a tidy work area is to clear away rubbish as it builds up in your work area. This will keep the area uncluttered and safe, and will prevent trips and falls. This is called good housekeeping.

Safe manual handling techniques

In carpentry and joinery, you may have to move large or heavy items such as long pieces of timber or large sheets of plywood. It is important to make sure that you lift these items in a safe, controlled manner. This will reduce the risk of **musculoskeletal** injuries.

Take the time to plan your lifting task and follow these steps.

1 Get your body (i.e. your waist) as close as possible to the load.
2 Adopt a stable position with both feet shoulder-width apart and knees bent.
3 Make sure that your back is straight and get a secure hold of the load. Use the whole of your hand, not just your fingertips.
4 Straighten up slowly without twisting.

Always make sure that you can see where you are going and stop for a rest if you need to.

Cleaning tools

Make sure that you clean your tools immediately after you use them. A clean and well-maintained tool is easier to use than a tool that has been poorly maintained. Often, they are also safer. For instance, a sharp chisel is safer to use than a blunt chisel as you need to use less force to cut timber with it. A blunt chisel may even fly off course because it cannot cut into the timber efficiently.

Safe use and storage of tools and equipment

You should always maintain a clean and tidy storage area. Store timber neatly in racks with heavy timber sections at the bottom of the rack, and smaller timber sections at the top of the rack. You should not store timber above shoulder height if you are handling it without equipment.

You should store carpentry and joinery tools in an organised way so you can easily identify them and get them out safely. The storage area should be lockable for security reasons. You should return tools to their storage place as soon as you have finished with them, ready for the next person to use.

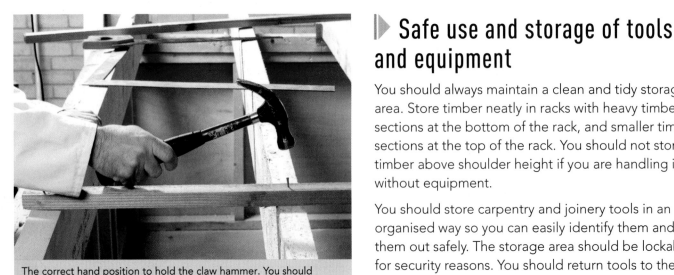

The correct hand position to hold the claw hammer. You should always use tools correctly. It makes you safer and often requires less effort too!

Assessment activity 6.1

1 You are an apprentice in a joinery shop making wooden window frames. Your supervisor has asked you to produce a list of the tools and equipment needed to measure, mark out and cut the timber for the job. Remember to give reasons for your choices.

2 Now that you have listed the tools and equipment, you have been asked to create a leaflet for other apprentices about the PPE needed for this job.

Tip

The best answers will **evaluate** the tools that they have selected. This means that you explain why you would use each particular tool, and then bring all this information together to form a conclusion about your choice. Remember that your conclusions should always be supported by evidence.

Learning aim B **TOPIC** **B.1**

▶ Health and safety

Introduction

In this topic you will learn about health and safety practices in carpentry and joinery. Health and safety can seem quite dull but it is really important that you take it seriously, especially when working at height or with electric cutting tools.

▶ Identifying hazards and risks

Before starting your work, you will have to do a risk assessment. This involves identifying the hazards in the workplace.

A hazard is something that has the potential to cause harm. For example, the workshop floor may be messy with bits of timber that people could trip over. This is a hazard.

A risk is the level of danger that a hazard poses. For example, a very messy workshop floor where lots of joiners are working means that there is a high risk of an accident happening.

Some hazards in joinery can be physical, chemical or just down to human error:

- physical hazards include storing timber incorrectly so it is likely to fall over or be tripped over
- chemical hazards could occur from the type of wood glue that you are using, and you control the risk by wearing protective gloves
- human error can also cause hazards – for example, a person not using a chisel correctly.

▶ Identifying people at risk

As part of the risk assessment process, you need to look at who might be harmed or affected by the hazards you have identified on the work you are about to perform. People at risk may be:

- operatives such as carpenters and joiners or others working on site
- employees
- employers
- visitors
- the general public.

Did you know?

The Health and Safety at Work etc. Act 1974 requires employers and employees to take reasonable care of themselves and others. For people to do this, there has to be a safe system of work in place.

Discussion

You tutor has told you a timber delivery has arrived. You need to unload the long timber planks from the lorry to the timber store at your training centre.

- What hazards are there in doing this?
- What could be done to prevent accidents?

Key term

Identification – in this context, this means looking at and accounting for all the people who may be affected by a hazard.

Control measures

When you have identified all of the hazards in your work, you should work out the level of risk for each. If the risk is high, you may need to use control measures to bring it down to an acceptable level.

Wearing PPE is one control measure. This includes:

- safety boots to protect feet and toes from dropped timber or tools
- a safety helmet to protect your head when moving around scaffolding and from falling objects
- eye protection such as safety glasses and goggles to protect your eyes from dust caused by cutting timber
- a dust mask to prevent you from breathing in wood dust when cutting timber
- hearing protection such as ear plugs or ear defenders to prevent hearing damage
- knee pads to prevent damage to the knees caused by kneeling while working
- gloves to prevent splinters and abrasion to the skin, as well as giving better grip when handling materials on site. They should also be used when using glues.

When working on site, you should also wear high-visibility clothing so that other operatives can see you, especially those operating machinery and heavy plant.

PPE used in carpentry and joinery.

Remember

Never use ear plugs that have been used by someone else.

Discussion

How do the hazards you face in the workshop differ from the hazards you might face on a construction site?

Link

See page 158 for more detail about safe manual handling techniques.

Safe working practices

Safe working practices can be as simple as maintaining a tidy work area, using safe manual handling techniques or having a positive attitude towards health and safety.

Case study

Lewis is working at a bench alongside Tom and Hasan. Tom and Hasan have not tidied their working area and are messing about with the chisels from their toolbox. Lewis asks them to help tidy up and reminds them of the need for appropriate behaviour. They tell Lewis he is boring and ignore him. Soon afterwards, Tom cuts his hand on a chisel and has to go to the first aid room.

1 Discuss in groups what Tom and Hasan should have done.
2 Did Lewis do the right thing? What else could he have done?
3 In your group, draw up a code of conduct. When you have finished, compare your code with that of another group.
4 Why is it important to have clear guidelines for appropriate behaviour?

Activity 6.3

Before any construction activity starts, you need to carry out a risk assessment. Take a look around your workshop and answer the following.

1 Identify and list the potential hazards you see around you.
2 Assess the level of risk (high, medium, low) for each potential hazard.
3 What control measures can you use to reduce the risk?

Construction of a timber frame

Introduction

In this topic you will learn how to construct a timber frame using four different types of joint.

Timber joints

There is a great variety of timber joints, some of which are specific to certain uses or sizes of timber. You will have to use four different joints in the frame that you produce.

Housing joint

This joint 'houses' another piece of timber. The size of the housing is related to the thickness of the timber you are using. The housing joint could be used to make a bookcase. The shelves would be housed into the side of the bookcase.

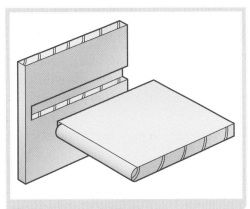

Figure 6.1 A housing joint.

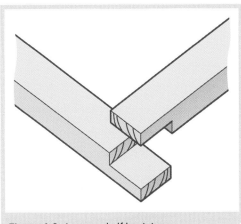

Figure 6.2 A corner half lap joint.

Corner half lap joint

This joint forms a right angle and could be used to form a simple frame, such as a timber frame supporting a bath panel. In this joint, half of the timber thickness is removed from both pieces of the two parts of the joint.

 Did you know?

Furniture from Egyptian tombs shows that the ancient Egyptians used dovetail joints.

Tee halving joint

A tee halving joint forms the shape of a 'T' when it is completed. Slots are cut in both pieces of timber so that they fit together.

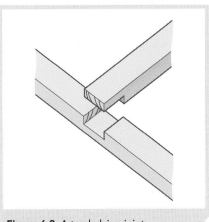

Figure 6.3 A tee halving joint.

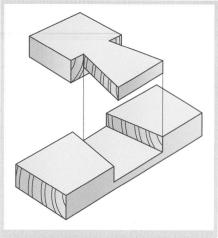

Figure 6.4 A dovetail halving joint.

Dovetail halving joint

This joint forms a right angle and could be used to form a simple frame. In this joint, half of the timber thickness is removed from both pieces of the two parts of the joint. The dovetail fits into the dovetail housing and will not pull out sideways.

Mortise and tenon joint

This joint is used to join two pieces of timber at right angles. It is one of the strongest joints and is often used in doors and windows. The mortise is the rectangular hole and the tenon is the part of the joint that fits into this. The thickness of the mortise hole is one-third of the thickness of the timber.

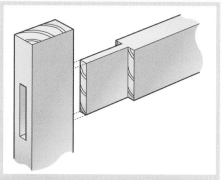

Figure 6.5 A mortise and tenon joint.

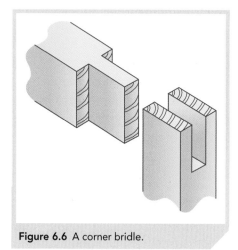

Figure 6.6 A corner bridle.

Tee bridle joint

The bridle joint is another way of joining two pieces of timber in a 'T' shape, like a tee halving. This type of joint is stronger than a tee halving joint. Figure 6.6 is a corner bridle. A tee bridle works in the same way but in the middle of a length of timber, not at the end.

Mitre joint

This is a joint between two pieces of wood that have been cut at the same angle. It can be used in picture frames or skirting boards.

Activity 6.4

Different joints have different uses and strengths. Describe the joints that you could use in the following frames:

- bath panel frame
- picture frame
- window frame
- door frame.

Marking out a timber frame

Your tutor will have given you a drawing or **setting out rod** of the timber frame you are going to make. A handy and easy method of marking out the timber is to use this drawing. Place the timber on the drawing and 'mark off' the length of the piece that is needed, using a sharp pencil. Also mark off the position of the joints on the timber. Next, use the pencil and tri-square to accurately transfer the mark around all the edges of the timber. Use hatched lines to mark clearly the part you are going to cut off.

Activity 6.5

A cutting list is a list that identifies all the different parts of a frame, their sizes and also their lengths. It will also tell you the type of timber to use.

1 Produce a cutting list for the frame you are going to make.

2 Using your list, calculate the total amount of timber you need. Add 10 per cent to the total amount calculated to allow for wastage.

3 Calculate the cost of the timber from two different timber suppliers and compare these.

The marking gauge is useful for scoring lines on the timber. It is easier to use the marking gauge to score lines when it is pushed away from your body. Putting the timber in a wood-working vice also makes it easier to use both hands to hold and control the marking gauge.

Useful techniques for cutting basic joints

It takes practice to use a saw correctly and accurately, so do not become frustrated. Every carpenter has had to learn how to saw straight.

- When holding your tenon saw, point your index finger along the saw blade in the direction you are going to cut.
- When you start the cut, gently score the timber with the saw blade.
- Always cut on the waste side of the line you have marked, otherwise you will take off more wood than you should do and your joint will not fit together properly.
- When using a bench hook, put it in the wood-working vice to prevent it from moving about while you are sawing the timber.
- Use the wood-working vice to hold pieces of timber when you are working on them, because this allows you to use both hands on the tools.

Assembling your timber frame

Before assembling the frame, all the inside surfaces should be cleaned up, as this is difficult to do after assembly. When your frame is ready to be put together, you should first assemble it with no glue to check everything fits properly. Then glue the frame together on a level surface and hold it together with sash cramps until the glue sets.

Your frame needs to be diagonally square. To check this, measure the diagonal measurements of your frame. The two diagonals should be the same length once assembled. If this is the case, your frame is square and all the corner angles are right angles or 90°. If the diagonals are not the same length, this means that one of the parts of your frame is either too long or too short.

Discussion

If a frame was made and one of the sides was short, would the diagonal measurements be the same length?

Key term

Tolerance – this is the amount of error that is acceptable in an object that is fit for purpose. If a joinery firm makes a lot of window frames that turn out to be the wrong size, the tolerances they have used are too broad. Huge gaps around a window frame are not acceptable tolerances!

Assessment activity 6.2   *Maths English*

Produce a 300 × 300 mm timber frame to the specification given to you by your teacher or tutor. The frame will include four different types of joints. It must also be square to at least 3 mm and have a joint gap **tolerance** of ± 3 mm or less.

Tips

To achieve the merit or distinction criteria, you need to ensure that:

- your frame is dimensionally square to 2 mm for merit or 1 mm for distinction
- your frame has a joint gap tolerance of ±2 mm for merit or ±1 mm for distinction
- your frame is not twisted.

The best way to prevent your frame from twisting is to mark out carefully from your setting out rod.

WorkSpace

▶ Kirsty Black

Carpentry foreman

I work for a carpentry and joinery firm, where I'm responsible for a team of four carpenters. Our firm specialises in interior fit-outs of shops and offices. The carpentry projects usually take three or four weeks, including weekends. We work on projects all over the country, meeting lots of different people, which makes my job very varied and interesting.

At the start of a job, I read and interpret the drawings that I have been given by the contract manager. I also make sure that we have all the necessary materials on site. When the carpenters and labourers turn up on site, I assign them their work. I also oversee the standard of their work, which means that at the end of each day I assess the standard of the work that has been done and give the carpenters any feedback.

I love my job because carpentry projects vary a lot. One week I might be working on an office refurbishment and the next I might be fitting kitchens for a housing association.

Think about it

1 Why are communication skills important to Kirsty's job?

2 What skills would you need to develop to become a carpentry foreman?

3 The carpentry project that Kirsty is in charge of is behind schedule. What could she do to finish the job on time?

Introduction

The oldest bricks in the world used to construct houses are over 6,000 years old. We have used mud mixed with water and dried in the sun to construct buildings for thousands of years. It is a cheap and quick method of constructing a building to shelter from the weather.

Do you have any thoughts about what skills you need to lay bricks? Have you wondered whether maths will be one of these skills? Laying bricks takes a great deal of skill. This unit will allow you to practise the techniques needed so you can build up speed and accuracy in brickwork and blockwork.

You will need to use quite a bit of maths in bricklaying. You have to organise the materials and work out how many courses are required for the plans you have been given. A finished wall should look correct horizontally and vertically, with bricks lining up correctly. This will help ensure a client is pleased with the work you have done.

As a bricklayer, you will have to work in all weathers when bricks can be laid and you will be working mainly outside. You will need to be physically fit but it is rewarding, skilled and satisfying work.

Assessment: You will be assessed by a series of assignments set by your teacher/tutor.

Learning aims

In this unit you will:

A understand tools, materials and equipment used for brickwork and blockwork

B develop practical skills and safe techniques to construct brickwork and blockwork.

I'd like to be a bricklayer, so I'm doing a BTEC First in Construction and the Built Environment and then I want to go on to an Apprenticeship. I want to work on commercial buildings that everyone will notice. I love the thought that loads of people will be able to see and admire my work – plus it'll keep me fit. I don't mind the thought of working in all weathers – I'll enjoy the sun in the summer and wrap up warm in the winter!

Mohammed, *17-year-old aspiring bricklayer*

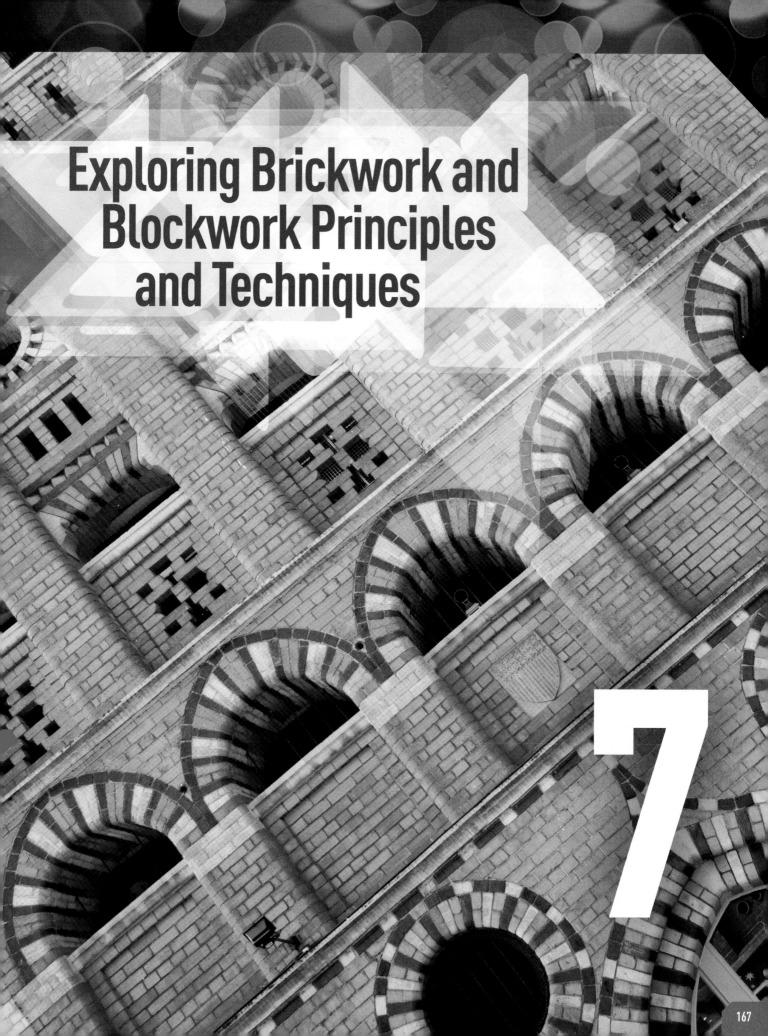

Exploring Brickwork and Blockwork Principles and Techniques

7

BTEC
Assessment Zone

This table shows what you must do in order to achieve a **Pass**, **Merit** or **Distinction** grade, and where you can find activities in this book to help you.

Assessment criteria			
Level 1	**Level 2 Pass**	**Level 2 Merit**	**Level 2 Distinction**
Learning aim A: Understand tools, materials and equipment used for brickwork and blockwork			
1A.1 Identify the purpose of tools and equipment, and the use of materials for brickwork and blockwork.	**2A.P1** Explain the selection and use of appropriate tools, materials and equipment for brickwork and blockwork. **See Assessment activity 7.1, page 172**	**2A.M1** Justify the selection of tools, materials and equipment for a specified brickwork and blockwork task. **See Assessment activity 7.1, page 172**	**2A.D1** Evaluate the use of alternative materials for a specified brickwork and blockwork task. **See Assessment activity 7.1, page 172**
1A.2 Outline the safe use and storage of brickwork and blockwork tools, materials and equipment.	**2A.P2** Explain the safe use and storage of brickwork and blockwork tools, materials and equipment. **See Assessment activity 7.1, page 172**		
Learning aim B: Develop practical skills using safe techniques to construct brickwork and blockwork			
1B.3 Identify hazards and control measures prior to commencing brickwork and blockwork activities.	**2B.P3** English Carry out a risk assessment prior to commencing brickwork and blockwork activities. **See Assessment activity 7.2, page 180**		
1B.4 Work safely using personal protection equipment with guidance.	**2B.P4** Comply with safe working practices including using appropriate personal protection equipment. **See Assessment activity 7.2, page 180**		
1B.5 Maths Construct a cavity wall to a given specification, with a minimum of six courses of bricks and two courses of blocks (450 mm high), with guidance.	**2B.P5** Maths Construct a cavity wall to a given specification with a minimum of nine courses of bricks and three course of blocks (675 mm high). **See Assessment activity 7.3, page 184**	**2B.M2** Maths Construct cavity walls to a given specification, with a minimum of nine courses of bricks and three courses of blocks (675 mm high), with an appropriate joint, where: • both faces of the wall are plumb to a tolerance of ±10 mm per m height and length • face plane deviation to both faces of the wall is accurate to ±10 mm. **See Assessment activity 7.3, page 184**	**2B.D1** Maths Construct a cavity wall to a given specification, with a central feature in the brick face using contrasting or recessed bricks, where: • brickwork is clean with bricks selected, blended and laid with an appropriate joint • both faces of the wall are plumb to a tolerance of ±5 mm per m height and length • face plane deviation is accurate to ±5 mm. **See Assessment activity 7.3, page 184**

English	Opportunity to practise English skills	Maths	Opportunity to practise mathematical skills

How you will be assessed

This unit is internally assessed by one or two assignments set by your tutor or teacher. These will cover a range of the theoretical assessment criteria for this unit. The assessments will contain a scenario to help you focus on what to include in your written evidence in support of the grading criteria. The second learning outcome will be workshop based; you will produce practically built models of a cavity wall that contains brickwork and blockwork with wall ties.

The assessments will contain an opportunity to work towards merit and distinction level for your final grade. You will need to extend many of the topic areas in order to achieve these higher grades. In the practical models, this will be measured in terms of accuracy against the given drawing. Make sure that you meet the assessment deadlines in order to receive positive feedback from your assessor. The unit specification will give you additional guidance as to the evidence requirements for each grading criterion.

▶ Tools and equipment used to construct brickwork and blockwork

Introduction

Laying bricks takes a great deal of preparation. You need the right resources, the bricks and blocks stacked to the right height, the mortar set up on a spot board and the right tools for bricklaying. All this time spent preparing will help you ensure a good level of quality in the work you produce.

You will need to use many different tools to construct and finish off a cavity external wall. You will lay the bricks using a walling trowel, and when you have laid enough, you then **point** the wall. This section looks at some common bricklaying tools you will use and practise with. These can be categorised into the different way the tools are used:

- measuring and setting out
- walling and pointing
- cutting brickwork and blockwork.

▶ Setting-out tools and equipment

The quality of the brickwork and blockwork will depend on how accurately you set it out. Using a spirit level that is accurate will ensure that your mortar joints are horizontal and that the face of the wall is vertical. Brickwork is often 'laid to a line'. This is the string line that is stretched along the top of the bricks, so they can be laid and tapped down into the position shown by the string line.

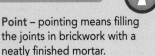
Key term

Point – pointing means filling the joints in brickwork with a neatly finished mortar.

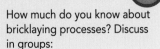
Discussion

How much do you know about bricklaying processes? Discuss in groups:

1 Would the bricklayer prepare the working area?

2 Who would mix the mortar for laying bricks?

3 How would a bricklayer check for quality as they build?

4 What tools will a bricklayer need?

Now find out what other groups thought and see whether their answers are different from yours.

Key term

Gauge – the depth of a brick or block plus one bed joint. For example, a brick is 65 mm depth + 10 mm = 75 mm gauge.

Measuring tape You use this to measure and check coursing of brickwork and calculation of quantities.	
Gauge rod You use this to check **gauge**. It is often a piece of planned softwood timber with saw cuts within it every 75 mm. This indicates the brick plus a joint dimension.	Gauge rod
Spirit level You use this to check the brickwork or blockwork both vertically and horizontally.	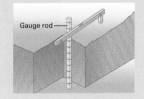

Builder's line and pins

You insert the pins into joints when corners are formed. You stretch the line from pin to pin and bricks can then be laid to this line.

Corner blocks

You use these with a string line. They allow the line to be clipped to a corner and stretched across. They work in the same way as pins.

Building profiles

You attach these to corners where walls meet. They allow you to build a length of wall without having to complete the corners first.

Tingle plates

This is a plate that clips on to the builder's line and rests on top of a brick. It supports the line in the middle and stops it from sagging, which would affect the quality of the horizontal line.

Activity 7.1

The use of profiles can be quite complicated. Undertake some research to find out how they are fitted to a corner.

Remember

Everyone can see the quality of the brickwork when it is finished. This quality will only be as good as the time and care taken to set out, check and measure.

▶ Hand tools and equipment

Walling and pointing tools

You will use lots of different tools in your work and they all have different functions. You will need to know what each one is for.

Walling trowel

A walling trowel is manufactured from stainless steel and has a non-slip handle.

Pointing trowel

This is smaller than a walling trowel and is used for forming weather-struck pointing to brickwork.

Jointing iron

This is used to form a 'bucket handle' joint to the mortar surface.

Wheeled recessed jointer

This is a hand tool that has an adjustable pin in it. This is run up and down the joints to remove excess mortar and recess the joint, forming an architectural feature.

Key term

Bucket handle – a joint that is rounded, forming a concave shape to the mortar joint in the brick wall. It is the most common joint.

Key term

Stretcher – the dimension of a brick along its length, normally 215 mm.

Cutting tools

Facing brickwork and internal skins of blockwork often have to be cut where a full **stretcher** cannot be fitted in the running length of a wall. These bricks are commonly cut using hand tools, but you can also cut them with a petrol rotating saw and a diamond blade for a clean, smooth cut.

Brick hammer You use this to dress or clean the brick that has been cut free of any raised points on the face of the cut.	
Club hammer You use this with a brick bolster to cut bricks.	
Bolster chisel You use this with a shield to cut bricks.	

Research

Look on a tool manufacturer's website at the different hand tools that you can use to cut bricks. See if you can find a petrol saw with a diamond blade. What do you think are the advantages of the petrol saw?

Remember

Cutting often involves the use of a bolster and hammer. You should wear safety gloves and goggles in case of flying brick chips. Always ensure that the head of the bolster is sharp and not rounded over. This rounding over is caused by being hit by the hammer; the bolster gradually forms a mushroom on the end. Any part of this can then break off and fly into someone's face.

Assessment activity 7.1

1 You are working as a trainee with a bricklaying firm. They have asked you to produce a fact sheet for new trainees about the sort of tools and equipment they will be using. In the leaflet, explain the tools, materials and equipment you would select for the construction of stretcher bond facing brickwork. Make sure that you explain the safe use and storage of each described tool and material.

2 A client has asked for the mortar joints on their brickwork to the house to be weather-struck on the north side and recessed on the south-facing side next to the external patio area. You will need to use a pointing trowel and a recessed tool. Justify the two tools that will be required for each of the two pointing tasks by explaining why these are used.

Tips
Remember, to justify means to give reasons of evidence to support opinion in order to show how conclusions have been arrived at.

▶ Materials used for constructing brickwork and blockwork

Introduction

Bricks have been made from local clays for hundreds of years. These are then fired in a kiln to make them into a useful facing brick product. Because of the different local materials, they are available in lots of different colours and textures.

▶ Bricks

There are lots of different bricks used for facing work. They are made for different applications and locations. For example, bricks used below a damp-proof course need to be hardwearing and dense to resist the increased moisture and the effects of freezing. Typical bricks are:

- common bricks – these are cheap clay bricks. They are mass produced and are often used in locations where they cannot be seen
- engineering bricks – these are used in very moist areas. They are especially designed to be used for manhole construction in drainage and in foundations below damp-proof courses
- **facing bricks** – these are decorative bricks with a face that is often coloured or has a different texture. They are often used with a coloured mortar to provide a decorative and architectural feature to the facing brickwork.

 Key term

Facing bricks – bricks with a decorative face to provide an attractive wall.

Can you think of any examples of decorative brickwork in your local area?

▶ Blocks

Blocks are a cheap way of constructing walls quickly and easily. They are equal to six bricks in area and are normally covered with a plaster finish. As such, work involving these is not called 'facework' as it is not seen. Typical blocks are as follows.

- Solid blocks are used in areas of high loading, as they can support heavier loads than a lightweight block. Solid blocks are denser and heavier and harder to cut.
- Insulation blocks are made from cement and an **air entraining** agent that forms millions of tiny bubbles within the block. These bubbles trap air, increasing their insulation properties, which helps reduce heat loss from a building.
- Fair faced blocks have one face that is smooth and even. This means they can be used in places like sports halls, where they can be laid and painted to provide an economical finish.

Table 7.1 shows some possible locations for using bricks and blocks.

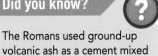
Table 7.1 Locations for the use of bricks and blocks

Material	Internal location	External location
Bricks	• Decorative feature walls, for example, fireplaces • Structural work, for example, supporting the ends of steel or concrete beams	• Skins of cavity walls forming the outside skin of facing brickwork • Manholes, inspection chambers used in drainage and below damp-proof courses
Blocks	• Internal plastered walls which separate rooms • Can be used from the internal foundation within the sub-structure	• The internal skins of cavity walls that are plaster finished • Can be used from the sub-structure strip foundation up to dpc as an internal skin

Activity 7.2

A local bricklayer has been asked to propose some alternative materials for a new housing scheme being built in the area. They have suggested thin joint masonry and brick slips. Evaluate the advantages and disadvantages of each material and present your conclusions in the form of a report.

▶ Materials used in preparing mortar

Mortar bonds bricks together and is a combination of several different materials as follows that are mixed together.

- Building sand or soft sand is the major element of mortar.
- Cement reacts with the water that is added (see below) and sets solid, binding the grains of sand together.
- Lime or plasticiser helps the mortar become workable, letting each particle of sand roll and making it easier to spread and level.
- Water is used to start the chemical reaction of the cement and the setting process.

Did you know?

The Romans used ground-up volcanic ash as a cement mixed with sand to form a mortar.

Mortar is mixed in different proportions according to the strength required. For example, you might add less sand, or more cement. Typical mortar mixes and proportions commonly used are:

- 1:3 cement / sand – this is a high-strength mix used to increase the strength of a wall and its load-bearing capacity
- 1:1:6 cement / lime / sand – this is a normal mix used for common brickwork walls.

▶ Materials used in forming cavities

Wall ties are used to hold together the two skins of an external cavity wall. They stabilise each skin and make the wall safer. They have to be placed within a wall 900 mm apart horizontally and 450 mm apart vertically. Wall ties are also used to hold any cavity insulation in place, using clips that slip on to the wall tie. Types of wall ties include:

- wire – a straight wire with a hook at each end, bedded in mortar
- double triangular – a triangle is formed at each end, bedded in mortar
- butterfly – a traditional wall tie that looks like butterfly wings
- fishtail – a split-end tie that looks like a fish tail
- polypropylene – these wall ties are made of polypropylene plastic, which can be manufactured from recycled plastics.

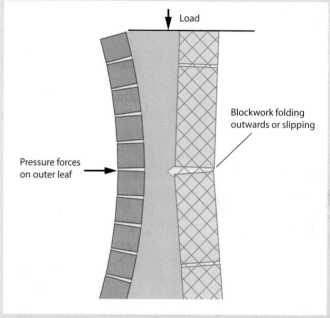

Load

Blockwork folding outwards or slipping

Pressure forces on outer leaf

Figure 7.1 Without wall ties, a cavity wall could be damaged by the load it has to bear.

▶ Material properties of bricks and blocks

The material properties are what make bricks and blocks fit for purpose within a location.

- Structural strength is very important for an external or load-bearing internal wall. These walls support the loads of the floor joists and roof trusses, and carry them down to the foundations.
- Durability is a material's ability to resist the weather over its lifecycle. This is often linked to the initial cost of the material and the quality of manufacture. For example, a brick wall is only as good as the mortar that holds it together.
- Aesthetics is the final look created by the wall. A good-quality, well-constructed wall with coloured mortar can give a lasting impression in terms of quality.
- Porosity is the ability of a material to absorb and let moisture through it. For example, a thermal block will absorb more water (due to its air bubbles) than an engineering brick.

 Just checking

1 Where might you use facing bricks?
2 What is 'facework'?
3 Where might you use engineering bricks?
4 Why would you include lime or plasticiser in mortar?
5 Name two kinds of wall tie.

▶ Safe use and storage of tools, materials and equipment

Introduction

Producing good-quality brickwork and blockwork relies on the safe use of the hand tools and equipment you use. Brickwork tools are expensive, so you should look after them, clean them after use, and repair and maintain them to extend their useful life.

Appropriate behaviour is also very important to ensure people's health and safety in construction. Careless behaviour on a construction site can be very dangerous and you could be suspended from working on-site because of this.

Why do you think it is important to use the correct PPE in different situations?

▶ Personal protective equipment (PPE)

In your working environment, you may need to use personal protective equipment (PPE). This includes:

- safety boots – these will protect your feet from any damage, for example if you drop a brick during laying
- hard hat or safety helmet – bricklayers often have to climb scaffolding when working, and this will protect your head when walking along scaffolding as well as protecting you from falling objects
- high-visibility jacket – this will make sure others on site can see you
- safety gloves – wear these when handling bricks and cement to prevent contact with sharp edges and to avoid your skin reacting to the cement
- safety glasses – wear these to stop flying debris or dust getting in your eyes while cutting bricks using a bolster
- barrier cream – put this on your hands to stop any absorption of chemicals and to stop materials sticking to your skin.

You may also have to use task-specific PPE. You should always choose this after carrying out a risk assessment. This will ensure that the PPE you use is the right equipment to reduce the risk.

Safety spectacles (top) give less protection than safety goggles (bottom). This is because they do not fully enclose the eyes.

Activity 7.3

You are an apprentice working for a local bricklayer. You have been asked by your college to prepare a list of PPE for other apprentice bricklayers.

1 Consider and list the risks that you might come into contact with on a construction site.

2 Explain how these risks can be reduced by using PPE.

▶ Maintaining a clean and tidy work area

Having a clean and tidy work area will help you avoid any hazards from slips, trips and falls. Brickwork is often constructed off scaffold platforms. Any debris from cutting and laying brickwork or blockwork must be cleared to get rid of any trip hazards which could cause an injury. You can reduce these hazards by:

- cleaning the platform regularly
- not over-stacking bricks and blocks
- making sure a clear walkway is left.

▶ Safe manual handling

Manual handling hazards are mainly due to weight, size, handling, grip and any trip hazards while moving bricklaying materials. You can reduce the risk from manual handling brickwork materials and equipment by:

- wearing appropriate PPE – safety footwear, hard hat, safety glasses, overalls and gloves as mentioned earlier
- using rough terrain forklifts to move bricks, blocks and mortar tubs
- stacking bricks and blocks properly next to the working area
- making sure bricks and blocks are kept dry so their weight is not increased before laying
- laying brickwork and blockwork when it is not raining or icy, so you do not slip on wet or frozen surfaces.

▶ Using tools and equipment correctly

If you use a bricklaying tool properly, you will extend its useful life, reduce wear and make sure no accidents or injuries happen.

Often bricklaying involves cutting bricks. Using a club hammer and bolster is the right way to make sure a brick is cut safely and cleanly. Many bricklayers use the edge of their walling trowel to achieve a cut across a facing brick. This is not a recommended method, so do not do it, but they do it because it is quick and cheap.

Link

See page 158 for more detail about safe manual handling techniques.

Did you know?

Under the Manual Handling Regulations, you should always undertake a risk assessment before moving or lifting an object.

Remember

Check that the bolster has a safety guard attached to the shaft and that the end has not been burred over as this can cause a hazard.

Cleaning tools after use

You should clean bricklaying tools at the end of the day to remove any spots of cement mortar. If you do not, the cement mortar will harden overnight and be much harder to remove the next morning. Washing down with water is an ideal method, but make sure you dry the tools properly to prevent rusting.

Take great care with the bricklaying level to make sure mortar does not set in the bubble observation window on the level as this would stop you being able to use the level.

Activity 7.4

You need to comply with safe working practices when using tools and equipment.

Imagine you have spent the day laying bricks and blocks to a cavity wall.

1 What would you do with your tools at the end of the day?
2 What would you do to the work area?
3 What condition would you leave a scaffold in?

Storing your tools

You should store brickwork tools correctly to avoid any injuries from sharp edges and points. Always keep bricklaying levels in their protective sleeves. Store trowels, hammers and bolsters in a suitable tool bag or box so you can carry them safely.

Taking time at the end of a working day to clean, maintain and store tools properly will save time and money on repair, replacement and maintenance in the future.

Storing bricks, blocks, sand and cement

- Bricks and blocks are normally delivered to a construction site banded and shrink-wrapped in polythene. This allows a forklift truck to pick them up and put them next to the working area where they are needed. The polythene protection keeps the materials dry and free from any mud or dirt that would spoil their appearance.

- Sand is normally delivered as a loose material as it is transported in bulk or in large bags weighing about 1 tonne. This needs to be tipped next to the cement mixer on a flat, clean surface. This prevents soil being mixed in with the sand, which would spoil the sand.

Why is it important for materials to be stored neatly on site?

- Cement for the construction of small areas is normally delivered in bags of 25 kg each. These should be stored above the ground to prevent any damage from frost or damp, which can make the cement set in the bag. Cement reacts with water, so open bags should be protected from rainfall. You will need to rotate the bags of cement, so that the bag on the bottom is not left there and fresh bags placed on top of it.

Did you know?

Cement is bagged as a 25 kg weight as this is the heaviest amount suggested by safety regulations to avoid any muscle or strain injuries.

Learning aim B   **TOPIC**   **B.1**

 # Health and safety

Introduction

Brickwork often involves working at height from scaffolding platforms that are constructed to support people and materials safely. Falls from height are the greatest cause of fatal accidents in the UK construction industry. You must take great care when working at height. Working conditions often change due to the weather, and rain and snow will turn a working platform into a slip hazard.

Link

This topic has links with all the practical units, including plumbing, electrical, joinery, painting, carpentry and joinery, in the identification of hazards, risks and appropriate control measures.

Identifying hazards and risks

Identifying hazards is the first step in preventing accidents. A **hazard** is something that could cause harm. For example, cement dust could cause an irritation if it enters the eyes. A **risk** is the result of any accident or event caused by the hazard. For example, burns to the eye caused by the cement dust.

Table 7.2 lists common hazards associated with brickwork and blockwork, and the risks that can develop from each hazard.

Key term

Musculoskeletal injuries – injuries affecting our muscles and bones.

Table 7.2 Hazards and risks of brickwork and blockwork

Hazards	Risks
Poor housekeeping	Slips, trips and falls can occur due to waste materials on the working platform.
Tools and equipment	Sharp edges and points of tools can cause cuts and puncture injuries to the skin.
Abrasive materials	Wind-blown sand can irritate the eyes.
Lime	This causes burning if it comes into contact with moisture in the eyes or throat.
Cement	This can cause burning when it comes into contact with moisture and human tissue.
Falling objects	Somebody could be struck by an object (such as a loose brick) as it falls, causing serious head injuries.
Untidy work area	Tools and materials left lying around could trap people's feet and therefore cause falls and injuries.
Lifting and moving	Manual handling strains and stresses can be caused by lifting and moving heavy objects in an incorrect way. This includes **musculoskeletal injuries**.
Flying debris from cutting	Injuries can be caused to the eyes when using a bolster and hammer or an abrasive wheel saw.

When you are about to work in a workshop environment, you need to be aware of the risks in the workshop.

Spend some time observing the workshop space you will be working in. Make a list of hazards you have identified.

Identifying people at risk

As part of the risk assessment process, you need to look at who might be harmed or affected by the hazards you have identified on the work you are about to perform. People at risk may include:

- operatives
- employees
- employers
- visitors
- the general public.

Using control measures

What hazards can you see in this photograph? What control measures is this bricklayer using?

When you have identified all of the hazards in your work, you should work out the level of risk for each. If the risk is high, you may need to control it to bring it down to an acceptable level. You must always reduce the risk as much as you can, using practical methods and procedures.

Control measures in brickwork and blockwork operations may include wearing:

- safety boots to protect feet and toes from dropping brickwork materials
- safety helmets to protect your head when moving around scaffolding and from falling objects
- gloves to give grip when picking up bricks and to protect your hands from the chemical reaction of cement
- overalls to protect your skin from mortar and other construction debris
- safety glasses and goggles to protect your eyes when cutting bricks.

The following items of PPE have been given as control measures in a risk assessment:

- goggles used when cutting bricks with a bolster
- mask worn when emptying bags of cement.

For each, identify why wearing this PPE is safe practice and how it reduces the risk from the hazard.

Observe a practical bricklaying activity. Remember to think about personal protective equipment (PPE) as well as the tools that are in use.

Now identify five hazards associated with this work and the risks that could develop from the hazards. Present your findings as a risk assessment.

▶ Cavity walls

▶ Preparing and setting up the work area

You will need to prepare the working area before the brick or block laying commences. The items you will need to prepare are:

- spot boards – plywood boards which you put mortar on before laying, and these need to be supported on blocks so they are at the right level for you to reach
- materials – you need to stack bricks and blocks to the right height so they are next to the line of laying and reduce the number of movements.

▶ Setting out the work

You would normally do this after looking at the architects' drawings that show the external dimensions of a building. From these, centre lines of walls are often plotted on to profile boards. You need to set out bricks on a 'facing wall' so all of the joints and courses are evenly spaced and 10 mm wide. Architects' dimensions do not always work to exact bricks so you may have to do some cutting.

Accurate setting out for the face and horizontal levels are the two most important tasks, along with making sure that corners are square.

Setting out can involve using specific items of equipment that can help with the process of laying bricks or blocks.

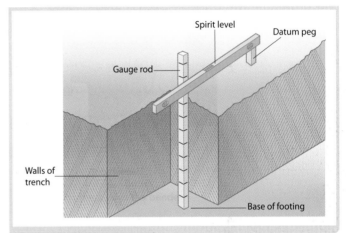

Figure 7.2 Using a gauge rod.

For example, a gauge rod helps you to work out the right height. Figure 7.2 shows how you would use a gauge rod in trenches to work out the right depth of the footing up to damp-proof course (dpc) level.

Corner profiles make it easier to construct corners without having to first build or 'raise' the corners and stretch a string line between them.

Figure 7.3 shows the use of pins, a tingle plate and a string line to keep the bricklaying level. The line pins are placed into a joint and the string line pulled between them. The corners have to be raised to start with. You can then lay to the level of the line.

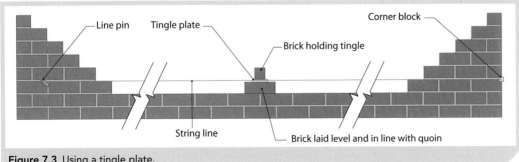

Figure 7.3 Using a tingle plate.

Figure 7.4 A tooled bucket handle joint.

Trowel skills

As you practise the skills discussed in this unit, you should start to lay bricks and blocks faster. Bricklayers are often paid not only by the hour but by the quantity of bricks that they lay, so speed and quality are essential. These two qualities are required for:

* rolling mortar – you have to roll mortar on the spot board so you can prepare it and pick it up on the trowel
* spreading and preparation of the bed joint – this involves getting sufficient mortar on the trowel, running it along the joint and spreading it out
* application of mortar to vertical joints – you have to 'butter' the ends of bricks with mortar and then place them in position
* finishing joints with a tooled 'bucket handle' joint – Figure 7.4 shows an example of this joint, which is often used to finish the joint and make it weather-tight.

Activity 7.7

Set up your mortar board and practise rolling the mortar. When you are ready, pick up a trowel of mortar and spread it evenly for a bed joint.

Figure 7.5 Stretcher bond.

Stretcher bond

Stretcher bond is generally used for low-rise domestic and commercial developments. This is because it is the only bond that can be used with the outer leaf of a cavity wall construction.

As you can see in Figure 7.5, the bricks are laid lengthways one after the other with a 10 mm joint between at the ends. Each course is shifted half a brick so the brick courses bond together.

Laying and bedding bricks and blocks to line

To build a wall without using corner profiles, you have to build the corners first and then fill in the wall. Building the corners enables you to fix a string line between each corner, which will act as a guide when laying bricks or blocks in between.

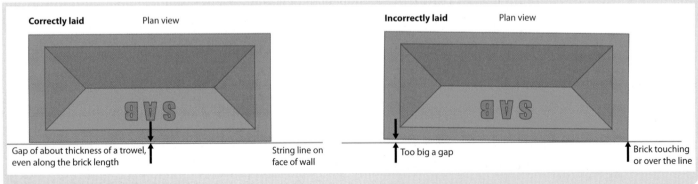

Figure 7.6 Laying to line.

Half-brick wall in stretcher bond

As the name suggests, this is a brick wall that is half a brick wide (100 mm), built in stretcher bond. A cavity wall consists of a half-brick wall in stretcher bond which is then joined using wall ties to a block wall to form the completed cavity external wall.

By constructing a half-brick wall as a practice model, you can try different pointing techniques on each face of your wall.

Block walling in stretcher bond

A cross-section through a typical modern house would show the use of a cavity external wall. The cavity is the space between the two skins of the wall. As shown in Figure 7.7, this cavity is nowadays completely filled with insulation to reduce heat loss.

The first stage of building a cavity is to construct the internal leaf of blockwork to an acceptable height, normally four or five blocks high. The stainless steel wall ties are then inserted. This allows the insulation to be clipped or secured around the wall ties as required. The front skin of facing brickwork is then added to complete the wall, with the wall ties incorporated into the wall as the work proceeds.

Forming cavities

A cavity or space is formed when you build two leaves of brickwork and blockwork and join them together using stainless steel wall ties. If you work on older houses, you will notice that traditional cavity walls did not contain any insulation, but these days the whole cavity is filled with insulation.

A cavity is designed to stop damp and moisture crossing it and getting into the building. However, as you can see in Figure 7.8, mortar has collected on a wall tie and at the base of the cavity. This mortar forms a 'cold bridge' and allows damp to cross the cavity. This is why the cavity insulation must be kept free from mortar splashes and drops.

There are two methods of ensuring that the cavity is kept clean from mortar splashes. The first method uses a batten that is the same width as the cavity. As you can see in Figure 7.9, this batten is suspended within the cavity and catches any extra mortar. You lift the batten up in stages as the work proceeds and the wall gets taller.

The second method involves leaving some bricks out at the base of the wall. The cavity is then cleaned manually through these gaps, to remove all of the mortar which may have dropped down inside the cavity. After this, the missing bricks are inserted and the wall is finished.

Remember, these diagrams do not include any cavity insulation.

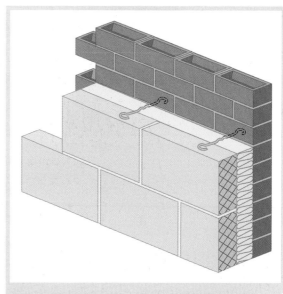

Figure 7.7 External cavity wall filled with insulation.

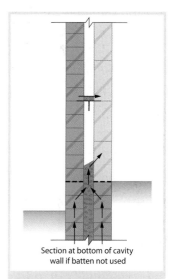

Section at bottom of cavity wall if batten not used

Figure 7.8 A cold bridge.

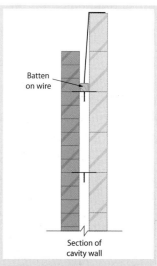

Batten on wire

Section of cavity wall

Figure 7.9 Using a batten to keep the cavity clean.

▶ Wall ties

Wall ties are essential to make a cavity wall stable. They tie both skins together, preventing any stability problems that a tall slender skin might face. The correct wall tie spacing must be followed according to the Building Regulations. This is shown in Figure 7.10.

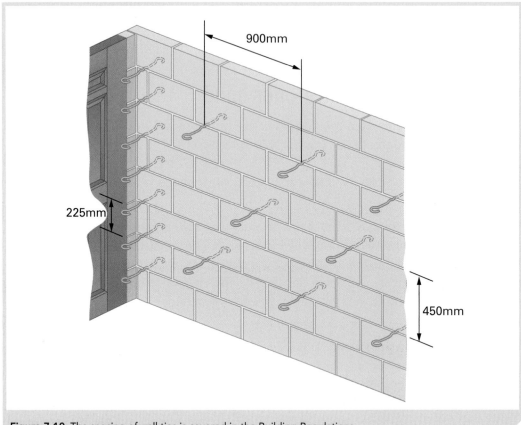

Figure 7.10 The spacing of wall ties is covered in the Building Regulations.

Where there are openings such as doors or windows, the wall tie spacing is reduced to 225 mm to provide additional support to the opening.

Assessment activity 7.3 *Maths*

You are a newly qualified bricklayer. You have been asked by a contractor to construct a sample of your bricklaying that is 675 mm high. The sample should be a cavity wall nine courses of bricks long and three courses of blocks high.

Tips

When constructing your cavity wall, try to ensure that:

- the wall is vertical to a tolerance within +- 10 mm of plumb for Merit or +- 5 mm of plumb for Distinction
- the wall's overall length is within +- 10 mm for Merit or +- 5 mm for Distinction
- the face of the wall does not deviate by +- 10 mm for Merit or +- 5 mm for Distinction
- the quality of your work is clean and jointed well.

To really show off your skills, include a central feature in the brick face of your wall using contrasting or recessed bricks. This could be a raised or sunken pattern.

WorkSpace

▶ **Frederick Bluku**

Bricklayer

I qualified as a bricklayer over six years ago, having completed levels 1 to 3 at my local technical college. During my last year at college, I got a bricklaying Apprenticeship with a local building company. This was the best way to apply my knowledge and understanding of brickwork on the construction of traditional houses.

I like working as a bricklayer, as it's mainly outdoor work, constructing cavity and internal walls for semi-detached and terraced houses. I always want to do the best work possible, as it could be seen for hundreds of years. It also has to stand up to the rain and the cold – I know because I work in those conditions!

With timber-framed buildings, the brickwork is a skin that is attached to the timber frame using stainless clips. This is a quicker way of producing an efficient building but still uses traditional brickwork.

Often I work on features at the gables where different-coloured and corbelled brickwork is used to enhance the appearance of the outside walls and gable ends. This has to be done right to achieve the quality needed.

The best bit of my job is when I've finished a whole wall of a home in different-coloured mortar and facing brickwork. I can stand back and appreciate the effort I've put into the wall to make the client happy.

Think about it

1 Would you want to work all year outdoors?

2 What job satisfaction does Frederick get from his job?

3 How could Frederick move into a supervision role later?

Introduction

What impact do colour and decoration have on your everyday life? We are surrounded by colours, textures, patterns and designs, and the effect this has on us cannot be underestimated. For example, colour can affect a person's mood. You may not have thought about it before, but there is a strong chance that your own lounge at home is decorated using yellow, red or orange base colours. This is because these are warm colours and they can make a room feel cosy.

To become a painter and decorator takes skill, dedication and a keen eye for detail. But achieving high-quality finishes, like that on the front door of 10 Downing Street also needs expert knowledge about the tools, materials and processes used.

Demand for good decorating skills is greater than ever, and this unit will help you develop the skills and knowledge needed to prepare for a career as a painter and decorator.

Assessment: You will be assessed by a series of assignments set by your teacher/tutor.

Learning aims

In this unit you will:

A understand tools, materials and equipment used in painting and decorating

B develop practical skills using safe working techniques to complete surface preparation tasks and apply surface finishes.

I've always been passionate about colour and texture, and wanted to use that passion to build myself a career. I really enjoy exploring how different colours and textures make us feel. This unit gave me the opportunity to improve my practical skills while also learning about the range of tools and materials that decorators use. When I've finished training, I want to run my own business as a decorator.

Lucy, 15-year-old aspiring decorator

Exploring Painting and Decorating Principles and Techniques

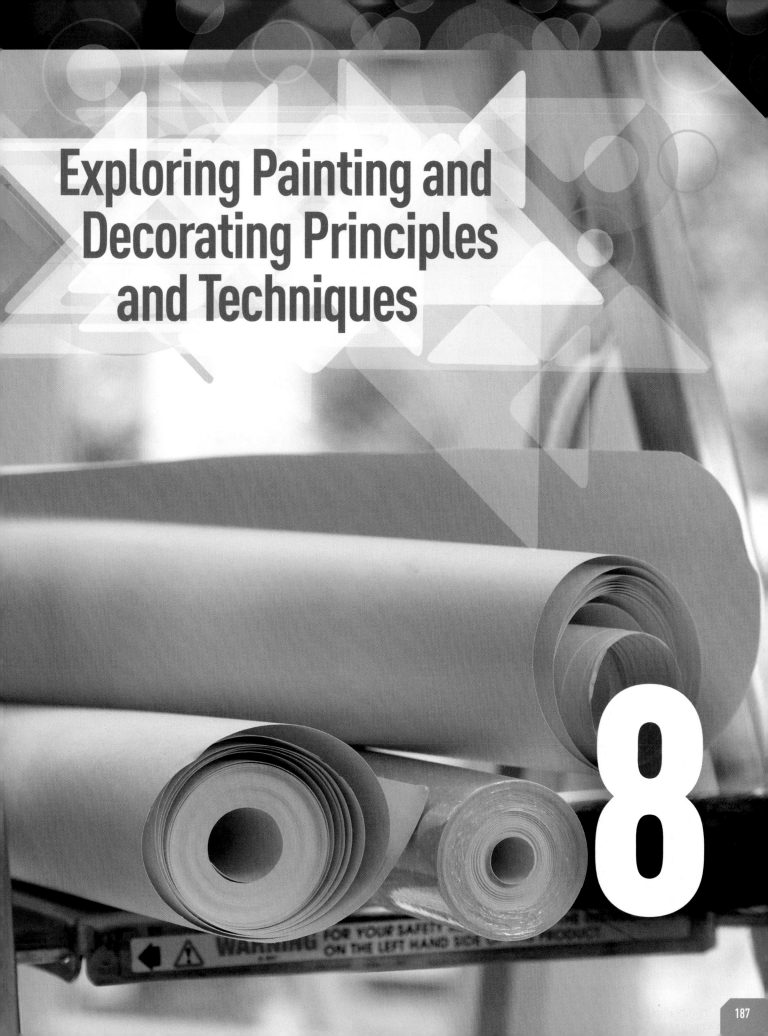

8

Assessment Zone

This table shows what you must do in order to achieve a **Pass**, **Merit** or **Distinction** grade, and where you can find activities in this book to help you.

Assessment criteria

Level 1	Level 2 Pass	Level 2 Merit	Level 2 Distinction
Learning aim A: Understand tools, materials and equipment used in painting and decorating			
1A.1 Identify the purpose of tools and equipment, and the use of materials in painting and decorating.	**2A.P1** Explain the selection and use of appropriate tools, materials and equipment in painting and decorating. **See Assessment activities 8.1 and 8.2, pages 193 and 203**	**2A.M1** Justify the selection of tools, materials and equipment for a specified painting and decorating task. **See Assessment activities 8.1 and 8.2, pages 193 and 203**	**2A.D1** Evaluate the use of alternative materials for a specified painting and decorating task. **See Assessment activities 8.1 and 8.2, pages 193 and 203**
1A.2 Outline the safe use and storage of painting and decorating tools, materials and equipment.	**2A.P2** Explain the safe use and storage of painting and decorating tools, materials and equipment. **See Assessment activities 8.1 and 8.2, pages 193 and 203**		
Learning aim B: Develop practical skills using safe working techniques to complete surface preparation tasks and apply surface finishes			
1B.3 Identify hazards and control measures prior to commencing painting and decorating tasks.	**2B.P3** English Carry out a risk assessment prior to commencing painting and decorating tasks. **See Assessment activity 8.3, page 208**		
1B.4 Work safely using personal protection equipment with guidance.	**2B.P4** Comply with safe working practices including using appropriate personal protection equipment. **See Assessment activity 8.3, page 208**		
1B.5 Prepare surfaces to receive undercoat, gloss and emulsion surface finishes by cleaning and removing dust.	**2B.P5** Prepare surfaces to receive undercoat, gloss and emulsion surface finishes by filling and sanding large surface defects.	**2B.M2** Prepare surfaces to receive undercoat, gloss and emulsion surface finishes by filling and sanding large and minor surface imperfections.	**2B.D2** Prepare surfaces to receive undercoat, gloss and emulsion surface finishes by: • filling and sanding large and minor surface imperfections • sanding smooth with no visible scoring or scratching of the surface.

Assessment criteria

Level 1	Level 2 **Pass**	Level 2 **Merit**	Level 2 **Distinction**
Learning aim B: Develop practical skills using safe working techniques to complete surface preparation tasks and apply surface finishes			
1B.6 Apply undercoat, gloss and emulsion surface finishes by brush and roller with: • minimal roller skid marks • no bristles visible on the finished surface.	**2B.P6** Apply undercoat, gloss and emulsion surface finishes by brush and roller with: • no bristles or roller skid marks visible on the finished surface.	**2B.M3** Apply undercoat, gloss and emulsion surface finishes by brush and roller with: • no brush marks or roller skid marks • minimal orange peel effect • neat cutting in • no more than one run, or sag visible on the finished surface.	**2B.D3** Apply undercoat, gloss and emulsion surface finishes by brush and roller with no visible defects: • no brush or roller skid marks • no orange peel effect • neat cutting in • no runs or sags visible on the finished surface.
1B.7 Maths Measure and cut wallpaper to required length, allowing 75 mm at each end for trimming, prior to hanging.	**2B.P7** Maths Measure and cut wallpaper to required length, allowing 50 mm at each end for trimming, prior to hanging.		
1B.8 Maths Hang patterned wallpaper to straight walls with: • no gaps or overlaps >5 mm • no air bubbles, creases or wrinkles • no pattern mismatch >5 mm.	**2B.P8** Maths Hang patterned wallpaper to straight walls with: • no gaps or overlaps >3 mm • no air bubbles, creases or wrinkles • no pattern mismatch >3 mm.	**2B.M4** Maths Hang patterned wallpaper to straight walls with: • no gaps or overlaps >2 mm • no air bubbles, creases or wrinkles • no pattern mismatch >2 mm.	**2B.D4** Maths Hang patterned wallpaper to straight walls with: • no gaps or overlaps • no air bubbles, creases or wrinkles • no pattern mismatch >1 mm.

English Opportunity to practise English skills

Maths Opportunity to practise mathematical skills

How you will be assessed

This unit will be assessed by a series of internally assessed tasks that will cover both the practical and written outcomes. These will be designed and marked by your tutor. You will be expected to show an understanding of the tools and materials used to apply paints and wallpapers to surfaces. You must also demonstrate the techniques you have learned to reach the standards needed. Your evidence for this unit could be in the form of:

- presentations
- practical tasks
- written assignments
- case studies
- risk assessments.

▶ Tools for painting and decorating

Introduction

There are many tools used for painting and decorating, and each one has a specific purpose. They can be broadly classified as preparation tools, paint application tools and wallpaper hanging tools.

▶ Surface preparation tools

Surface preparation is key to producing a quality finish that will last. You must prepare all surfaces correctly, whether they are new or previously painted. A lot of people wait until a surface is unsound before thinking about repainting, but it takes more time and money to fix an unsound surface. For example, all the paint might have to be removed, whereas a sound surface may only require a light rub down.

Scrapers
These are used for scraping away loose or flaking paint, or for removing old wall coverings, with a pushing motion. They have 2- to 4-inch blade widths and hardwood handles. Heavy-duty or blade scrapers have a very sharp blade and can be up to 6 inches in width. Be careful when using this type of scraper because it has a razor-sharp blade, and make sure you do not damage the surface.

Filling knife
This is used to apply fillers to cracks, holes and other surface **imperfections**. It is used in the opposite direction to a scraper, being pulled across a surface. It is like a scraper but has a thinner, more flexible blade.

Putty knife
This is used to apply and smooth putty when glazing. It is also great for filling corners or edges. It is similar to a scraper but has one straight edge and one curved. This makes it ideal to push filling materials into holes or cracks.

Shavehook
These are used in a pulling motion to scrape paint or varnish off surfaces. They usually have a wooden handle and can vary in shape at the end. Which one you choose depends on the job you are doing. For example, you might use a triangular shape for flat work, and a combination shavehook for more detailed work.

Caulking board
This has a plastic blade with a wooden handle across the top. It is used to apply fillers to larger areas, for example filling over plasterboard joints when **dry lining**. It is also used to smooth down vinyl wallpapers and remove air bubbles.

Hacking knife

This is used to remove old putty from around the glass when replacing window panes. It is used with a hammer, and has a sharp blade and a leather handle. This absorbs some of the impact, making it more comfortable to use.

Hot air stripper

This is mains powered and is used to remove old surface coatings that are usually unsound. It works like a hair dryer, although at a much higher temperature (up to 600°C). When burning coatings off with this, it is common to use the shavehook mentioned earlier. You should only use a hot air stripper after you have been trained.

Dusting brush

This is used to remove dust and loose debris from a surface before applying paint. It is an important tool used by the decorator to ensure a grit-free paint finish.

Sanding block

A sanding or rubbing block is used with various abrasive papers (such as sandpaper) when rubbing down. They make the preparation process easier. However, they should only be used on flat surfaces, as they would remove too much paint from raised or sharp areas.

 Remember

Burning off is the process of using heat to remove old paint films. As this gives off fumes, you must make sure that there is adequate ventilation and you are wearing the correct personal protective equipment (PPE).

 Did you know?

Until the mid-1960s paints contained lead, so you should take extra precautions if you ever need to burn off or prepare coatings on older buildings. Lead poisoning can cause damage to the kidneys, heart and nervous system. You would need to rub down affected surfaces wet, rather than dry, as this reduces the hazard from breathing in paint dust.

Case study

Water-based paint technology has come a long way in the last few years. This gives customers an even greater choice when choosing paints for the home or commercial buildings. Paint companies even have apps that can match paint to an existing colour.

Darren has worked for himself for a number of years and has noticed the changes that have happened since the Volatile Organic Compounds in Paints, Varnishes and Vehicle Refinishing Products Regulations 2012 came into force, especially because the cost of paint has increased as it has been developed to meet the new standards.

1 Why do you think water-based paints are becoming more popular?

2 What advice would you give to a client if they asked for the advantages and disadvantages of water-based and solvent-based paints?

3 Find out more about the VOC 2012 Regulations and how these relate to solvent-based paints.

Cutting in – painting a neat line between surfaces that touch each other – for example, the line between the wall and ceiling or where the skirting board meets the wall.

Ferrule – a metal band that secures the filling (bristles) to the handle.

Pile length – the length of the material used for the roller sleeve. Long pile sleeves are used for heavily textured or rough surfaces. Short pile sleeves give the best finish on smooth surfaces.

Orange peel – this occurs when a long pile roller sleeve is used on a smooth surface. It leaves the surface slightly textured, like an orange.

▶ Paint application tools

Selecting the correct application tools is vital to the success of a job. Not only does a paintbrush have to be the correct size for the job you are doing, it also has to have the correct bristle or filling type.

Paintbrushes

These are used to apply paint. They come in a range of sizes from 12 mm to 100 mm, and usually have natural or synthetic bristles (filling). Brushes are also used for **cutting in** when applying paints to large areas by roller. The better-quality brushes have a hardwood handle and stainless steel **ferrule**.

Cutting in using a natural-bristled brush.

Natural bristles come from animal hair, usually a hog, and are best for applying solvent-based paints. This is because they hold more paint and are generally stiffer than synthetic brushes.

Synthetic bristles are made of nylon and polyester and are lighter in colour than natural bristles. This type of brush is better for water-based paints, because the filling does not absorb water and it keeps its shape, producing a better finish.

People working on heritage buildings are not allowed to use rollers. This is because when the work was originally done, rollers had not been invented, so only a brush finish is allowed.

Paint rollers

A roller is used to apply paint to large areas quickly. They can be used on flat or textured surfaces. Rollers have a frame and a sleeve. The sleeve is available in different widths and **pile lengths**. If a long pile sleeve is used on a smooth surface, it may result in an **orange peel** effect. An extension pole can be inserted into the handle to allow you to paint high areas while standing on the ground.

Roller tray

This is usually made from plastic and holds the paint. The paint is poured into the trough section, leaving the front part to roll on to. This makes sure the right amount of paint is loaded on to the sleeve.

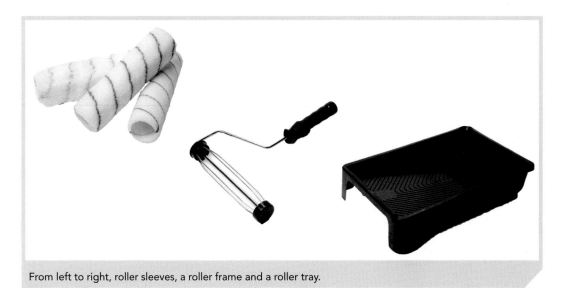

From left to right, roller sleeves, a roller frame and a roller tray.

Paint kettles and scuttles

Paint kettles are used to hold paint when using a brush. They are made from either plastic or galvanised steel. Plastic is most popular because all the dried layers of paint can just be peeled out.

Scuttles are usually made from plastic and can hold more paint than trays. They can have hooks or attachments that are helpful when working at height.

Assessment activity 8.1

Your employer has given you the following information about a job:

1 An exterior panel door is to be painted. It is in sound condition with the exception of the bottom two panels, which are flaking in places.

2 A hallway that has been previously painted is dirty and has some small cracks. It is to be finished in vinyl matt paint.

Produce a tool list for these jobs and explain why you have selected them.

Tips

- Name the tools and equipment needed to complete the job and why you have chosen each. You could also write a specification for all the materials needed for the preparation and painting tasks.
- Explain how you would safely use the tools, materials and equipment, and how they should be stored.

Research

Research the different types of roller fabrics available and the advantages of each.

Find out the name of the roller that has a 100 mm-wide sleeve and a long handle.

▶ Wallpaper hanging tools

Wallpapering needs a different range of tools from painting. Each one is designed to perform a specific job. Again, surface preparation is vital to get a quality end result.

As with all tools, paperhanging tools must be kept clean to keep them working correctly and to avoid damaging the face of the wallpaper.

Tape rule
This is used to produce accurate measurements when measuring a wall or ceiling before cutting the paper.

Paperhanging shears
These are used to cut and trim paper, both on the paste table and on the wall. They have sharp stainless steel blades and plastic handles. Take care when using or cleaning them, to avoid cuts. Shears can become blunt if they are not cleaned regularly during use.

Trimming knife
This is used with a decorator's straight edge to produce a neat cut when trimming paper. It has an extremely sharp blade that can be snapped off in sections to keep the blade fresh. This should be done using the slot at the back of the knife. The blade must be pulled in when not in use.

Decorator's straight edge
This is a metal bladed tool, similar to a caulk board, which helps create a straight cut and prevents the paper from tearing when it is being cut. The trimming knife cannot be used successfully without using a straight edge.

Plumb line
This is a length of string attached to a cylindrical weight held against the wall. This produces a perfect vertical line that is marked before hanging wallpaper. It is vital with patterned wallpaper to make sure that after working around a room, the last piece aligns with the first.

Spirit level
This is used to create vertical and horizontal lines. They are especially useful if using a split paper or for borders. Lengths of 600-1,000 mm are ideal for a decorator, as these are longer than the width of most wallpapers.

Paperhanging brush
This is made from natural bristle with a hardwood handle. It is used to smooth all types of paper on to a wall or ceiling. You need to apply pressure when using it, to remove air bubbles.

Paste brush

This is used to apply paste to wallpaper or to the wall and comes in sizes ranging from 125 mm to 175 mm. It has long bristles for speedy application and can be used for applying **size** to wall areas. It usually has a hardwood handle, natural bristles and a copper ferrule.

Paste table

This gives a long flat surface, around two metres in length. It offers support to wall coverings while you are measuring, cutting, pasting and folding.

Paste bucket

This is a large plastic bucket with measurements on the side to aid the paste-mixing process. You can fasten a piece of string across the top to give a resting place for the paste brush.

Seam roller

This is rolled down the joints when papering to make sure the joints are stuck down firmly. You must take care not to use it too much as this can cause **delamination**. The roller head can be made from plastic, hardwood or rubber.

Decorator's sponge

This is essential to keep papers and nearby surfaces free from paste. If paste is not removed, it dries shiny on a surface and can cause some paints to flake off.

Key terms

Size – a coating applied to a surface to make it less absorbent. Thinned-down paste can also be used for this job.

Delamination – when the two layers of paper separate. This can be caused by over-soaking the paper or using a seam roller too much.

Activity 8.2

Measure up your work area or classroom for wallpaper.

As a guide, find the area of the walls and divide the measurement by five. This will tell you how many rolls you will need. The 5 m² is the area that one roll of wallpaper will cover, allowing for wastage.

Take it further

The method outlined in Activity 8.2 for estimating wallpaper quantities is not the only method. Do some research to find another method that you can use.

▶ Materials in painting and decorating

Introduction

There is a vast number of different paints and wallpapers on the market today and the choice can be very confusing. Think about the last time you visited a DIY store. Did you notice aisles of paints, stacked from floor to ceiling, and rows of wallpapers, patterned and plain, smooth and textured? In this topic you will learn about the materials available and when and where they are best used.

Flaking can be caused by a number of reasons, including a poorly prepared or powdery surface.

Materials used by the decorator can be broadly divided into surface preparation materials and finishing materials.

▶ Surface preparation materials

Surface preparation materials are used to make surfaces ready to receive **paint systems**. They are used to make sure the surface is clean, smooth and has a **key**.

The existing condition of the surface will decide the extent of the preparation needed. The range of preparation includes the complete removal of broken-down paint, using heat or liquid paint removers, scraping off flaking paints, filling cracks, holes and other surface imperfections, washing dirt or grease off a surface, or just rubbing it down.

Coated abrasive papers

Abrasives are used to key, smooth or flatten a surface. There are various types and grades available. Abrasive papers are known as coated abrasives, and the size of abrasive particles decides the grade of the paper.

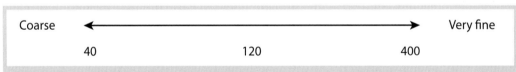

Figure 8.1 Common grades of abrasive papers in use

The most popular abrasive paper used by decorators today is aluminium oxide. This is usually green or yellow and is available in grades 40 to 120. The benefits of this type of abrasive are that it lasts longer than traditional sandpaper and is anti-clogging due to being **open coated** during the manufacturing process.

Activity 8.3

Find out what types of abrasives are available, what surfaces they would be used on and the grades used.

Some coated abrasives, such as silicon carbide, have a waterproof backing paper and can therefore be used wet or dry. This type of abrasive is usually used for finer work, with grades 120 to 400 used by the decorator.

For preparing surfaces in very poor condition, you could choose a 60 grade paper. Abrasive papers graded as 400 have very fine particles and would be best for preparing an undercoated surface before applying a high-quality gloss finish.

Abrasive powders and compounds

Abrasive powders are rubbed on to the surface and perform the same job as coated abrasive papers. However, these have mostly been replaced by coated abrasives.

Liquid paint removers

Paint systems that have broken down may require complete removal. If this is the case, using liquid paint remover is an option. This is applied thickly to the area to be removed and left for a period of time, depending on the type and thickness of coating to be removed. The paint remover breaks down the paint film, causing it to blister. The blistered area is then scraped off and washed down to neutralise the surface. Some liquid paint removers are self-neutralising and do not need any washing.

The main disadvantage of this process is that the paint remover is expensive and the work is labour intensive. You must take care when using this product to avoid contact with other areas and your skin. You need to wear PPE at all times, including gloves and safety glasses or goggles.

Detergents

You may need to wash some surfaces to remove dirt and grease before painting. You can do this with detergents and washing materials such as sugar soap.

Fillers

Fillers are used to **make good** surface imperfections and are available in either powder or ready-mixed types. Table 8.1 shows the type, use and properties of the main types in use today.

Table 8.1 Filler types, uses and properties

Filler type	Use	Properties
Powder-based	Filling holes and cracks in plaster and woodwork	• Easy to sand down • Shrinks on drying
Ready-mixed (fine surface)	Filling minor imperfections mainly in woodwork such as a window board	• Rubs to a very fine finish • Should only be used on shallow imperfections
Two pack (ready mixed)	Filling holes, cracks and surface imperfections in woodwork	• Very strong • Quick drying • Expensive
Caulk (tube filler)	Filling internal angles such as top edges of skirting and architrave	• Flexible • Fast application

Fillers should be stored off the floor, in a cool, dry environment. Powder fillers are the most sensitive to storage requirements. They are supplied in sacks of up to 10 kg, so you need to use correct manual handling techniques for lifting them.

Did you know?

Nicotine needs to be washed off a surface or sealed. If this does not happen, the colour of the nicotine will bleed through when a water-based paint is applied to the surface. This will keep happening, no matter how many coats are applied.

Key term

Make good – prepare a surface to be painted.

Discussion

In small groups, discuss the advantages and disadvantages of:

• filling flush or level with the surface
• filling proud (leaving the filler raised on the surface).

Filling using caulk.

▶ Types of paint

Paints are available in a wide range of different finishes and thousands of colours. Most paints used by the decorator are either water-based or solvent-based. Water-based paints are thinned with water and solvent-based paints are thinned with white spirit.

You cannot put just any paint on any surface. Paints have a very different function within a paint system. For example, an undercoat is designed to build up a paint system with high **opacity**.

Table 8.2 Common types of paint and their uses.

Name	Water- or solvent-based	Use	Properties
Primer	Water or solvent	• The first coat of paint that is applied to a bare surface	• Specific primers are needed for different surfaces, e.g. ferrous and non-ferrous metals or wood • Good adhesion to the surface
Acrylic primer/ undercoat	Water	• Can be used as a primer on bare wood or as a water-based undercoat	• Quick drying • Can usually see brush marks
Undercoat	Solvent	• Applied over primers or a previously painted surface, before the gloss	• High build with good opacity • Bonds well to primers or prepared surfaces
Eggshell	Water or solvent	• Mainly used as a finish on internal woodwork • Can also be used on walls and ceilings	• Dries to a mid-sheen finish • Can be wiped clean
Gloss finish	Water or solvent	• Mainly used on internal or external woodwork	• Very shiny finish • Hard-wearing • Good resistance to weather and abrasion
Emulsion	Water	• Internal walls and ceilings	• Available as a matt (flat) • Easily marked or damaged • Mid-sheen • Silk (high sheen) can highlight textured finishes

Paints are quite expensive and therefore need to be stored correctly. They should be kept in a secure locked area that is cool and well ventilated. Water-based paints also need to be protected from frost or they will turn lumpy and be ruined.

Application methods

Usually, paint is applied by brush and roller. An even application and the right amount of paint applied are essential for a good quality finish. There are three basic techniques that any painter and decorator must master.

1 Laying the paint onto the surface and spreading it out to ensure an even coverage of paint.

2 Cutting in – using brushes to paint areas of a surface that are too tight to be reached by rollers (such as where a wall meets the ceiling or another wall).

3 Laying off – this is when you use the tips of the brush to reduce or remove brush marks from the paint. It also evens the paint up on the surface.

▶ Wallpaper types and use

Wallpaper can be broadly classified as either preparatory papers or finished papers. Preparatory papers are usually classed as lining papers but can also include woodchip, Anaglypta™ and some blown vinyls. Finished papers do not require painting once hung and include washables, vinyls and flocks.

Lining papers

These create a surface of even **porosity** and help to hide minor surface defects. Lining paper is an ideal base for a finished paper or for painting. It is available in a range of grades, and in single, double and quadruple rolls. The standard width is 560 mm.

When **cross-lining** before hanging a finished paper or painting, it is important to put enough pressure on your hanging brush to avoid getting air bubbles.

Activity 8.4

In pairs, look around your classroom or workshop and make a list of all the materials you can see and surfaces that are painted. Now jot down whether you think they are porous or non-porous. Think about which materials would be most and least porous.

Lining paper comes in grades from 600 to 1,400. The thicker grades would be used for walls and ceilings in poor condition.

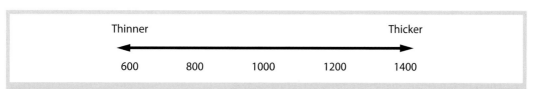

Thinner				Thicker
600	800	1000	1200	1400

Figure 8.2 Common grades or weights of lining paper in use

Did you know?

Acrylic matt paint is becoming very popular for use in homes because it is much harder-wearing than traditional vinyl emulsions.

Key terms

Porosity – a surface's ability to absorb moisture.

Cross-lining – hanging lining paper horizontally.

Did you know?

If you are lining and then painting the paper, you should hang it vertically instead of horizontally and the joints need to be butted (when the edges are touching).

Relief coverings

Anaglypta™ has a raised pattern and once painted, it creates a hard-wearing surface. Anaglypta™ comes in a standard roll size of 10.05 m by 0.53 m and is used to give a textured look. This means it can cover minor defects or walls in poor condition.

When applying Anaglypta™ you must take care not to over-soak it or apply too much pressure, as this will flatten the pattern.

Woodchip is classed as a relief paper and consists of two layers of paper with small bits of wood sandwiched between. It is available in a standard roll size and is hard-wearing once painted. There is no pattern to match, so it is easy to hang. However, you can only cut it with shears. Woodchip is not as popular as it used to be.

Blown vinyl consists of a paper backing with expanded PVA (polyvinyl acetate) on the surface, which is used to create the patterns. It is available in standard roll sizes and can hide ceilings and walls in poor condition. As it is a relief paper, it already has a flat back and therefore is not easily flattened on application. Blown vinyl is spongy and easily damaged once applied.

Washable wallpapers are usually a single layer of paper with a design printed on them and then coated with PVA to allow light cleaning. Used in domestic situations, they can create a high-quality look.

Paperback vinyl is smooth or slightly textured PVC (polyvinyl chloride) that is bonded to a backing paper, producing a hard-wearing washable surface. Vinyls can be used on most surfaces, including kitchens, bathrooms and high-traffic areas, as it can be scrubbed down.

Vinyl paper comes in a standard roll size of 10.05 m by 0.53 m, but it is also available for commercial use with widths of up to 1.3 m.

Flock is a backing paper or material that has fibres stuck to adhesive on the surface. It gives a luxurious feel to a room and is popular for feature walls due to its large bold patterns. It comes in a standard roll size and individual boxes to prevent it being crushed.

Why do you think blown vinyl could be used to mask minor surface defects?

Where would you be most likely to use a vinyl wallpaper?

Why might you choose to use flock wallpaper?

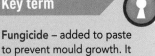
▷ Wallpaper adhesives and use

There are three main types of adhesive in use today as shown in Table 8.3. Cellulose and ready mixed are the most popular. Most adhesives contain **fungicide** so take care when using pastes – wash your hands after use and before you eat. Keep adhesives away from small children and pets.

Table 8.3 Types of adhesive in use

Adhesive type	Use with	Characteristics	Storage
Cellulose	• Lightweight vinyls • Lining papers • Washables • Woodchip • Anaglypta™ or blown vinyl	• High water content • Contains fungicide • Does not stain the paper • Inexpensive	• Only lasts a few days when mixed • In boxes in a cool, dry area
Ready mixed	• Heavyweight papers and vinyls • Flock • Washables	• Very good adhesion • Medium to low water content • Expensive	• Lasts a long time • In a cool dry area
Starch	• All preparatory papers • Medium-weight papers	• Some contain fungicide • Can stain the face of paper	• Once mixed, it should be used within two days

Application methods

Adhesives can be applied by brush, roller or paste machine. Brush is still a popular method for domestic work. However, when applying ready-mixed tub paste to the wider vinyls, it is most suitable to use a roller.

When pasting, it is important not to miss any areas as this will cause blisters and lifting edges. You also need to check the label that comes with wallpaper for information such as the pattern type, match and pasting instructions. International wallpaper symbols and their meaning can be found in Figure 8.3.

Figure 8.3 International wallpaper performance symbols. Why wouldn't these instructions just be written on the packaging?

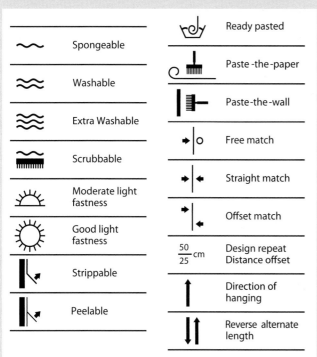

	Spongeable	
	Washable	
	Extra Washable	
	Scrubbable	
	Moderate light fastness	
	Good light fastness	
	Strippable	
	Peelable	
	Ready pasted	
	Paste-the-paper	
	Paste-the-wall	
	Free match	
	Straight match	
	Offset match	
	$\frac{50}{25}$ cm	Design repeat Distance offset
	Direction of hanging	
	Reverse alternate length	

Discussion

What do you think are the advantages of ready-mixed adhesive?

Did you know?

More and more papers now have a fabric backing, which means you can paste the wall and not the paper. Using Figure 8.3, find and draw the symbol you would find on a label for this.

Just checking

1 Is emulsion water-based or solvent-based?

2 Where would you use eggshell paint?

3 What sort of paint would you use on woodwork?

4 List three kinds of relief coverings.

5 What should you bear in mind when mixing up cellulose adhesive?

6 Why is fungicide used in adhesives?

▶ Equipment for painting and decorating

Introduction

This topic looks at the types and purpose of personal protective equipment (PPE), and the types of access equipment you will use while working on this unit.

Did you know?

The risks from both painting and paperhanging can be greatly reduced by wearing appropriate PPE.

▶ Personal protective equipment (PPE)

Essential PPE for the decorator is overalls and safety footwear. However, depending on what you are doing, you will need to wear other items.

Safety footwear
Safety boots or trainers are designed to protect the feet, should anything drop on them. They also give good grip when using access equipment.

Overalls
These are usually white and are designed to protect your body and clothes from dirt, paint and minor cuts. Overalls are either bib and brace or white trousers. Both have handy pockets for tools and personal belongings.

Hand protection
The thicker types of safety gloves are used when burning off, or when moving rough materials. These protect your hands from abrasions. Latex gloves are used to prevent paint from getting on your hands.

Eye protection
You should use safety goggles or glasses to protect your eyes when there is a chance of flying debris. You should also use them when removing paints.

Dust masks
These prevent the inhalation of dust that may be hazardous. They must be a good fit and be replaced regularly. You should wear them when rubbing down paints and fillers. Respirators protect against the inhalation of solvents. They should be used when applying solvent-based paints in confined or unventilated areas.

Barrier cream
You should use barrier cream when performing any painting tasks, especially when using solvent-based paints. It prevents harmful chemicals from entering the skin.

Activity 8.5

You are about to start decorating a client's house. One room is to be decorated using wallpaper and the staircase also needs to be painted. The room needs the old wallpaper removed and the surfaces prepared. The staircase is to be prepared and have emulsion applied to the ceiling and walls. The woodwork is to receive one coat of undercoat and one coat of gloss.

1 What sort of PPE do you think you might need? Give reasons for your choices.

2 What precautions should you take when working on these two tasks?

▶ Access equipment

As a decorator you often have to work at height. This may be just to reach the top of an interior wall or at greater height when working outside. When working at height internally, low-level access equipment is usually enough and includes stepladders, hop-ups and trestle working platforms.

Stepladders

Stepladders are the most common type of access equipment used. They come in a variety of different sizes, are used for various tasks and can be used internally and externally. Stepladders should be in good condition, fully open and placed on a firm, level base. Make sure your knees are always below the top of the stepladder when using it. Stepladders are used on their own if you are papering a wall or cutting-in, or you can use two with a plank spanning between them when papering a ceiling.

Hop-ups

These are ideal for low-level work. They provide a little extra height, usually around 400 mm off the ground. This makes them well suited for use in modern properties with lower ceilings of around 2.4 m in height.

Trestle working platforms

Trestles are used with a staging board to access large areas or a long run of work. Trestles, like stepladders, are made from aluminium or wood and the same safety procedures apply.

Assessment activity 8.2

You have been asked to recommend a paper with a raised pattern. The job is a staircase in a house that was built in the 1970s.

1 Compare two different papers with a raised pattern.

2 What type of wallpaper would you recommend for this situation? Give your reasons, highlighting the advantages and disadvantages of choices available.

What safety precautions should you take when using access equipment such as a stepladder?

 Remember

Never use damaged or faulty equipment. Instead you should report it to whoever is in charge.

 Did you know

All access equipment should be stored in a cool dry environment and checked before use.

 Take it further

Evaluate the proposed use of a flock paper in the entrance hall of a large and busy public building, and research some alternative materials. Remember that evaluating means you need to review the information you gather, so that you can come to a conclusion.

Health and safety

Introduction

It is very important when working to ensure the health and safety of yourself and others around you. You will need to be able to identify the hazards in your workplace and complete a risk assessment to record these correctly.

The health, safety and welfare of employers, employees and members of the general public must be protected at all times during work operations. This is covered by a number of key acts and regulations, the main ones being:

- the Health and Safety at Work etc. Act 1974
- the Control of Substances Hazardous to Health (COSHH) Regulations 2002.

Activity 8.6

Look around your work area and make a list of any hazards you can spot.

Risk assessment

Risk assessments are produced before a job starts. They are needed by law and are used to identify potential hazards on a job. A hazard is anything that has the potential to cause harm, while a risk is the result of any accident that happened because of the hazard. It is an employer's responsibility to complete risk assessments.

For the practical part of this unit, you will need to produce a risk assessment on the practical tasks of preparing surfaces, applying paints and hanging wallpaper.

Activity 8.7

1 Consider a typical construction site, such as a new housing site or an extension to your school or college. How many potential hazards can you identify? Produce a poster that warns the employees of a construction company about all the potential hazards on a construction site.

2 Imagine that you are a health and safety manager for a construction company. Write a set of rules that could apply to **all** of your construction sites.

Identifying hazards and risks

Hazards in painting and decorating must be identified, assessed and then controlled. You should always assess the hazards of any practical task that you are going to do. Carrying out a risk assessment makes sure that you look at the task and analyse it carefully.

Table 8.4 Hazards, risks and control measures encountered in painting and decorating

Hazard	Risk	Control measure
An untidy work area	Slips, trips and falls.	Make sure that your work area is kept tidy, as this will reduce the number of trip or slip hazards.
Sharp tools	Cuts, injuries or ailments caused by tools and equipment.	Always handle scrapers and trimming knives carefully, and make sure that your technique is as safe as possible.
Abrasive materials, solvents, fungicidal pastes, dust	Irritation to skin, eyes and respiratory system. For example, if white spirit is used to clean hands, it can dry out the skin and eventually lead to dermatitis. If solvents or dust are breathed in, they can damage your respiratory system.	Use of suitable PPE such as gloves, goggles and dust masks to prevent contact with hazardous substances.
Falling objects	Injury or concussion. Falling objects could include paint tins.	Make sure that your work area is kept tidy, especially when working at height or on a working platform. Hard hats may also be worn.
Repetitive bending or stretching, or heavy lifting	**Musculoskeletal injuries** and muscular strains.	Make sure that you use the correct lifting technique when lifting paints, paper and bagged materials.

Remember

As well as being a hazard, an untidy work area can look unprofessional when dealing with clients and it can make a job take longer.

Key term

Musculoskeletal injuries – injuries affecting our muscles and bones.

Link

See page 158 for more detail about safe manual handling techniques.

Once you have identified a list of hazards, you should then assess the control measures that you can use. This allows you to see whether the risk rating is reduced to an acceptable level.

▶ Identification of people at risk

You should always think about the different people who may be at risk from the hazards you have identified. This needs to be included on a risk assessment and should include **all** the people who could be affected.

People at risk could include:

- the general public
- visitors to the site – such as clients and local planning officers
- employers
- employees – either directly employed or subcontractors.

Control measures

When a hazard has been identified, you can use control measures to reduce or remove the risk posed by the hazard. PPE should be the last resort and is used only if the risk cannot be removed in any other way. Control measures may include:

- safety boots to protect feet and toes from paint tins and other items falling on feet
- gloves and overalls to keep paint, paste and dust off your skin and clothing
- safety glasses or goggles to protect the eyes from dust and flakes of paint or wallpaper as they are removed. They also protect the eyes from splashes of paint and paste.

Activity 8.8

Richard employs a small team of decorators and specialises in high-quality domestic work. Since starting his Apprenticeship at 16 years old, he has always taken pride in his work. Richard is decorating a lounge in a Victorian property, which has high ceilings. The job needs the ceiling to be lined with lining paper and painted, the walls are to be cross-lined and a finished paper hung, and the woodwork is to have two coats of solvent-based eggshell.

1 What is the best way for Richard to access the ceiling while hanging the lining paper?

2 What PPE would he require for this job?

3 What technique or approach would he use to make sure the first piece of wallpaper is straight?

TOPICS   B.2   B.3

Preparing surfaces and applying paints

Introduction

In this topic, you will develop your practical skills by preparing already-painted surfaces to receive paints and wallpapers. You will also learn about selecting and applying water-based and solvent-based paints to these surfaces, using the right techniques.

Before starting any decorating tasks, you should set the job up safely. Place dust sheets flat and check your tools and equipment.

Table 8.6 shows what preparation and paint systems you need for the surfaces you will be working on.

Table 8.5 Preparation and paint systems needed for different surfaces

Surface	Condition	Preparation needed	Paint system
Wood	New unpainted	• Lightly rub down to smooth, clean and remove sharp edges • Apply two coats of **knotting**	• Prime with water-based or solvent-based wood primer • Apply one or two coats of undercoat • Apply gloss finish
	Previously painted in sound condition	• Rub down to make sure surface is smooth and keyed • Surface may also require washing to remove dirt and grease • Fill if needed	• Apply undercoat • Apply gloss finish • Two coats of eggshell finish can be used if working internally
	Previously painted in unsound condition	• Remove all traces of paint by burning off or using liquid paint remover • The surface can then be treated as new	• Same as new unpainted
Ferrous and non-ferrous metals	New	• Clean with white spirit to remove all traces of grease • Apply appropriate primer	• Apply appropriate primer • Apply undercoat • Apply gloss finish
Plaster	New unpainted	• Scrape over with a broad scraper to **de-nib** the surface • Fill where needed, wetting the area with water first • Rub down filler	• Apply a thin coat of matt emulsion • Apply two coats of emulsion or acrylic paints
	Previously painted	• Lightly rub down to make sure the surface is clean and smooth, with no loose or flaking material • Fill where needed	• Apply two coats of emulsion or acrylic paint

Key terms

Knotting – a preparation liquid substance or solution of shellac and methylated spirit. It is applied to knots in timber to stop the resin leaking out and damaging the paint film.

De-nib – removing any bits or plaster splashes from a surface.

Activity 8.9

Find out how much paint you will need to complete your practical task, remembering to think about the preparation materials you will need.

Hanging wallpaper

To prepare the surface for paperhanging, you must first remove the old wallpaper and get rid of the paste from the surface by washing it down. Make good the surface in the same way as preparing for painting. If the surface is bare plaster, you must apply a coat of size.

Measuring, cutting and applying paste to wallpaper

Once you have set up your paste table, you will need to cut your lengths. Always add an extra 100 mm on the length to allow for trimming at the top and bottom.

Apply the paste down the centre of the length and then out to the edges. Make sure the paper is to the edges of the paste table, otherwise you will get paste on the board and then on the face of the wallpaper.

What is the best technique for applying paste to wallpaper?

Hanging wallpaper to a straight wall

Plumbing a line is important to keep the paper running straight. Mark out from the edge of the wall 510/520 mm, then run the plumb line through the mark. Mark behind the string line every 300 mm from the top of the wall to the bottom so you have a series of marks. You are now ready to hang the paper.

Apply the pasted paper to the wall, following the plumb line. Use your hanging brush to smooth the paper down, first down the centre and then out to the edges. Trim the paper at the top and bottom. Apply the next piece in the same way, making sure the edges touch the previous piece.

When hanging wallpaper, it is important to clean paste off the adjoining surfaces such as ceilings, door frames and skirting boards. This will make sure it does not leave a stain.

Assessment activity 8.3 — *English*

You employ five qualified members of staff and one apprentice. You complete risk assessments before each job. Your next job is a staircase in a private house that needs emulsion on the walls and solvent-based paint on the woodwork. The hand rail also needs stripping back to bare wood.

1 What hazards will you have to include on the risk assessment?

2 Why are risk assessments important?

3 Who could be affected during this painting job?

4 Complete a risk assessment for this job or before starting your practical tasks in the workshop.

Tips
- Identify the hazards that could be present and the control measures that need to be put in place.
- Complete a risk assessment to include all risks, those affected and the level of risk that each task poses.

WorkSpace

▷ Jack Fowler

Painter and decorator

I'm a qualified painter and decorator, working for a high-quality small company. My day-to-day responsibilities include:

- communicating with clients, keeping them up to date with progress and access requirements
- ordering and collecting materials from suppliers
- producing the quality of work expected by my employer and clients
- working and communicating with my colleagues
- helping to train and offer advice to our apprentice.

I love my job and get a lot of job satisfaction from transforming customers' houses. I've even helped some clients choose colours for their rooms, which adds extra responsibility to my job.

My main role is painting and decorating. This includes preparing surfaces, applying water-based and solvent-based coatings, and hanging wallpapers. The work we're doing a lot of at the moment is removing old wallpapers, lining the walls and painting. Feature walls papered in bold patterns are also very popular.

To be successful in this job you need to work hard, have good communication skills, be able to work as part of a team and be trustworthy.

Think about it

1 Why are good communication skills important in Jack's working day?

2 What have you learned during this unit that will help you if you want to further your career in this trade?

3 What would be the next step for Jack if he wanted to progress his career further?

Introduction

Can you imagine living without clean water to hand when you need it? Why do we need a clean supply of water for our homes and schools and hospitals and workplaces?

Clean quality water is vital to use as drinking water, and for washing, bathing and heating our homes. Although water falls to the ground as rain and is collected from rivers and reservoirs, it has to be treated so that it is safe for us to use.

Modern commercial and domestic buildings have a network of pipes that carry hot and cold water to our kitchens, bathrooms and toilets. This supply needs to be installed so it does not leak or get contaminated or wasted.

Plumbers have to know how to carry out good-quality plumbing installation work. In this unit you will explore the different tools, equipment and materials that you will need when cutting pipework, forming plumbing joints, and bending and connecting pipework.

For part of this unit you will form a practice pipework frame. This will let you demonstrate your skills in cutting, bending and connecting pipework together using soldering or compression fitting techniques. You will need to be accurate when you measure, mark and cut pipework. You will also demonstrate how you form clean soldered joints on your work.

Assessment: You will be assessed through a series of assignments set by your teacher/tutor.

Learning aims

In this unit you will:

A understand tools, materials and equipment used for plumbing operations

B develop practical skills using safe techniques to undertake plumbing operations.

> During my first week of training I learned that in plumbing installations you need to use the correct hand tools for the materials you're using. Having the right sharp and well-maintained hand tools makes the work much easier to do. I'm learning about the different ways of joining pipework and the tools I'll need for this. I watch experienced plumbers to see different techniques and then they let me try these myself, so I learn as I work. Every day is different as we get all sorts of jobs to do.
>
> Simon, *16-year-old aspiring plumber*

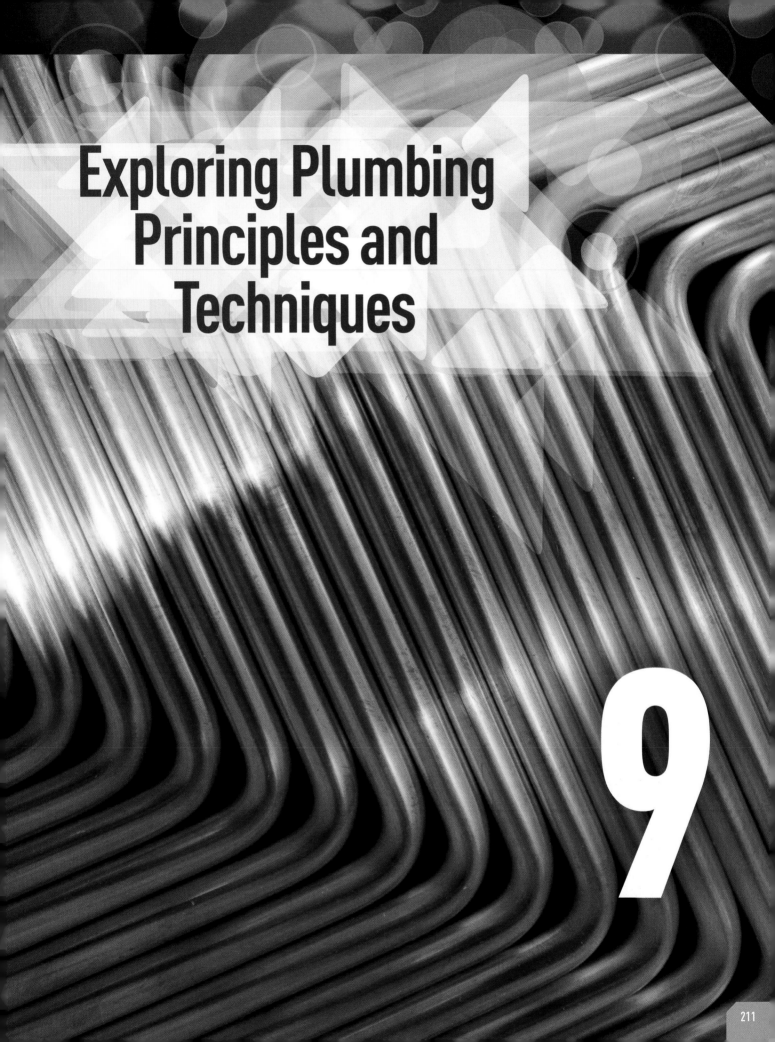

Exploring Plumbing Principles and Techniques

9

BTEC
Assessment Zone

This table shows what you must do in order to achieve a **Pass**, **Merit** or **Distinction** grade, and where you can find activities in this book to help you.

Assessment criteria

Level 1	Level 2 **Pass**	Level 2 **Merit**	Level 2 **Distinction**
Learning aim A: Understand tools, materials and equipment used for plumbing operations			
1A.1 Identify the purpose of tools and equipment, and the use of materials for plumbing operations.	**2A.P1** Explain the selection and use of appropriate tools, materials and equipment for plumbing operations. **See Assessment activity 9.1, page 224**	**2A.M1** Justify the selection of tools, materials and equipment for a specified plumbing operation task. **See Assessment activity 9.1, page 224**	**2A.D1** Evaluate the use of alternative materials for a specified plumbing operation task. **See Assessment activity 9.1, page 224**
1A.2 Outline the safe use and storage of plumbing operations tools, materials and equipment.	**2A.P2** Explain the safe use and storage of plumbing operations tools, materials and equipment. **See Assessment activity 9.1, page 224**		
Learning aim B: Develop practical skills and safe techniques to undertake plumbing operations			
1B.3 Identify hazards and control measures prior to commencing plumbing operations.	**2B.P3** **English** Carry out a risk assessment prior to commencing plumbing operations. **See Assessment activity 9.2, page 232**		
1B.4 Work safely using personal protection equipment with guidance.	**2B.P4** Comply with safe working practices including using appropriate personal protection equipment. **See Assessment activity 9.2, page 232**		
1B.5 **Maths** Measure and mark out materials for a pipe rig framework to a given spec with guidance.	**2B.P5** **Maths** Measure and mark out materials for a pipe rig framework to a given spec, accurate to 5 mm. **See Assessment activity 9.2, page 232**	**2B.M2** **Maths** Measure and mark out materials for a pipe rig framework to a given spec, accurate to 3 mm. **See Assessment activity 9.2, page 232**	**2B.D2** **Maths** Measure and mark out materials for a pipe rig framework to a given spec, accurate to 2 mm. **See Assessment activity 9.2, page 232**
1B.6 **Maths** Construct a simple pipe rig framework with compression and soldered joints, with guidance.	**2B.P6** **Maths** Construct a simple pipe rig framework with: • compression • manual bends • soldered joints • tested to 1 × the operating pressure. **See Assessment activity 9.2, page 232**	**2B.M3** **Maths** Construct a simple pipe rig framework to: • ±5 mm in length and ±5 mm in height measured against the rig drawing • tested to 1.5 × the operating pressure. **See Assessment activity 9.2, page 232**	**2B.D2** **Maths** Construct a simple pipe rig framework to: • ±5 mm in length and ±5 mm in height measured against the rig drawing • pass a pressure test standard 2 × operating pressure. **See Assessment activity 9.2, page 232**

English Opportunity to practise English skills   **Maths** Opportunity to practise mathematical skills

How you will be assessed

The unit will be assessed by a series of internally assessed tasks. You will need to demonstrate your understanding of the tools, equipment and materials that are used safely in the installation of plumbing operations. You will need to demonstrate practical skills when you construct the pipe rig frame. This test piece will contain a number of different joints and fittings. These skills should include working safety, accuracy and cleanliness. The ability to form watertight joints is essential for you to advance onto the plumbing operations unit.

Your assessment could be in the form of:

- a written assignment
- an observation record of your practical performance
- the production of a practical test piece.

▶ Tools and equipment used for undertaking plumbing operations

Introduction

In this topic you will learn about the different tools and equipment used in plumbing installations. These include the hand tools, power tools and other equipment that is used to cut, bend and connect pipework together.

There are lots of different plumbing tools that are used for plumbing. From blow torches to adjustable spanners, the range is very wide. You need to know which tools are right for the job.

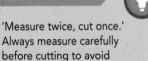

Discussion

When you start your training as a plumbing apprentice, you will need a tool bag with all the tools and equipment that you will use when installing.

What tools would you buy first for your start-up tool kit?

Remember

'Measure twice, cut once.' Always measure carefully before cutting to avoid wasting pipe.

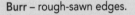

Key terms

Burr – rough-sawn edges.

Cutting wheel – a hardened steel wheel that is gently rotated and tightened against the copper pipe and slowly cuts through it.

Perpendicular – the pipe is cut at 90° to its length, or cut 'square' across its length.

▶ Hand tools, power tools and equipment

There are many different hand tools used in plumbing operations. These can be divided according to how the tools are used:

- cutting
- bending
- measuring
- holding.

Cutting

You need to cut copper and plastic pipes when installing them in a home as they are made in standard lengths. Cutting accurately and cleanly will make jointing the pipes easier. For example, if you use a junior hacksaw to cut copper pipe, you need to clean the cut by filing to remove the rough-sawn edges or **burrs**, so the joint fitting can push over the end of the cut pipe.

Tube cutters These have a set of rollers and a cutter head that revolves around the copper pipe. A **cutting wheel** is tightened against the copper pipe as it revolves, gradually cutting the pipe clean with no burrs.	
Wheel cutters These are used to cut different diameter pipes using a wheel-shaped blade. The cutter head is a wheel that is fitted over the pipe and then rotated around the pipe, pulling the cutting wheel into the pipe and cutting as it rotates. The cutting wheels come in different sizes.	
Pipe cutters These are used for slicing plastic water pipes cleanly and with a straight end that is **perpendicular** to the pipe.	

Junior hacksaw

This is not as accurate at cutting as the above two hand tools, so it is up to the user to achieve an even cut. It can be used to cut several different materials.

Half round file

This is used for removing any burrs that may be formed when cutting copper pipes.

Take it further

There are many ways of cutting copper pipes using the types of cutters mentioned here. Try each one to see which you are comfortable using and which gives the best cut.

Bending

You may often need to bend copper pipework as this is faster than cutting, preparing and soldering two pieces together. To do this you must use specialist pipe benders so the pipe does not become distorted when it is bent.

Tube bending machine

This is hand-operated and has a back guide. It holds the copper tube in shape as it is bent around the **former**.

Remember

Cutting often involves the use of a sharp edge, wheel or blade. You need to choose the best tool to cut a copper pipe so it does not leave any sharp edges or burrs.

Measuring

Spirit level

A spirit level is used to check that surfaces are level. A small **boat level** can easily be used on short **runs** of pipework and in tight areas to make sure that runs are level.

Measuring tape

This is used to measure lengths of pipework before cutting.

Key terms

Former – this is the radius part of the pipe bender, which holds the correct diameter pipe in position as it is bent around the former. This gives the correct radius for the pipe that is being bent. Normal-sized formers are 15 mm and 22 mm.

Boat level – a small short level used for awkward areas where a large level is not practical.

Runs – a length of pipe in a run from one point to another.

Did you know?

A hand bender works on the principle of leverage. The handles act as levers, allowing you to easily bend the copper pipe around its former. You would struggle to do this by hand.

215

Holding

Often you will need to hold plumbing items securely so you can fit them, tighten them or take them apart. Since we cannot do this with just our hands, we have to use tools to do this safely.

Spanners
These are used to tighten the locking nuts on compression fittings. The most useful is an adjustable spanner, which has one fixed jaw and one that moves up and down. This lets you adjust the spanner to fit any size of nut.

Wrench
This is used to secure compression fittings by gripping the outside **flanges** of the compression nuts and allowing them to be turned until tight.

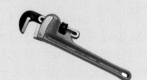

Pipe grips
These are used to grip manually onto any plumbing material to turn or tighten it.

Bench vice
This is used to hold any pipework securely so it cannot move during jointing or cutting.

Key term

Flange – a projecting flat rim for strengthening, guidance or attaching to something else.

General plumbing

Other general plumbing tools include power tools, screwdrivers and blow torches.

Power tools
These are the low-voltage power tools that are used to fix pipe brackets and for fitting plumbing appliances. For instance, hammer drills (right) are used to drill holes through brickwork for plumbing waste outlets. Cordless drills are used to attach fittings such as sinks to walls.

Screwdrivers
These are used to turn screw-threaded bolts and screws to tighten them – for example, a pipe bracket is screwed to a block wall to support a pipe. Slotted and Pozidriv® screwdrivers are used when installing and securing plumbing pipework and fittings.

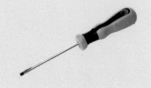

Blowtorch
A gas-operated blowtorch is used to heat up a joint so it can be soldered.

Activity 9.1

1 A plumber often has to light a blow torch several times when soldering plumbing fittings. Do you think they have to carry matches?

2 Now carry out some independent research into the commercial blowtorches that are available. You could use the internet or visit your local builders merchants.

Remember

A blowtorch can be a very dangerous tool. Always follow the instructions about its use and remember that even when switched off, it will remain hot.

Just checking

1 What tools could be used to cut 15 mm copper pipework to a measured length?

2 What tool is used to form a made bend in copper pipework?

3 Name two tools that you might use to hold pipe and other plumbing items securely.

Did you know?

The temperature in the flame of a propane blowtorch can reach 2000°C.

TOPIC   A.2

▶ Materials used in plumbing operations

Introduction

For a long time copper has been used to carry water around our homes, as it does not react with water and can easily be soldered to join pipes. Modern fittings now include plastic push-fit fittings, which join together using a push-fit coupler with no soldering. This is quicker and faster than installing copper pipework.

Remember

With any material used for plumbing, you should always read the manufacturer's data sheets first. This will help you install items properly, and make future problems or issues less likely.

▶ Copper

Copper pipe is used for plumbing operations as it is safe to carry drinking water. Copper is **flexible** and will expand without cracking when heated. However, it can fail if frozen, as ice can form and expand, and split the copper pipe. Copper is easy to cut, bend and joint using a **solder** that is melted into a joint to form a watertight seal.

Copper pipe is available in standard sizes, including:

- 15 mm diameter for branches and final feeds to appliances
- 20 mm diameter for major distribution, supplies to baths, and central heating primary pipework. For example, filling a bath using hot water would take longer using 15 mm diameter copper pipe, so 20 mm diameter is used.

Key terms

Flexible – changes shape easily.

Solder – this is a metal that melts at the temperature of the blowtorch. It fills the gaps between two copper surfaces and bonds to them, forming a watertight joint.

Normal water pressure means 15 mm diameter copper pipe and fittings can be used to supply all the cold water services within a home. Pipes with bigger diameters are used for commercial applications such as hospitals, where pipework carries water for several buildings.

▶ Copper fittings

There are three different types of fitting that are used with copper pipework to change angle and to join different diameter pipes together. Copper pipework can be joined together using the following styles of fittings.

- Soldered joint using end feed fittings – solder is fed in from the end of the fitting, which needs the copper pipework and fitting to be cleaned using steel wool. A **flux** is applied to let the solder flow and bond as it is fed into the joint.
- Copper solder ring fittings – the solder is kept in a ring. All pipework and the fitting should be cleaned using wire wool. A flux-applied heat then melts within the pre-soldered fitting and flows around to seal the joint.
- Push-fit fittings – these use an O-ring and a grab ring to hold the push-fit fitting onto the pipe and form a watertight seal. No hot work is needed and new technology in these fittings means you can take them apart and reuse them.

Generally, all the fittings above are produced in standard fitting types, such as:

- elbows, which are 90° changes in direction
- straights, which are couplers which join two pipes together in a straight line
- 'T-junctions' which allow a third pipe to join two others so it looks like a 'T'.

Copper pipe comes in many different sizes.

Typical copper fittings. What types can you see?

Key term

Flux – this helps the soldering process by stopping the cleaned copper from oxidising and stopping the solder from bonding to the copper.

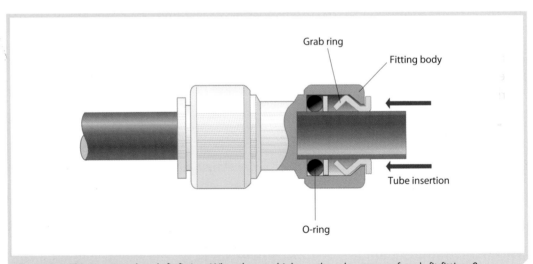

Figure 9.1 This is a typical push-fit fitting. What do you think are the advantages of push-fit fittings?

Soldering is the traditional method of jointing pipework. This uses a 'soft solder', which is a metal that melts easily when a blowtorch is used on it. By melting and flowing into a soldered fitting, it bonds the fitting to the pipe to form a waterproof joint. The solder is normally supplied in a roll that is unwound as it is used.

When you use plain-end feed fittings, the solder is fed in from a reel. With pre-soldered fittings, the solder is already in the fitting and melts when heated. A flux is applied to the area to be joined, which must be cleaned to prevent any **oxidisation** as this would stop a good joint forming. The flux further prevents oxidisation of the copper while the joint forms.

Activity 9.2

You have been asked to write down the procedure for soldering a copper joint using capillary end feed fittings.

Write a sequence of steps that other learners could use as a checklist when planning to solder a joint. Carry out the steps and take a sequence of photographs that you can add to your checklist.

Brass fittings

Brass is an alloy or mixture of copper and zinc. Brass does not rust as it contains no **ferrous** compounds and so it is ideal for fittings that will be used with water. Brass is also safe to use with drinking water.

A range of brass compression fittings are available for many applications and different pipe diameters. Compression fittings are normally made of brass. They contain a component called an **olive**, which is slipped over the copper pipe to be joined to the compression fitting. The compression nut is then tightened against the fitting. This forces the olive onto the copper pipe and forms a watertight seal. No soldering is needed at all in this process.

Compression fittings allow a joint to be taken apart for repairing or maintenance. They are especially useful where using a blowtorch may cause damage to any fittings or nearby features.

Plastic pipe and fittings

Plastics are being used more and more for water supply distribution in domestic homes because they are cheap. They are used for waste water systems that connect to the external drainage system.

Plastic pipes can be easily placed in a home and can be bent around corners without being damaged. Plastic is safe to use with drinking water supply and does not need hot work to form any joints. Plastic pipes are made from a range of plastics that are chemically resistant to water and often contain a barrier to prevent light affecting water quality. Water pipework in the ground is normally blue, and in homes it is grey.

Plastic pipes are joined using the 'push-fit' system shown in Figure 9.1, on page 218. These push-fit fittings allow quickly and easily constructed joints to be formed. The pipework is cut with pipe shears, forming a perpendicular cut to the plastic. The fitting is then pushed over the end of the pipe and a seal is made when the pipework is pressurised with mains water pressure.

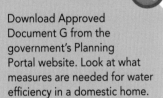

Solvent-welded joints are usually used in waste pipework. The solvent can take up to 24 hours to set fully.

Waste pipework

Waste supply pipework is normally available in two standard sizes for domestic connections. These are 32 mm or 40 mm internal diameters. The larger diameter is used for showers and bath wastes where a larger quantity of water needs to flow to the drainage system.

Plastic wastes and traps are used to connect the outlets from sinks, baths and showers. WCs use a larger-diameter connection to a soil stack (the pipe that takes all the waste away).

All waste systems must comply with **Building Regulations** and a waste trap must be supplied. This stops smells and gases from the drainage system from entering back into a building. This trap is usually a U-bend in the waste pipework that retains a water seal of 75 mm depth.

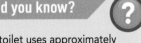

Research

Download Approved Document G from the government's Planning Portal website. Look at what measures are needed for water efficiency in a domestic home.

Plastic waste pipes can be joined in two ways:

- using a push-fit fitting that contains an O-ring that fits tightly to the pipework – a lubricant is normally needed to push the fitting over the pipe
- using a solvent-welded system where a solvent is painted onto both surfaces to be joined and forms a chemically bonded seal.

Just checking

1 What is a compression fitting? What are the benefits of using compression fittings?
2 Why might you use 20 mm copper pipe instead of 15 mm copper pipe?
3 You have uncovered a grey plastic pipe in the ground. What is grey pipework used for?
4 Where would a brass fitting be used?
5 Can plastic pipework be used for drinking water supplies?
6 What two methods can be used to join plastic pipework for a waste to a sink?

▶ Appliances

If you look around your house or school or college, you will find lots of different appliances connected to water and water waste.

In the kitchen, appliances normally include a kitchen sink with a primary drinking water supply, a dishwasher connection, a washing machine hot and cold water supply connection, and a fridge ice maker connection.

Did you know?

A toilet uses approximately 30 per cent of the total water consumption in a house.

In the bathroom, fittings usually include a wash hand basin (whb), a bath and a shower, all needing hot and cold water supplies. The toilet needs only a cold water connection.

Take it further

Find a local plumbing supplier or plumbing showroom and look at a range of appliances and fittings that would be installed in a domestic home. Work out what all the supply requirements are and the different connections that will be needed to install each item.

HANDY PLUMB

Job no.: .....051...

Location: .....115 Home Street, Claxton.........

Labour	Time Started	Time Finished	Cost (Office use)
Ellen Kingston (Plmb)	10.15	11.15	
Total hours		1hr	£

Materials	Quantity	Cost (Office use)
Pillar tap	1	
Tap washers	1	
Total cost		£

Equipment	Quantity	Cost (Office use)
Van	1 hour	
Total cost		£

Total cost of job: ....

Figure 9.2 Job sheets should always be completed for every plumbing task

Case study

Ellen is a plumber and has been asked to install a replacement tap to a kitchen sink within a home. She has to complete a job sheet for each task she carries out.

1 Why does Ellen have to complete a job sheet?

2 What do you think might happen if Ellen did not complete one for a job she had done?

Activity 9.3

A kitchen sink is going to be installed into a pre-cut opening within a worktop. Produce a job sheet for this operation and include:

- the tools and equipment needed for this operation and how they will be used
- what materials will be needed to install the sink and how they will be used.

Safe use and storage of tools, materials and equipment

Introduction

This topic looks at the safe use of the tools and equipment used for plumbing operations, to ensure that no harm or injury results from their use. Cutting and jointing involve the use of sharp edges and hot working. You can reduce the risks from both of these by wearing the right personal protective equipment (PPE).

Key term

COSHH – the Control of Substances Hazardous to Health Regulations 2002.

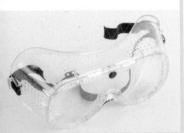

Why do you think it is important to ensure that you have the most suitable PPE for each individual task?

Remember

There are many types of gloves. You will need to select the right sort for the task you are doing.

Before you use any tool, material or equipment, you should read and understand the instructions that are given. It is essential to read safety data sheets, especially when it comes to handling and using plumbing materials. You may also need to do a **COSHH** assessment before using solders, fluxes, solvents and push-fit lubricants .

Personal protective equipment (PPE)

In a working environment you may need to use PPE. This can include:

- **safety boots** – worn to prevent any damage to your feet, toes or soles of the feet either by impact from above or puncture from below
- **hard hat** – prevents damage from falling objects on a construction site
- **high-visibility jacket** – it is vital to wear this on a construction site so that you are highly visible to people operating machinery on site
- **safety gloves** – often worn when handling materials, plant and equipment to stop the materials you are using from coming into direct contact with your skin
- **safety glasses** – worn to prevent flying debris or dust getting into your eyes while cutting, drilling or doing any other activity where particles could enter your eyes
- **barrier cream** – this cream is rubbed into the hands and prevents any absorption of chemicals or materials sticking to your skin.

You may need special PPE for specific tasks, such as hot working or cutting. You should always choose this PPE after carrying out a risk assessment. This will ensure that you use the right equipment to reduce the risk.

Blowtorches

When you use a blowtorch, it heats the copper pipework or fitting in order to melt the solder that needs to flow into the joint. It is best to hold the pieces to be joined in a vice while this is done. You should leave the heated components to cool before picking them up and storing them, including the blowtorch. You should carefully consider which gloves are most appropriate when using a blowtorch. The gloves must not retain heat and must prevent heat transfer to the skin.

Cutting

When using a hacksaw to cut any pipework, you need to remove any sharp edges using a half round file or emery paper. This will prevent cuts to the hands. Always wear

appropriate gloves to prevent sharp edges from injuring your hands and causing cuts which could become infected.

Positive attitude towards health and safety

Some plumbing operations have particular associated hazards. You will need to act and behave sensibly, and have the right attitude when doing these operations. As a plumbing apprentice you may well enter customers' and clients' buildings, where you must behave with complete professionalism. Good behaviour earns respect from customers and clients, and leads to more business.

Maintaining a clean and tidy work area

You must keep your work area clear of waste materials and free from any trip hazards which could cause an injury. Always use an appropriate tool bag to keep your equipment safe. Sweep up and leave the site as you found it.

Safe manual handling

Manual handling **hazards** are mainly due to the weight, size, handling, grip and any trip hazards while transporting the object. The **risks** from manual handling plumbing materials and equipment can be reduced by:

- wearing appropriate PPE
- keeping the work area clean and tidy and free from any obstructions
- knowing how heavy an object is that you are going to lift
- using mechanical lifting wherever possible
- using the right lifting techniques.

Using tools and equipment correctly

For many plumbing operations you will need to use specialist tools and equipment. A plumber's tool kit must be maintained to make sure that all tools and equipment operate safely, that everything is stored properly and maintained or repaired when needed.

A plumbing tool must be used for the purpose it is designed for. If you look at the manufacturer's safety data sheets that came with a tool when it was bought, these will give very helpful guidance about how to use it properly.

You must always take care when using tools – for example, grips can slip, and a blowtorch has a range of hazards linked with its use.

Cleaning tools

You should keep plumbing tools clean and free from too much grease or oil, as this would make them difficult to grip and use. When cleaning a plumbing tool, you should inspect the tool for any defects as required by the Provision and Use of Work Equipment Regulations 1998 (PUWER). These should be reported and the tool either repaired if possible or marked defective and replaced.

You also need to consider the sharpness of tools carefully, and replace blunt cutting wheels, edges or blades regularly so that the tool operates cleanly and properly.

Key terms

Hazards – things that have the potential to cause harm, such as a naked flame.

Risks – these result from hazards, such as someone burning themselves with the naked flame.

Link

For more about safe manual handling techniques, see page 158.

Did you know?

The Provision and Use of Work Equipment Regulations 1998, also known as PUWER, applies to all people and companies who own, use or control work equipment. It means that employers have to make sure that work equipment is safe to use, maintained safely and used only by people who are trained to use it.

Take it further

The Health and Safety Executive (HSE) has many leaflets on guidance on the regulations – for example, PUWER (Provision and Use of Work Equipment Regulations). You can download these from the HSE's website.

Carrying your tools in a suitable belt or bag makes carrying tools easier and safer. It will also help stop them from getting damaged.

Key term

Malleable – able to have its shape changed by flattening, bending or denting out of shape.

Storing tools

A plumbing tool should be stored correctly so it does not:

- become a hazard
- get damaged
- need extra maintenance.

If the tool came with a storage box, sleeve or container, you should put it back in this after you have finished using it. Power tools have appropriate secure and cushioned boxes that prevent any damage while they are carried between tasks.

If you get out a plumbing tool and find it is broken, you should not just put it back again. Damaged tools can cause serious injuries. Report it to a supervisor and have the tool repaired, or disposed of and replaced.

Storing pipework, appliances and fittings

You need to think how you are going to store your equipment. Copper is **malleable** and will bend out of shape easily. Therefore any dents are a point of weakness where a failure could occur. Copper pipework is normally transported flat in a tube on a roof rack or carried in a bundle. It should be stored flat in a suitable storage rack. You should leave plumbing fittings and appliances in their packaging until you need them. This prevents any accidental damage, which could be expensive to repair or replace.

Just checking

1 Give two reasons why it is important to keep your working area tidy.
2 What sort of PPE might you use while cutting copper pipe? Give reasons for your choices.
3 What is the correct method of storing copper pipe?
4 Do you need to leave a blowtorch to cool before putting it away?
5 How should you store power tools?

Assessment activity 9.1

You are preparing to plumb in a toilet using the tools, materials and equipment of your choice. Your Apprenticeship supervisor needs a written work report for this job.

This report should contain:

- an identification of the tools, materials and equipment that you will need for this job
- an explanation of why you have chosen what you have chosen
- an explanation of how each is used safely, and how they should be stored
- a justification as to the selection of tool, material and equipment
- an evaluation of any alternative materials that you could use for plumbing in the toilet.

Health and safety

Introduction

Health and safety is very important in construction, as there are lots of hazards on a construction site. As a plumber you need to be made aware of these through the site induction that you receive before starting work on the site. Regular 'toolbox talks' with colleagues will also keep you up to date with any changes on the site that may affect you.

 Link

This topic has links with all the practical units of brickwork, electrical, joinery and painting, in the identification of hazards, risks and appropriate control measures.

 ## Identifying hazards and risks

A hazard is something that has the potential to cause harm, while a risk is the result of any accident that happened because of the hazard. Plumbing hazards must be identified, assessed and then controlled through the use of a risk assessment. You should assess the hazards of any practical task that you are going to do.

Table 9.1 Some of the hazards and risks of plumbing operations

Hazard	Risk
High temperatures and hot working	Can cause burning to the skin if hot pipework comes into contact with it
Bottled gas	Fire and explosion from bottled gas
Sharp tools	Cuts and grazes from sharp tools not handled correctly
Untidy work area	Slips, trips and falls
Dirty tools and equipment	Infection caused by waste water bacteria and viruses transmitted through inhalation, absorption or ingestion

To reduce the risk from a hazard, you should carry out a risk assessment. The process of doing a risk assessment makes sure that you look at the plumbing task you are about to do, and analyse it for any hazards.

It includes identifying who may be at risk from the hazards, such as employees and clients. Once you have identified a list of hazards, you should then assess the control measures that you can use. This allows you to see whether the risk rating is reduced to an acceptable level.

James is working for a plumbing company that installs drinking water fountains in offices. The work involves making a supply for the fountain, and fitting a water softener and water filter to the supply. The drinking fountain, which is a free-standing unit, is then connected by a flexible hose to the new supply.

James has been asked to do a risk assessment for the work but is not sure if there are any hazards present.

1 Is spilled water a hazard in the office?
2 Will James be subjected to any hazards?
3 What precautions should he take?
4 Are there any hazards with the connection of the new supply to the drinking fountain?

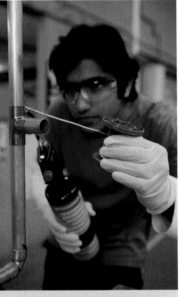

Gloves and eye protection should be used when using a blowtorch. Why do you think this is?

Control measures

Control measures are used to reduce the chance that the hazard will cause harm to someone. The measures include:

- adoption of safe working practices or safe systems of work
- isolation from the hazard
- removal of the hazard
- the wearing of PPE.

The use of personal protective equipment (PPE) must always be the last resort when you are considering control measures. The reduction or removal of the hazard is always the best course of action.

Well-maintained tools and equipment will prevent any possible injury from their use, and wearing appropriate gloves will prevent any infection or contamination from occurring.

Activity 9.4

You have been asked to replace an existing toilet cistern and pan. This will involve a new plumbing connection for the cold water supply. Carry out a risk assessment for this task, remembering to:

- identify three hazards associated with this work
- work out the risk associated with each hazard
- examine the control measures that you will put in place for each hazard
- describe the personal protective equipment that you would use for this task.

Just checking

1 Should a risk assessment be undertaken for all plumbing operations?
2 What is the hazard associated with bottled gas?
3 What does a control measure do?

Developing pipe bending and jointing skills

Introduction

As part of the assessment for this unit you will be given a drawing of the pipe rig to make. A **pipe rig** is a small-scale model of an arrangement of pipes that will let you show you can bend and join all of these together. It contains a range of different fittings that you have to assemble using the skills set out in this unit.

Marking out and manual bending of pipework

Before a plumber can mark out their pipework, they need to be able to interpret the drawing to establish the lengths of pipework and fittings needed. This may involve using a scale ruler or any dimensions that are on the issued drawing. You will need to know what typical symbols mean and be able to work out what lengths of pipework you need from the drawing.

If the pipework is for a kitchen, you will need to keep in mind that a typical base unit is 600 mm or 1000 mm wide and from this you should be able to determine the lengths of pipework to service a kitchen sink. Often you may have to do a site survey before starting work, to overcome any problems.

Activity 9.5

Your tutor will give you a drawing for a small kitchen extension showing the location of the incoming cold water supply from the street. Determine the total length of pipework you will need to order for the cold water supply.

When you mark out pipework to cut, remember to check twice and cut once, as this will make mistakes less likely. Copper pipe is expensive and must not be wasted. Also, the more joints you place in a pipe run because you had to join shorter incorrect lengths together, the more friction there will be, and the less pressure at the tap.

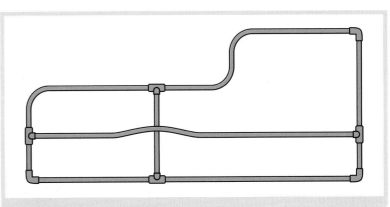
Figure 9.3 A typical practice pipe rig frame.

Your pipe rig frame needs to include a bend made using a manual hand bender. You will need to work out the length of pipe needed for the bend. The radius of the bend is usually four times the pipe diameter. For example, if you were bending 15 mm diameter pipework, this would be 4 × 15 = 60 mm radius.

The following simple formula will help you prepare the length of pipe needed for the bend:

$$\frac{\text{Radius} \times 2 \times 3.14}{4}$$

Link

For more on maths in construction, see *Unit 3: Scientific and Mathematical Applications for Construction*.

Worked example 9.1

Salma is working on a pipe rig and has to work out how much pipe she needs in order to form a bend. She is using 10 mm pipe.

10 × 4 = 40 mm

$$\frac{40 \text{ mm} \times 2 \times 3.14}{4} = 62.8 \text{ mm}$$

Salma needs 63 mm of pipe to form the bend.

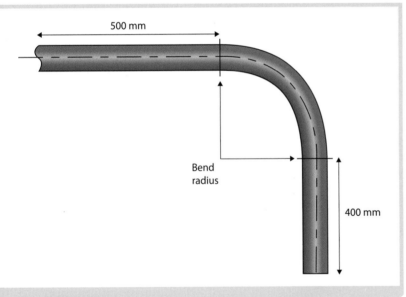

Figure 9.4 Finding the length of pipe required to form a bend

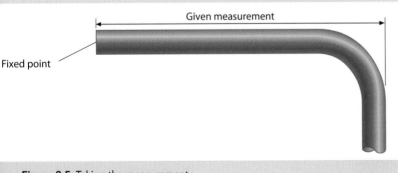

Figure 9.5 Taking the measurement

In Figure 9.4, you can see that the total length of pipe Salma needs is 400 mm plus 500 mm, plus the 63 mm that is needed for the bend.

When you have worked out the lengths of pipe you need, mark these and cut them to length. Use a black felt marker so this can be seen and easily recognised as the cut line.

Remember to allow for the parts of the pipe that go inside the fittings. Use the actual fittings as guides to cutting pipes to length, to make sure you are as accurate as possible.

Always measure twice and cut once. This will make your work more accurate and waste less material.

Forming manual bends

A hand bender will usually be used for the type of bends you will be forming. The copper pipe is marked from a fixed point to establish the 'given measurement'. This is the measurement from a fixed point to the back of the bend.

Figure 9.5 shows the taking of this dimension. The fixed point could be where the end of the tube fits into a fitting. Mark the end point of the given measurement onto the copper pipe using a pencil, as shown in Figure 9.6.

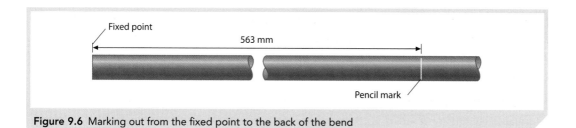

Figure 9.6 Marking out from the fixed point to the back of the bend

After placing the pipe into the manual bender and holding it in place with the tube stop, use a 90° set square to work out the position of the pencil mark relative to the outside former.

Pull the bend with the back guide in place until a 90° angle is formed.

Figure 9.7 shows how to position the pipe in the bender.

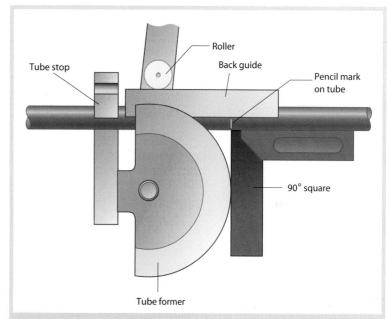

Figure 9.7 Positioning the pipe in the bender

Activity 9.6

You have been asked by the safety manager in the plumbing department of a construction company to produce a safety leaflet. This leaflet is to be about the safe cutting of pipework to the measured and marked-out lengths, and the different methods people could use. Produce a leaflet that will inform people about:

- the recommended way and tools used to cut pipes
- any PPE needed when cutting
- the need for maths skills in marking out
- alternative methods of cutting.

Formation of a soldered joint

Research

What sort of precautions should you take when soldering?

Soldering is a method of joining metals. It uses an alloy with a low melting point to join the metals together. This alloy is the solder. A soft-soldered joint can be formed using two types of fittings:

- integral solder ring – this is pre-loaded into a fitting and melts when heat is applied to form the joint
- end feed fitting – this does not have any solder in the joint; it has to be fed into the end of the fitting from a reel of solder.

The soldering process

Remember

Apply the flux using a clean brush and not your fingers. This is because you might transfer natural oils from your hands onto the cleaned joint, and this could weaken the soldered joint.

1 The copper pipe should be cut **perpendicular** to its length. The pipe is then cleaned and de-burred using a file if needed. You should use steel wool to remove any **oxidisation** from the outside of the pipe. The inside of the fitting is also cleaned using steel wool.

Step 1 Clean and de-burr the pipe.

2 Flux is applied onto the inside of the fitting and the outside of the pipework. This prevents further oxidisation of the copper surface that the solder will bond with. It also helps keep the joint clean.

Step 2 Apply flux using a brush.

Discussion

Why would you flush out a newly soldered water pipework supply?

3 The joint is assembled and heat is applied using a blowtorch. If you use the integral solder ring fitting, a ring of melted solder should appear at the end of each fitting. If you use an end feed fitting, you need to feed solder into the joint until a ring of solder is seen around the whole joint.

Step 3 Apply heat to the fitting.

▶ Formation of a compression joint

A compression joint is formed using a brass fitting. The pipe is first cut square across its length and the securing back nut slid over the pipework followed by an olive, which is slipped onto the pipe. An olive is also known as a compression ring and this is the part that tightens onto the pipe when the compression fitting nuts are tightened. The compression back nut is tightened clockwise until the olive bites into the pipework and forms a sealed joint. Compression joints are quick, easily formed and can be taken apart to maintain plumbing equipment. Figure 9.8 shows a typical compression t-fitting. The brass or copper olive is vital to make sure that the joint stays watertight. The olive must not be damaged and it must be free from defects.

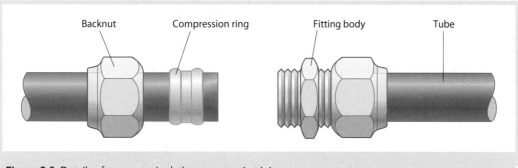

Backnut   Compression ring   Fitting body   Tube

Figure 9.8 Details of a non-maniuplative compression joint

Pressure testing

You need to pressure-test the pipe rig you produce for assessment to check the quality of the joints that you have formed. You will do this using a hydraulic pressure tester. The pressure used when testing is higher than the operating pressure. This means that the system can take more pressure than it actually needs to.

1   Cap the ends of any open pipes, leaving only one open end. Fill the rig with water to make sure that most of the air has been replaced, and connect the hydraulic pressure tester. Normally a flexible connection hose is used that is attached to the tester and the rig. It has screw couplings on it that fit onto the test rig using a compression fitting.

2   Fill the reservoir in the pressure tester with water to the indicated level. A valve on the hydraulic tester allows water from the reservoir to be pumped into the test rig and you can see the water pressure of the pipe rig on the tester's pressure gauge.

3   Increase the pressure using the hand pump to the testing pressures of 1 ×, 1.5 × and 2 × **operating pressure**. You can release the pressure once you have finished the test.

Activity 9.7

Your test rig has failed at 1.5 × operating pressure. Analyse what may have caused the failure and explain what you could do to avoid the same thing happening next time. Discuss with other learners.

Just checking

1   Why do you have to be accurate when marking out pipework?

2   What two types of soldered joint are currently used?

3   What does an olive do in a compression joint?

Discussion

Why should you pressure-test your pipework?

Remember

Pressure testing equipment must be used in accordance with the instructions and training that you have been given.

Key term

Operating pressure – the pressure of the water within the pipe that normally would be produced when in use. Your tutor will set the operating pressure that the test rig's starting pressure will be set from.

Assessment activity 9.2   *English, Maths*

You have been asked to carry out kitchen and bathroom installations in a local development. The supervisor wants to see a sample of your work before contracting you. You are going to mark out and construct the pipe test rig shown in Figure 9.9 as a sample. You should:

- carry out a risk assessment
- think about the kinds of personal protection equipment you will need
- measure and mark out your rig, accurate to 2 mm
- test your rig to 1 ×, 1.5 × and 2 × the operating pressure.

Record the results of your test. If your test rig fails, evaluate the failure.

Tips

- Make sure that your risk assessment is written clearly, and check it for spelling and grammar once it is complete.
- 'Evaluate' means bringing together your information and reviewing it to reach a conclusion. Do this by identifying where the rig failed and what pressure it was under when it failed. You can then come to a conclusion and work out what you need to do differently next time.
- Make sure you read the numerical values on the pressure testing dial accurately.

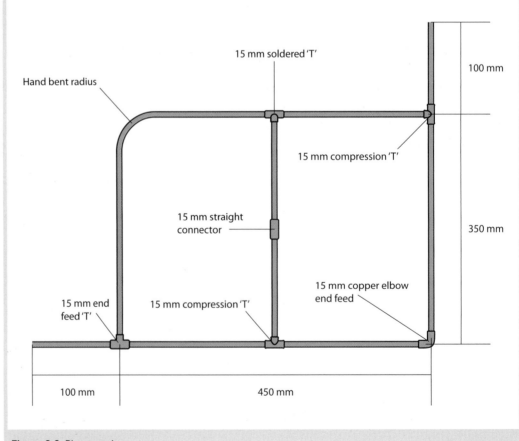

Figure 9.9 Pipe test rig.

WorkSpace

▶ Nicky Gibson

Plumber

I work for a housing association and respond to call-outs from tenants who've logged plumbing defects. I have to fix lots of different plumbing items, including tap washers that need replacing, sink wastes that need unblocking and toilets that won't flush.

My work is very varied and I get to meet a lot of different people who live in our housing association premises. My routine varies with the seasons – as you can imagine, there aren't so many problems with heating during the summer!

During the winter, I have to sort out stuck thermostatic radiator valves and malfunctioning central heating boilers. At this time, heating repairs are my highest priority because lots of the tenants are elderly and so more affected by the cold. During the summer I work mainly on upgrading bathrooms and kitchens, disconnecting old appliances and suites, and installing new ones.

I can't work on gas appliances yet, as I'm still working towards my Gas Services qualification. This will let me register with the Gas Safety Register so that I can work safely on gas appliances. One day I'd like to run my own plumbing business, so I want to get as much experience as I can in my current job.

Think about it

1 Why are social skills important in Nicky's working day?
2 Why is it important that Nicky can work to deadlines and targets?
3 Why are gas regulations important?

Introduction

Electricity is an essential part of our everyday lives, and most of us cannot imagine living without it. How many of the objects you use each day are powered by electricity? From the digital alarm clock that wakes us up in the morning to the streetlights that light our roads at night, electrical items are now essential to our society.

Electricity is supplied through copper conductors encased within cables. These conductors supply power from the fuse board to electrical appliances and lighting around the home. Because electricity is potentially dangerous, electrical installations must be done by a qualified and approved electrician.

In this unit, you will install electrical cables and sockets in a test circuit. This will allow you to demonstrate your skills in correctly wiring in accordance with current wiring regulations and health and safety standards. You will also test your circuit to make sure it is earthed, safe and wired correctly.

Assessment: You will be assessed by a series of assignments set by your teacher/tutor.

Learning aims

In this unit you will:

A understand tools, materials and equipment used for electrical operations

B develop practical skills using safe techniques to undertake electrical operations.

> I love working on my BTEC course as I get to do some practical work as well as learning about different electrical tools and materials. Because we will be working with electricity, we also have to learn about health and safety, as well as writing a risk assessment for the task we're going to do. Then we can get going on wiring our test circuit, which I'm really looking forward to doing!
>
> Ranjit, *16-year-old aspiring electrician*

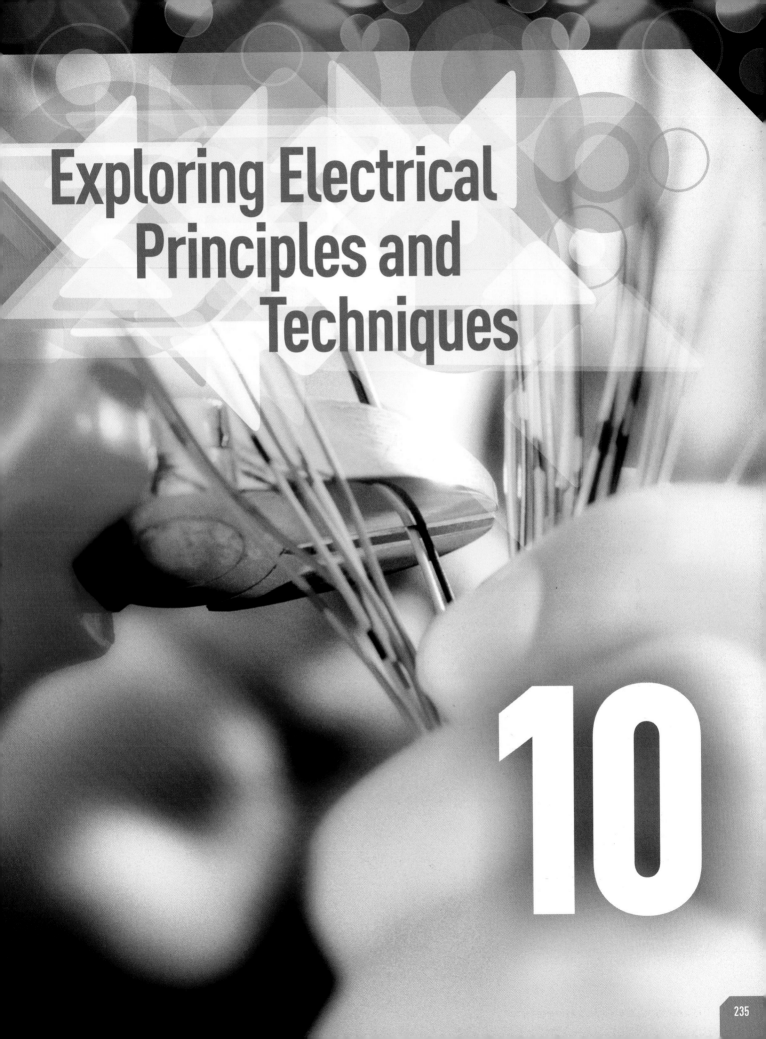

Exploring Electrical Principles and Techniques

10

BTEC
Assessment Zone

This table shows what you must do in order to achieve a **Pass**, **Merit** or **Distinction** grade, and where you can find activities in this book to help you.

Assessment criteria

Level 1	Level 2 **Pass**	Level 2 **Merit**	Level 2 **Distinction**
Learning aim A: Understand tools, materials and equipment used for electrical operations			
1A.1 Identify the purpose of tools and equipment, and the use of materials in electrical operations.	**2A.P1** Explain the purpose and use of appropriate tools, materials and equipment for electrical operations. **See Assessment activity 10.1, page 247**	**2A.M1** Justify the selection and use of tools, materials and equipment for a specified electrical operation task. **See Assessment activity 10.1, page 247**	**2A.D1** Evaluate the selection and use of tools, materials and equipment for a specified electrical operation task. **See Assessment activity 10.1, page 247**
1A.2 Outline the safe use and storage of tools, materials and equipment for electrical operations.	**2A.P2** Explain the safe use and storage of tools, materials and equipment for electrical operations. **See assessment activity 10.1, page 247**		
Learning aim B: Develop practical skills and safe techniques to undertake electrical operations			
1B.3 Identify hazards and control measures prior to commencing electrical operations.	**2B.P3** **English** Carry out a risk assessment prior to commencing electrical operations.		
1B.4 Work safely using personal protection equipment with guidance.	**2B.P4** Comply with safe working practices including using appropriate personal protection equipment.		
1B.5 **Maths** Measure and mark out cables and conduits to produce a test rig circuit with guidance: • to a given specification with guidance • accurate horizontally to 10 mm.	**2B.P5** **Maths** Measure and mark out cables and conduits to produce a test rig circuit: • to a given specification. • accurate to 3 mm deviation from straight. **See Assessment activity 10.2, page 252**	**2B.M2** **Maths** Measure and mark out cables and conduits to produce a test rig circuit: • to a given specification • accurate to 2 mm deviation from straight • no insulation damage by hammer or clips. **See Assessment activity 10.2, page 252**	**2B.D2** **Maths** Measure and mark out cables and conduits to produce a test rig circuit: • to a given specification • accurate to 1 mm deviation from straight • with no insulation damage by hammer or clips. **See Assessment activity 10.2, page 252**

Assessment criteria			
Level 1	**Level 2 Pass**	**Level 2 Merit**	**Level 2 Distinction**
Learning aim B: Develop practical skills and safe techniques to undertake electrical operations			
1B.6 Maths	**2B.P6** Maths	**2B.M3** Maths	**2B.D3** Maths
Construct a test rig circuit consisting of a ring final circuit with two sockets and one fused spur, with guidance with: • all sockets level, in position to within +/– 10 mm. The test rig must: • pass tests for continuity, insulation resistance and polarity.	Construct a test rig circuit consisting of a ring final circuit with two sockets, one fused spur and a single lighting switched circuit with lamp holder with: • all sockets level, in position to within +/– 3 mm • no exposed electrical conductors • all earth sleeving in position • correct colour coding. The test rig must: • pass tests for continuity, insulation resistance and polarity. **See Assessment activity 10.2, page 252**	Construct a test rig circuit consisting of a ring final circuit with two sockets, one fused spur and a single lighting switched circuit with lamp holder with: • all sockets level, in position to within +/–2 mm • conduits neatly fixed to the circuit board • no exposed electrical conductors • all earth sleeving in position • correct colour coding. The test rig must: • pass tests for continuity, insulation resistance and polarity. **See Assessment activity 10.2, page 252**	Construct a test rig circuit consisting of a ring final circuit with two sockets, one fused spur and a single lighting switched circuit with lamp holder with: • all sockets level, in position to within +/– 1 mm • conduits neatly fixed to the circuit board • no exposed copper conductors • no exposed electrical conductors • all earth sleeving in position • correct colour coding. The test rig must: • pass tests for continuity, insulation resistance and polarity. **See Assessment activity 10.2, page 252**

English	Opportunity to practise English skills	Maths	Opportunity to practise mathematical skills

How you will be assessed

The unit will be assessed by a series of tasks set by your tutor. These tasks may be a combination of written assignments and practical hands-on electrical operations. You will need to show your understanding of the tools, equipment and materials that are used in electrical installations. Your practical skills will also be demonstrated when you construct your test rig circuit. These skills should include working safely, accuracy and cleanliness.

Your assessment could be in the form of:

● a written assignment

● an observation record of your practical performance

● the production of a practical test piece.

▶ Tools and equipment used for undertaking electrical operations

Introduction

An electrician uses a wide variety of specialist hand tools when installing electrical circuits. By the end of this topic you will be familiar with the most common tools and their uses.

Electrical tools can be classified into the following categories:

- measuring tools
- cutting and cable-**stripping** tools
- **fixing** and **termination** tools.

▶ Hand tools and equipment

Measuring tools

Measuring tools are vital when installing electrics. You may need to measure to position an electrical socket in the correct location. For example, with a wall-mounted television the client may not want to see the socket or the connecting cable, so your measurements, marking out and cutting need to be absolutely accurate.

Measuring tape	
This is used to work out accurately cable lengths and positions of sockets.	
Spirit level	
This is used to make sure sockets and appliances are fixed level and horizontal.	

Cutting and cable-stripping tools

When connecting cables to their sockets, appliances or fittings, they have to be correctly stripped of their insulation. This will expose the copper **conductors** that will need securing to the terminals that supply a light, socket or appliance. The insulation has to be stripped back in layers and to the correct length, exposing the minimum amount of copper conductor.

Cable cutters	
These are used to cut through different-sized cables to the needed length prior to stripping the insulation from the electrical conductor.	

Cable strippers
These are used to remove the insulation from the copper conductor.

Junior hacksaw
This is a small hacksaw used to cut conduit and heavier-duty cables to length.

Stripping knife
This is a short-bladed knife used for removing the primary insulation from the cable conductors. Its handle must be very well insulated.

Fixing and termination tools

The final connections of cables often need to be fixed to screw terminals. The tools used for this should always carry the **VDE** certification for safety when working with electricity.

Pliers
These are used to bend over the copper conductor to double its thickness and form a terminal for insertion into the terminal fixing.

Screwdrivers
These are specialist insulated screwdrivers used to fasten electrical conductors into their terminal blocks to make sure they are tight and cannot work loose.

Electrical testing equipment
This is used to detect and work out voltages in circuits. Mains testers can be plugged directly into a socket to test if a circuit is live. A multifunction tester is used to test for **continuity**, **insulation**, **current** and **impedance**.

Activity 10.1

1 Think about the tasks an electrician might carry out and make a list. Add the tools you think each listed task could need. Use the internet to help you research.

2 The standard that is used for electrician's tools is the VDE standard. What does this mean?

3 Obtain a multifunction meter. Under the supervision of your tutor, do a series of tests on a circuit to see if you can identify any faults.

Did you know?

A lot of electricians' tools have insulated handles, to prevent electricity travelling through the tool and shocking the electrician.

Key term

VDE – Verband der Elektrotechnik (the Association for Electrical, Electronic & Information Technologies) is one of the largest technical and scientific associations in Europe, and is a brand name for tested electrical tools.

Remember

Always use tools that are insulated, even if you think the circuit is not live.

Key terms

Continuity – the completion of a circuit without any breaks in the conduction of electricity.

Insulation – the plastic covering that surrounds the copper conductors.

Current – the amount of flow of electrical charge, which is measured in amps.

Impedance – the opposition of a circuit to the passage of electricity.

239

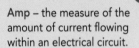

Materials used in electrical operations

Introduction

There are many different materials that are used for the installation of electrical circuits and terminal fittings within a domestic or commercial application.

This cable contains three copper conductors, which are all insulated individually. Which is the live conductor?

The choice of material is decided by the amount of current that it must carry. For example, higher-rated cables must be used to carry any extra load safely. Current is measured in **amps** and typically circuits carry the following ratings:

- lighting is usually 5 amps
- power circuits are normally 30 amps
- higher-voltage equipment such as electric cookers are usually 45 amps.

Cable

Electrical cable is used to distribute the supply around a domestic home or commercial business. This normally consists of a grey **PVC** cable, which is wrapped around the conductors. For single-phase AC installations, the live conductor is wrapped in a brown insulation and the neutral is identified by a blue insulation.

Lighting circuits are normally wired in cable that has conductors which are 1.5 mm^2 in **cross-sectional** area. This cable is rated for use in lighting circuits where there are no high current ratings from appliances, only low-energy light bulbs.

The ring main circuits are normally constructed from 2.5 mm^2 cross-sectional area conductors. These can therefore carry more current loading, which can be used by our modern appliances such as televisions and kitchen equipment.

Houses contain many metres of electrical wiring, which is usually hidden in the walls and partitions. The cable is chased into a solid wall and insulated to protect it, then the plaster finishes conceal its existence. Wiring can also be clipped inside hollow partitions and terminated in a plasterboard socket back box.

In commercial buildings, the wiring may be in a surface mounted conduit. This is a plastic tube in which single insulated electrical cables can be threaded and terminated. The conduits are secured by clipping them to the walls using screws. Rolls of single cables can therefore be used that only hold the red or blue insulation. The earth would also be a separate single conductor. Single cables, as the name suggests, only contain one electrical conduit. This is covered in one layer of insulation which is often colour coded to show whether it is live, neutral or earth.

For modern cabling colours:

- **live** is **brown**
- **neutral** is **blue**
- **earth** is **yellow and green**.

Activity 10.3

You are rewiring a kitchen ring main and have stripped the earth conductor cable. The earth conductor within a modern cable is normally not covered with a secondary insulation, and is bare and exposed when the grey insulation is stripped.

1 What size cable would you use for the ring main?
2 Why would you not use 1.5 mm² cable?
3 What two colours make up the earth protection?
4 What colour is the live conductor?

Electrical fittings

All cables eventually have to terminate at a **consumer unit**, **outlet** or a **joint box**. In domestic houses these fittings are often used as features with different-coloured face plates such as brass or chrome effects.

Sockets

Sockets that you plug an appliance into can be supplied as single or double sockets and switched or unswitched. A single socket only has one place you can plug an electrical appliance in; a double has two. These often have switches on them; if they do not, they are simply called 'unswitched'.

A switched double socket.

Flex outlets

A flex outlet is a socket that holds a direct wired appliance. The appliance cable is passed through a receiving hole in the socket face and clamped tight. This is then terminated appropriately on the face plate. Flex outlets can be switched and may have a rated fuse and a neon indicator when the current is on. These are often used for the wiring of permanently fixed electrical appliances – for example, a wall-mounted electrical convector heater would be fixed to a flex outlet socket.

Fused spur units

A fused spur unit is used to wire an electrical appliance that does not need a fused plug. The fused spur unit has a face plate with an access panel for the fuse to be maintained, a switch and a neon indicator. The appliance cable is fed directly into the rear of the socket box for direct connection to the power supply.

Appliance plugs

The final connection for an appliance is usually a 13 amp plug. These are mainly factory fitted and encased around the appliance's cable with an access cover for fuse maintenance. Where appliances are delivered without this facility, a plug will have to be correctly wired and the appliance tested.

Activity 10.3

Examine some of the appliances around you. Which are fixed to flex outlet sockets? Which of them have fused spur units?

Key terms

Consumer unit – the unit where the meter and isolation fuse feed into the domestic circuit. It has all of the fuses, residual circuit devices (RCDs) or miniature circuit breakers (MCBs).

Outlet – this could be a fused outlet where the cable from the appliance is directly wired into the ring main.

Joint box – used to connect two cables or more together safely.

Take it further

Visit a local electrical wholesaler supplier and look at the variety of sockets and face plates that are available for domestic applications.

▶ Lighting fittings

The modern home contains lots of different light fittings and these are used to make human occupation of rooms easier – for example, in the winter months during periods of darkness.

Ceiling rose

Normal domestic lighting cables are terminated within a **ceiling rose** or a conduit junction box. These are the two methods that can be employed to supply power to the light fitting. Often, the modern approach is to use the ceiling rose method, where a live conductor is looped into each ceiling rose. From this a switch wire travels down to the light switch and back to the light fitting. The neutral and earth are connected to the terminal block within the rose backplate.

With a metal light fitting, care must be taken to check that the manufacturer's instructions are followed with regard to earthing the metal fitting. This is because if a fault occurs, you should not receive an electric shock if you touched the metal of the fitting.

The ceiling rose has a backplate which fixes to the ceiling with screws. This contains a series of brass terminals to which the lighting feed is connected. A rose cover then screws onto the backplate to enclose any wiring safely. From this rose a central hole allows the lighting cable to connect to the lamp holder. The whole unit is known as a lighting pendant. Within the ceiling rose, cord grips secure the pendant cable to the backplate.

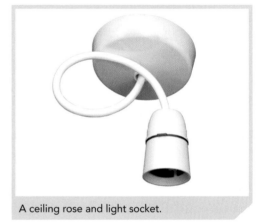

A ceiling rose and light socket.

Activity 10.4

1 Ask your tutor for a pendant light set. Unscrew all the parts to investigate how the lighting circuit cable is terminated within the ceiling rose.
2 Do some research on the different types of LED energy-efficient light bulbs.

Light switches

A light is operated by the use of a light switch. Single-way light switches turn a light within a room on and off. These are available in multiple switches for more than one light to be controlled. They can also be supplied as dimmer switches to lower the lighting intensity.

Batten lamp holder

Attached to a ceiling rose is the **batten lamp holder**. This is the socket that the light bulb fastens into.

There are two styles of lamp holder:

- a **bayonet** fitting – a bayonet light bulb has two pins in the top which lock into two holes in the batten lamp holder

- a **screw type** fitting – a screw type light bulb screws clockwise into the batten lamp holder and connects to the live and neutral terminals.

Two-way switching on a lighting circuit is used for a hallway and stairs application. It may be convenient to operate an upstairs or downstairs lighting pendant from either floor. In this case a two-way lighting circuit would need to be installed.

▶ Miscellaneous fittings

Conduit

Surface mounted conduit is normally supplied in 20 mm diameter lengths.

Where cables are to be buried within a wall chase, an oval conduit is used to protect the insulated cable from damage. The oval shape reduces the amount of chasing that has to be done so the plaster finishes cover the conduit.

Conduit junction boxes

These are used to connect lengths of conduit together and are especially useful where alteration work is needed and a ring main has to be 'broken into' to form a spur or circuit connection. Junction boxes, like cables, are rated for the amperage that they will be subjected to.

Activity 10.5

Examine a lighting switch face plate and a power socket. Work out which size socket box you would use for each so there is sufficient depth for the wiring.

Conduit elbows and T-junctions

Conduit lengths can be joined using connectors or junction boxes. At a junction box a removable plate allows access to the wiring encased within the conduit. Bends are achieved by the use of elbows, and T-junctions are also available.

Back box

Sockets rely on a back box that is fixed to the wall within a socket chase or plasterboard partition. This is a metal box that is screwed into the blockwork wall, and the socket face is screwed to the back box. It is this box that receives the ring main circuit cable. Within solid walls these boxes are constructed of galvanised steel. They have an earth terminal, which is a safety feature of the face plate. The socket face plate is screwed into the back box using steel screws. These screws are therefore linked to the earth protection circuit so any contact with them immediately switches off the current, should a fault occur.

As the cable enters a back box it should pass through a rubber **grommet** surrounding the back box inlet hole so any cable abrasion against a steel box is isolated and the integrity of the cable can be maintained.

Take it further

Go to your local DIY store and examine the range of different fittings that are now available for domestic use.

Did you know?

Conduit is available in heavy gauge plastic or in galvanised mild steel.

Key term

Grommet – a rubber ring that fits within the steel back box where the inlet has been formed and protects the cable from any sharp edges that could cut the cable insulation as the cable is pulled through.

Surface boxes

These are called surface boxes because they fix onto the surface of the wall. A socket box is used to house the back of the socket face plate where all the cable terminals are housed. They need to be selected with sufficient depth to hold the cables that enter the socket box. They are fixed to a solid wall using plugs and screws. Different-sized socket boxes hold single or double sockets. Within the socket box are adjustable lugs; these allow you to position the face plate straight so it looks aesthetically pleasing for a client.

When fixing sockets into a hollow plasterboard partition, you must use a plasterboard box. This has lugs within the box that clamp onto the plasterboard partition and a front lip that prevents the box from being pushed through into the partition void.

Surface boxes are normally used with exposed surface fixed conduit.

Conduit saddle clips

Conduit is fixed back to the wall using conduit saddle clips which are drilled, plugged and screwed to the wall using suitable screw fixings.

▶ Safe use and storage of tools, materials and equipment

Introduction

This topic examines the safe use of electrical tools, equipment and materials. Working safely with electricity is paramount to avoid any hazards and their associated risks.

▶ Use of general personal protective equipment (PPE) needed in the workplace

Appropriate personal protective equipment must be worn as a last resort when all other avenues of risk control have been explored through the risk assessment process.

- **Safety footwear** should be worn and maintained so the steel toecaps are not exposed and cannot come into contact with an electrical conductor.
- **Gloves** should be worn when handling sharp items or for manual handing.
- **Overalls** should be worn to create a barrier against your skin.
- A **hard hat** may be needed if you work on site, enter buildings below scaffolding or if there is any risk of materials falling on you.
- **Eye protection** may be needed if you are doing any cutting.
- A **high-visibility jacket** may be needed on some construction sites to make you visible to the plant operators on site.

> **Just checking** ✓
>
> 1 What is the difference between a single and a double socket face plate?
> 2 What colour would an earth conductor be?
> 3 When would you use a metal back box?
> 4 Why would you use surface fixed conduit?

...n electrician's PPE is designed to ...rotect against electric shocks.

Any specialist PPE should be used when using some fittings and tools. Manufacturers' safety data sheets will specify when this is needed.

Use of task-specific PPE when cutting cabling

When cutting electrical cable, it is always good practice to use the correct tool and to wear gloves. This will prevent any injuries caused by fingers or hands getting trapped.

If you are cutting metal conduit and are using an electric cutting saw, then you will need to wear overalls, eye protection and gloves.

Electricity must be treated with care. Inappropriate behaviour could lead to fatal accidents.

Appropriate behaviour

Working with electricity is hazardous. Great care and attention must be taken when installing electrical services so they are safe for the client to use and operate. They need to be installed so that they do not cause faults in a circuit that may have consequences for the occupant of a building – for example, faulty electrical wiring that overheats and causes a fire.

This means that care and attention to quality are essential to any electrical installation. You must make sure all exposed conductors are insulated correctly and all circuits follow the Institution of Engineering and Technology (IET) 17th Edition guidelines.

You must behave appropriately at all times when working with electricity, and have a positive attitude to health and safety. For example, you would not switch on the electrical current as a joke to give a friend an electrical shock. This could result in a fatal accident. Similarly, switching off the electrical current without telling a client or your colleagues can also have an effect – for example, it could shut down a production line and damage the machinery.

Did you know?

It only takes an electric shock of 100 milliamps to stop your heart. A typical computer port produces this level of current.

Discussion

Electrical hand tools have many safety features that protect you during their use, should you come into contact with a live conductor. Can you identify any of these?

Did you know?

The IET 17th Edition guidelines are the industry standard practice for a qualified electrician.

Just checking

1 Why should an electrician wear overalls?

2 Why is it important to behave appropriately when working with electricity?

3 Name the guidelines that set industry standard practice for qualified electricians.

Remember

You can avoid muscular injuries by carrying out appropriate manual handling assessments before starting any work.

Link

For more on manual handling techniques, see page 158.

Maintaining a clean and tidy work area

A tidy work area will remove many of the slip and trip hazards. Electrical work may often involve working at height from appropriate steps and platforms when fitting light fixtures and wiring. The removal of any waste materials is needed to maintain the workplace in an acceptable standard of housekeeping. A clean and tidy work area removes any risks from hazards.

Safe manual handling when lifting and moving

Cables often have to be pulled into position through the services voids, floors and ceilings of a building. These cables must be handled carefully to ensure they are installed correctly and safely. You should always allow for the weight of a cable drum and make sure it does not exceed the HSE guidelines of 25 kg, remembering to lift close into the body. Lifting heavy objects in an incorrect way can damage your spine and your back muscles.

Access into these voids, which could be classified as confined spaces, will also mean the appropriate safety measures must be followed – for example, consideration must be given to ventilation, adequate lighting and provision of access at height.

Using tools and equipment correctly

An electrical tool kit will consist of many of the tools explored in the opening topic of this unit. The manufacturer's instructions should be read and understood with regard to safe use during electrical installations. Tools must be used correctly. For example, the correct-sized head for a screwdriver must be selected for the size of the screw within a terminal block, or you may slip and cause damage to the screw head or nearby cable insulation.

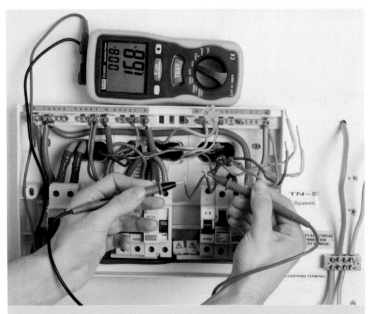

Why do you think it is so important for an electrician's tools to be well maintained?

Using the correct size of cable strippers will help produce a quality termination of a cable with the insulation stripped back evenly and without damage to any layers. This is a better outcome than trying to use a stripping knife to achieve the same quality.

Cleaning tools and reporting any defects

Tools should always be maintained by cleaning and any defective parts replaced or renewed, should they be beyond repair. Defects should always be reported to your supervisor, even if they appear minor.

Storing tools

Storage of tools is important to avoid any damage to them. If a tool was bought with its own storage container, then it should be returned there after use. Screwdrivers should be stored in a toolbox compartment and any cutting equipment kept separately so the VDE-approved insulation is not damaged when the toolbox is carried or moved. Any guards supplied with cutting knives or strippers should be in place when storing the tool.

Assessment activity 10.1

Your electrical company has started work for a new client and you have been chosen to help with this work. It is important that you make a good first impression on this client. The following questions will help you prepare for the work that you will do for this new client and need to be fully answered to make sure you will work safely and professionally, applying the knowledge that you have learned.

1 Explain what electrical tools you would select for the installation of an extension socket into a solid wall, the materials you would need, how you would use the tools selected and what other equipment you might need. The following tools, materials and equipment are going to be used for a light fitting installation:

- stepladders
- hole saw
- cable cutters
- wire strippers
- terminal screwdriver
- ceiling rose
- electrical cable.

2 Select one tool, material and item of equipment from the above list. Explain their safe use in installing the new light fitting.

3 Justify your selection of the tools, giving reasons why you have chosen them.

4 The client is considering the use of the following alternative materials:

- surface-mounted conduit to the light fitting
- low-voltage LED ceiling mounted fittings.

Evaluate the two alternative materials for this lighting installation.

5 Carry out a risk assessment for the installation of the new light fitting.

6 Identify and explain what PPE you would need to comply with safe working practices and record this on your risk assessment.

Tips

- Your justifications always need to state the reason why you have selected those particular tools, materials or equipment.
- Make sure that your evaluation of alternative materials includes the advantages and disadvantages of each material in some depth of description.
- You will need to devise a simple template for the carrying out of your risk assessment. The use of an observation record and some photographic evidence of you doing practical electrical operation would be of great benefit when identifying and explaining PPE.

▶ Health and safety

Introduction

You need to perform practical tasks in electrical operations and installations safely and efficiently, without harm to yourself or others. Working with electricity is hazardous and can cause serious injury. This is why health and safety is so important. In order to work on the practical installations, you must be able to identify the hazards in your work and complete a **risk assessment**.

A risk assessment identifies the hazards associated with the task and the people who might be affected. Any control measures already in place are then examined to see if they lower the risk from the hazard to an acceptable level. If they do not, further control measures may be needed.

▶ Identifying hazards and risks

The identification of electrical hazards can be done in a number of different ways, including:

- direct observation of the task
- using checklists
- using manufacturers' safety data sheets
- previous risk assessments.

The principal hazards associated with electricity could cover any of the following in Table 10.1, which shows the hazard with the associated risk.

Table 10.1 Hazards and risks associated with working with electricity

Identified hazard	Risk from hazard
Electricity	Electric shock, burns, death
Explosion	Gas cylinders used for soldering joints – burning, major injury, death
Hot work	Burns and blistering
Use of cable strippers and knives	Cuts to hands and fingers, entrapment by pinching using strippers
Use of tools and equipment	Cuts and injuries caused by tools and equipment
Untidy work area and poor housekeeping	Causing slips, trips and falls, back injuries, fractures
Working in confined spaces	**Musculoskeletal injuries**, strains, sprains, cuts, head injuries

▶ Identifying people at risk

As part of the risk assessment process, you must identify the people who are at risk. These could be employees, employers, students, visitors, delivery personnel and members of the public.

This is done so you can consider what control measures may be needed to protect them. For example, isolating an electrical supply before you work on it is very important. A safe system of work needs to be in place to make sure no one can switch the power on again early and electrocute a colleague.

Activity 10.6

Carry out a risk assessment for the following scenario.

An electrician has been asked to wire up a new hot water heater above a sink unit within an office. This will involve forming electrical connections to alter the mains supply feed for the new hot water heater.

Using control measures

A control measure is used to reduce the risk from a hazard down to its lowest level obtainable. The Health and Safety Executive (HSE) offers a **hierarchy** of control measures, or the order in which you should take steps to control the risk. This is shown in Table 10.2.

Table 10.2 The hierarchy of control measures, adapted from the HSE's Leadership and Worker Involvement Toolkit

Control measure	Method
1 Elimination	This means removing the risk entirely. An example would be removing old lead pipework and lead soldered joints, because lead can pollute drinking water and can cause serious illness.
2 Substitution	This means replacing one product or material for another less harmful product or material.
3 Engineering controls	This means finding a technical solution. For instance, you could use pre-soldered joint connectors at height so that you would have one hand free, which you wouldn't if you had to hold both a coil of solder and a blowtorch.
4 Administrative controls	This means using controls such as training and qualifications. This could include a site induction to prepare operatives who are new to the site and to give them information about the possible hazards they will face on site.
5 Personal protective equipment (PPE)	This should always be the last resort. For example, the use of gloves and eye protection when soldering will reduce the risk of burning.

Did you know?

The risk assessment process has five easy steps to remember: IDERR.

Identify the hazards.

Decide who might be harmed.

Evaluate the risk.

Record your findings.

Review the assessment.

Key term

Hierarchy – a ranking system according to the importance of each item listed in relation to the other items.

When using the hierarchy of controls to reduce risk, you should work from the top down in sequence until the risk is reduced to an acceptable level. Note that PPE is the last item on the list. This is because it should always be the last resort after all other options have been considered.

Remember

Always make sure the electrical supply is switched off and locked off while you are working on a circuit.

Key term

Polarity – the direction of a magnetic or electric field.

Just checking ✔

1 Identify an electrical hazard.

2 What are the five steps of a risk assessment?

3 Why do you have to complete a risk assessment before starting work?

4 How would you isolate an electrical supply?

▶ Adopting safe working practices

Isolation of electricity from a circuit is vital to safe working practice. It can be achieved in several ways.

- If you remove the fuse and keep it with you at all times, no one else can put it back into the fuse board while you are working.
- You could lock off the mains switch using padlocks, so each person has to place their lock on to the circuit.
- You could ask the electricity supplier to remove the mains fuse from the incoming main.

At all times you should observe the instructions and training from the IET Regulations about the installation of wiring. No exposed copper conductors should be allowed to come into contact with a human being or animal.

▶ Testing for continuity, insulation resistance and polarity

You should test for **continuity** to ensure that the circuit works and does not have any breaks in the conduction of electricity.

You will need to check for **insulation resistance** because electrical insulation starts to age as soon as it is made, and over time, it performs less effectively. This could cause risks to people's safety and also stop the equipment working. This means that it is important to identify this deterioration as quickly as possible so you can deal with it and replace if required.

You should also check for **polarity** to make sure all switches, fuses and circuit breakers are in the line conductor only, and sockets are wired correctly.

▶ Developing electrical operation skills

Introduction

In this topic you will carry out the wiring of power and lighting circuits accurately and without any errors so they function correctly.

▶ Marking out electrical runs and sockets

Sockets need to be marked out accurately for a number of reasons:

- to be at the height required in flood risk areas where sockets have to be a set distance above ground floor level
- to provide easy access for wheelchair users and the less physically able

- to hide services behind appliances so they are not visible
- to keep sockets level and make them aesthetically pleasing to the occupants
- to maintain safe distances from sources of water.

Interpreting requirements from drawings

You must be able to read, interpret and understand dimensions from drawings supplied by an architect or services engineer. You use the key shown on the drawing to identify what each symbol means – for example, a light fitting and its light switch position.

Marking out and cutting required lengths of cable and conduit

Marking out the sockets and cable routes needs to match the drawn information. There is a certain amount of flexibility with the adjustable tabs in socket boxes to level the socket face plates before finally tightening them. A cable is normally pulled into a circuit from a cable drum and cut to length when the required amount has been pulled into and through the service voids. You may have to estimate the lengths of cables needed, then measure and cut these to length. Always measure twice to check your measurements and avoid wasting cables.

Surface-mounted conduit lengths can be measured from the position of the surface boxes, then cut to the required length, allowing for any insertion into the boxes.

Did you know?

Often, you may walk around with a client and mark out the positions of each electrical item to be fitted using a felt-tip marker. These will show the position of sockets and appliances in two dimensions. You may then have to interpret a specification to work out the height dimension.

Activity 10.7

Evaluate your current skills by examining your strengths and weaknesses. List the new skills you will need to develop for doing the practical electrical operations.

▶ Electrical installation

Figure 10.1 shows the wiring diagram for the circuits that you are going to have to construct. It includes a ring main, which is fed from a consumer unit with two sockets. A fused spur is fed from one socket. The diagram also contains a lighting circuit. This is also fed from the consumer unit to a ceiling rose and back to complete the circuit. From the ceiling rose, a switch wire is fed down to the light switch.

This drawn information needs to be interpreted and put on your test rig board in accordance with the dimensions that your tutor will supply for the sockets. The test rig will then be wired using surface-mounted conduits, socket boxes and face plates.

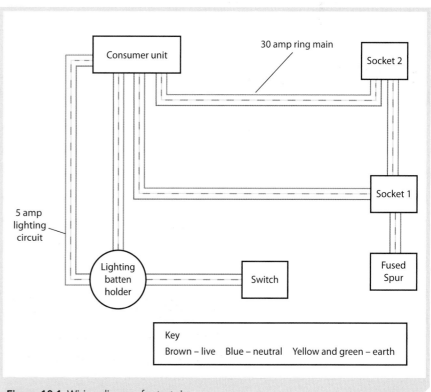

Figure 10.1 Wiring diagram for test rig

Key term

Sleeving – a separate sleeve that fits over the exposed earth conductor and covers up all of the copper conductor.

Activity 10.8

The final terminal connections are where accurate skills are needed, to strip back electrical cable, expose the conductors and partially remove the conductor insulation.

Practise these techniques by wiring a cable to an electrical plug.

emember, all testing must be done ith supervision by a tutor and with all upplies isolated.

The electrical supply to your test rig must be isolated and locked off for safety. The ring main and lighting circuit can be wired using singles cables as long as these are correctly identified by their colours.

Ring main

Socket back boxes should be screwed to the test rig board using correct length screws through the back of the socket boxes. Conduit gland connectors are fixed to the sides of the socket boxes to receive the 20 mm conduits. Make sure that you wire the socket faces correctly and that all earthing is done correctly, using **sleeving** to cover any exposed conductors.

Lighting circuit

The lighting circuit will use a lighting batten holder. This fits directly onto the terminal back box that contains all of the light circuit supplies.

Again, you must isolate the electricity supply before starting work. This circuit is also going to be wired within surface-mounted conduits.

Circuit testing

Your completed test rig will be tested to make sure that:

- the circuit has continuity with no breaks in any of the circuits
- the insulation of all conductors is in place, including the earth conductor to all back boxes and fittings
- the resistance of the circuit meets requirements
- the polarity of all the live and neutral socket pins is correct
- the quality and setting out of the circuit is within the necessary tolerances.

Testing is a very important stage of commissioning of an electrical installation. It makes sure that the occupants can use and operate appliances safely and without any faults.

Assessment activity 10.2   *Maths*

1 Marking out the position of your sockets may involve copying measurements from a drawing onto a wall, project board or ceiling. Practise using a tape measure to transfer these dimensions, then draw the outline of the sockets in pencil and level these correctly.

2 Fix your socket boxes to the test rig panel and then fix the conduit connectors to the boxes. Measure, mark and cut a conduit to fit between boxes, fittings or consumer unit.

Tips

- Using a sharp pencil will help you achieve the required tolerances. Tolerances are a way of checking how accurate you have been in setting out and fitting your electrical circuits, as compared to the original measurements.
- Look closely at the socket faces. You can see clearly the live, neutral and earth so you can identify where the cables need to terminate.
- When working on a ring main with cable going into a socket and out again, twist the conductors together using pliers. This will make sure they fit within the socket terminal better and will not fall out when the terminal is tightened.

WorkSpace

▶ Paula McCruick

Qualified electrician

I work as a maintenance electrician in a busy inner city hospital. I have to deal with the maintenance of all the electrical equipment and lighting, testing of power supplies, and refurbishment work to the hospital wards, corridors and offices.

I have to take great care when working around patients, making sure all supplies are maintained to their medical equipment and that no disruptions occur that could affect patients' comfort. Light fittings often have to be changed at night when the corridors and wards are less busy and it is safer to do this work. I need to make sure I'm not blocking access when using ladders in corridors to service light fittings, and often this is a two-person operation.

I have to work with my colleagues, the nursing staff and the facilities manager in organising my maintenance jobs during the day and often have to coordinate specific times when this work can be done. The intensive care unit needs lots of coordination and often involves pre-work meetings with all staff involved in the work area.

I really enjoy my work and it's great to know I have helped to keep the hospital running and operating safely.

Think about it

1 Why is the isolation of electrical supplies critical to Paula's job?

2 Why does Paula have to be aware of all of the people who might be harmed when completing a risk assessment for her work?

3 Why does Paula have to wear PPE?

Introduction

How much do you know about climate change and the effects it is having on the planet? Our climate is changing and this change is causing problems such as floods and non-renewable resources running out. People in the construction industry have to try to limit and overcome these negative effects of climate change. This can partly be done by building in a sustainable way, as this unit will show.

Sustainability is a broad concept and covers the physical, social and economic issues related to the design and construction of buildings. Using sustainable approaches will minimise the negative impacts of construction activities on the environment. Thinking about sustainability also means that places are created that communities can enjoy, as well as providing job and business opportunities.

There are various ways to achieve sustainability goals such as construction methods, site practices, use of alternative energy sources and use of sustainable materials. In this unit you will learn how these methods and techniques are applied during design, construction and use of a building development.

Assessment: You will be assessed using a paper-based examination lasting one hour and fifteen minutes.

Learning aims

In this unit you will:

A understand the sustainability issues of construction for the physical, social, and economic environment during the lifecycle of a development

B understand the techniques and methods used to reduce the impact of construction during the lifecycle of a development.

> This unit has given me a broader understanding of sustainability. Now I know it's not just about saving coal, oil and natural gas – it's about the local and global effects of construction too. This unit has really changed the way I look at buildings, because now I can see how they affect the environment around them.
>
> Zhang Yau, *17-year-old aspiring site manager*

Sustainability in Construction

11

▶ Sustainability concepts and benefits

Introduction

Over the past two decades, the words 'sustainable' and 'environmental' have been widely used in construction. Lots of buildings in the UK and across the world are being built following the principles of sustainable construction. In this topic, you will learn about the social, physical and economic benefits of sustainability.

Discussion

In groups, discuss what you know about sustainability. Why do you think it is so important in the modern construction industry?

▶ Key concepts of sustainability

Sustainability is about meeting the needs of the present without negatively affecting the needs and rights of future generations. In practical terms in construction, sustainability is about construction work that has minimal long-term impacts on the environment.

We all depend on natural resources to live on Earth. Construction projects use a number of these resources, such as fuel, water, timber, metals and aggregates. Some of these resources, such as fuel, are limited. Others can be renewed, such as water. This means that people have to use limited resources wisely so that they do not run out. Protecting the natural environment and using natural resources wisely will make sure that enough is available now as well as for future generations – in other words, that it is sustainable.

Did you know?

The UK construction industry uses over 420 million tonnes of resources every year.

This approach means that present and future generations should have a good-quality life. It also means that everybody has a responsibility to think about their actions and their impact on the wider world including people in the construction industry. The negative impact of construction has to be reduced from the first planning stages, during the construction process and through to completion and long-term use.

Activity 11.1

A new block is to be built in your school. Your head teacher has asked all learners to give proposals so that the new block is constructed in a sustainable manner. In groups, discuss the following:

1 What are your rights and responsibilities in relation to this project?
2 At what stage of this project would you like to be involved?
3 What would you expect to see as the project is developed?

Key terms

Biodiversity – this is made up of two words: biological and diversity. It means the variety of living organisms on the planet.

Infrastructure – includes physical structures and facilities such as roads, flood protection and power supplies.

Sustainability can be viewed in three ways:

1 **Physical sustainability** deals with environmental issues such as pollution, production of waste, appropriate use of land and **biodiversity**.

2 **Economic sustainability** includes all the costs involved during design, construction, use and demolition or reuse of a building. It also includes the cost of providing any **infrastructure**, as well as job opportunities for people.

3 **Social sustainability** is about creating projects to meet housing needs that give opportunities for community interaction. It aims to provide safe and comfortable spaces for the local communities.

▶ The benefits of sustainability

Following sustainable principles can help to protect the natural environment by using natural resources efficiently. For example, on a sustainable project, the timber used has to be certified from renewable sources.

A sustainable project should consider and resolve economic, social and environmental issues from the planning stage through to long-term use.

Many areas across the UK have been redeveloped or 'regenerated' for socially and economically deprived areas. Regeneration projects help to improve quality of life in the area as well as creating job opportunities for local people. This can help to reduce crime, which leads to people feeling safer, lower insurance costs and further commercial enterprises being attracted into a previously run-down location.

Remember

The Forest Stewardship Council (FSC) certifies sustainability managed forests around the world. Wood sold with the FSC logo means that it was grown in a certified forest.

Regeneration of an old industrial area harbour

A development containing a number of green spaces creates an aesthetically pleasing place for people to live, play and socialise. A sustainable project works best by involving communities in deciding these sorts of design and environmental features.

Thinking about environmental features and impacts can improve the environment – for example, by leading to cleaner air through reductions in pollution and, in turn, this improves the health of the local population. It can also mean a reduction in flooding and its impact.

In November 2012 alone, more than 200 flood warnings and alerts were in force in England and Wales.

Sustainability may also involve environmental protection of local habitats and resources, meaning the community can benefit from and enjoy these. This helps develop **eco-tourism** and brings benefits from associated commercial enterprises, and employment opportunities – for example, more opportunities in the local retail sector.

Just checking

1 List three advantages of involving local communities in the construction of a project.
2 List two ways in which regeneration can help in achieving social and economic sustainability.
3 Identify three ways in which waste can be disposed of safely.
4 Why is FSC certification needed for a sustainable project?

▶ Physical issues of construction

Introduction

Sustainability has three aspects: physical, social and economic. In this section, you will learn about the **physical** issues encountered when planning developments and during construction, as well as how to limit the negative effects of development locally.

▶ Physical issues

Resources

Buildings use a number of natural resources such as timber, fossil fuels and water during construction, use and demolition. These resources are finite or limited and should therefore be used wisely. If construction activities are not planned properly, they can damage the environment by using up these finite resources.

Pollution

The construction industry is known for having inefficient supply chains. This means that people order materials without considering factors like transportation which have an impact on the environment. If materials are ordered in bulk and local suppliers are used, less fuel will be used and there will be fewer carbon emissions. Parts of the construction industry also rely on machinery and equipment that cause a lot of noise, use more fuel and emit more carbon.

Climate change

Construction activities contribute to climate change by adding carbon emissions to the atmosphere, which is increasing the temperature of the Earth. For instance, the UK has experienced the worst floods in its history over the past few years, and this may be due to climate change. Sea levels are also rising.

Changes in climate also affect the structure of our buildings. For example, if there is no rainfall over long periods of time, the soil becomes very dry and can shrink, causing the ground to move and causing damage to the structures built on it.

Natural habitats

Construction can disturb or even destroy local natural habitats. This could have a negative impact on the natural environment, especially in conservation areas. These are areas whose natural features are protected. In such areas, permission is required to build, cut trees or demolish a building.

 # Land use

Because the population is increasing, more land is needed to construct buildings for people to live in. Traditionally, buildings have been constructed on **greenfield** sites. As a result, housing developments have led to the loss of woodlands and natural habitats in the countryside. If this trend continued with no change, there would be no land left to fulfil the population's housing needs.

Key term

Greenfield – a site where no construction has taken place before.

The more sustainable approach is to reuse land that has already been built on. Such sites are called **brownfield** sites and may have some structures that need to be demolished or soil contamination that needs to be cleaned up. In this way a site can be recycled.

To further protect natural habitats, wildlife areas can be relocated or sectioned off during construction. The cost of decontaminating the land and protecting natural habitats should be considered during planning.

Landfill waste disposal can also take up much-needed land space. This is why recycling as much waste as possible is so important, rather than relying on landfill.

How could the loss of greenfield sites affect the community?

Assessment practice 11.1

1 Identify two advantages and two disadvantages of developing on greenfield and brownfield sites. [4]

2 Paula is designing a development in an area where there are bats and newts. Identify two ways in which Paula can protect the bats and newts and maintain local biodiversity. [2]

Key term

Brownfield – a site that has already been built on.

Wastage

Waste is produced by:

- the extraction of raw materials during a material's manufacturing process
- the manufacturing process itself
- packaging materials
- the building process itself
- the demolition of existing structures
- the excavation of the building sub-structure.

The construction industry in the UK produces more than 100 million tonnes of waste. This includes both construction and demolition waste.

Waste is also produced once a building is complete. For instance, if a building uses traditional technology for lighting, heating and hot water, this wastes energy because it uses more energy to run than newer technology.

Waste is often disposed of by transporting it off site to landfill sites or by **incineration**. However, doing this causes environmental damage due to increased carbon emissions. Waste materials should instead be categorised so that they can be disposed of correctly, either at general or specialist disposal sites, or through recycling. It is essential to use a licensed disposal contractor to avoid **fly tipping**.

Pollution

Construction activities have the potential to cause various types of pollution, as shown by Figure 11.1.

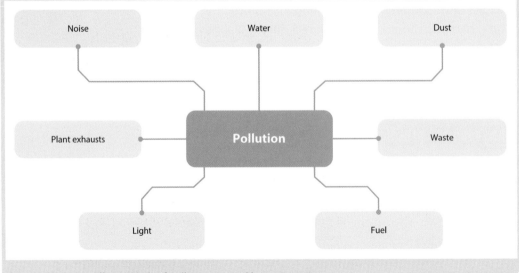

Figure 11.1 The different kinds of pollution created by construction

It is important to consider ways of minimising pollution, and Table 11.1 lists some of these.

Table 11.1 Sources of pollution and how to reduce them

Type and source	How to reduce?
Noise pollution caused by people, machinery and **plant**	• Use silencers for construction machinery • Maintain machinery so that less noise is produced
Emissions from construction traffic, plant and machinery	• Use fuel-efficient vehicles and equipment, which will generate less carbon emissions • Ensure regular maintenance and servicing • Use locally sourced materials as this will reduce the transportation and hence carbon emissions • Cut travel distances and the number of journeys to site by buying in bulk or ordering a variety of materials from one supplier
Carbon emissions created during the manufacture of high energy materials, such as plastics	• Use recycled materials as these need less energy to produce • Explore alternative materials that use less energy
Dust from excavation and demolition work	• Use water to damp the dust down • Ensure regular road sweeping and wheel cleaning • Use equipment that suppresses dust
Light pollution from site activities	• Use light shading to reduce the impact of site lighting • Use lower wattage lighting to reduce the impact of lighting
Land contamination due to fuel and oil spillages	• Use settlement tanks to filter debris (rubbish) • Use **bunded** tanks, **bund walls** and absorbent mats to minimise fuel and oil spillages
Pollutants at power stations	• Use filters and scrubbers such as fabric filters and **wet scrubbers**
Damage to the environment from the irresponsible disposal of materials	• Recycle materials where possible • Use specialist waste disposal services by trained and licensed contractors for hazardous materials such as asbestos • Minimise impact on local water sources and on-site drainage systems by responsible disposal of water used to wash out cement plant and equipment

Key terms

Plant – machinery used in the building process, such as diggers and bulldozers.

Bunded or **bund wall** – a structure that is built to hold any spillages.

Wet scrubber – a device that removes pollutants from gases.

Activity 11.2

In groups, see if you can think of any other methods that you could use to reduce pollution.

Did you know?

Transportation of building materials uses 10 per cent of all UK energy consumption.

Activity 11.3

Brian has been recently promoted to site manager. He is about to start work on his new site and wants to reduce the pollution to a minimum. There will be some weeks when work will be done during the night.

1 Identify two ways in which Brian can reduce noise pollution.
2 Identify two ways to reduce dust pollution.
3 Identify three types of pollution other than noise and dust and suggest ways to reduce these.

Remember

'Pre' means 'before' and 'fabricated' means 'made'. Prefabricated materials are made in a factory and brought to site for assembly only.

Key terms

Grey water – waste water from bathing, dishwashing or using washing machines. It can be recycled to be reused in other areas of the house, but is not used for drinking.

Sustainable Urban Drainage Systems (SUDS) – systems that make sure water is drained off in a sustainable manner.

Embodied (or embedded) energy – the energy needed to produce a material from extraction to its point of use.

Research

Investigate and identify two practices adopted by SUDS to make sure groundwater is protected.

⏵ Energy and water use

Construction projects need energy and water. This includes usage on and off site during pre-construction, construction and after construction.

Using prefabricated materials reduces the site operations and therefore the use of water. Storing and using rainwater and recycling **grey water** can also help to reduce water consumption.

Use of **Sustainable Urban Drainage Systems (SUDS)** helps to conserve the groundwater and its quality. This system makes use of materials through which water can seep into the groundwater. It also has a number of structures that allow storage of water as well as slowing down the water movement, which helps to avoid flooding.

Using recycled and local materials helps to reduce the **embodied energy** of a project. Good design features such as south-facing windows mean that less energy will be needed during the operation of a building.

It is important to think about the embodied energy of the construction materials used in any development. For instance, how much energy do you think goes into the production of cement?

Just checking

1 Identify three ways to reduce waste.
2 Identify three examples of how waste is produced during the lifecycle of a project.
3 Identify three ways to protect biodiversity.

Social issues of construction

Introduction

Sustainability has three aspects: physical, social and economic. In this topic, you will learn about the **social** issues encountered when planning developments and during construction, as well as how to limit the negative effects of development locally.

Social environment issues

Developments affect the people who already live there. Therefore their involvement in the planning, design, construction, use and demolition stages is very important. If the local community can express their needs these requirements can be embedded in the project at an early stage. Communities will also feel a sense of ownership of the development.

Involving the community also helps avoid overdevelopment of an area. This is when more buildings are constructed than are needed, resulting in vacant buildings, which may be vandalised.

Overdevelopment does not benefit the local economy.

Case study

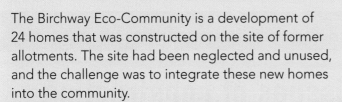

The Birchway Eco-Community is a development of 24 homes that was constructed on the site of former allotments. The site had been neglected and unused, and the challenge was to integrate these new homes into the community.

The project provides adequate parking, bicycle storage and communal green space for the residents. People living in these homes were asked to sign up to a 'green charter' which describes ways of running their home and their lifestyle that will have little impact on their environment.

Look at the Birchway Eco-Community website and then answer the following questions:

1 Do you consider the Birchway Eco-Community to be a socially sustainable project? Give two reasons for your answer.

2 What else could have been done on this project to achieve social sustainability?

Sustainability helps to use regeneration strategies to improve the quality of life in inner city, urban and run-down areas through the improvement of buildings and their surrounds. This results in reducing local crime rates and vandalism, which means that the community as a whole can feel safer.

A sustainable development provides indoor and outdoor areas and facilities for the community to use. This includes providing roads, drainage, open areas, nearby shops, schools, colleges, and health and recreational facilities. All of these improve the local community's social life.

Research

The Considerate Constructors Scheme (CCS) deals with areas of construction activity that affect the way in which society sees the construction industry.

- Visit the CCS website and identify four actions needed under the Scheme to ensure social sustainability.

- If you were the owner of a construction company, would you like to become a member? Could you provide two reasons in favour of becoming a member?

▶ Reducing the impact on the community

A new development can have a significant impact upon the community. A sustainable project uses site practices that minimise these impacts.

It is important to meet with the community to keep them informed about what is happening on the project. This involves:

- consultation events to get community involvement during the design stage
- the developer and community representatives meeting regularly
- sending regular newsletters and leaflets to the community
- making sure that the site is secure, clean and tidy.

Noise can have a huge impact on the community so noise reduction is important. This can be achieved through use of acoustic hoardings and noise reduction equipment.

The site layout should be carefully planned to minimise the impact of vehicles and workers accessing the site. One-way systems are ideal for managing site traffic. On-site parking facilities would mean no disturbance to the local people. The timing of deliveries and working hours could also be agreed with the local community.

Just checking

1 Identify two ways to involve communities in the design of a project.

2 Identify three ways to reduce noise on site.

3 Your site is next to a housing estate where most of the families have children of school age. What do you think are the two most important things you would consider during planning the construction stage?

▶ Economic issues of construction

Introduction

Sustainability has three aspects: physical, social and economic. In this section, you will learn about **economic** issues encountered when planning developments and during construction, as well as how to limit the negative effects of development locally.

▶ Economic issues

Providing sustainability on projects comes at a cost. Financial returns, or profits, are needed on most developments. During the design stage, all costs are considered. They are then monitored during the construction and use of a building. The cost is based upon running a building over its full life, from initial construction to final disposal or reuse. This is called lifecycle costing.

As instances of **flash flooding** appear to be increasing, the cost of flood defence improvement should be included in projects, as well as associated infrastructure development costs.

Employment and training opportunities

Sustainable projects bring employment opportunities for local communities as well as opportunities for new businesses, such as installing solar panels. Businesses that provide sustainable solutions are flourishing.

To make sure that such businesses can run, training has to be provided so that a skilled workforce becomes available. Many colleges have included sustainability as a theme in courses. Training opportunities exist in a number of areas, such as:

- wind turbine installation
- heat pump installation, such as ground source heat pumps
- solar and photovoltaic panels installation
- combined heat and power (CHP) installation.

Employment opportunities will also increase for planners who have experience or formal qualifications in town planning and have awareness of green agendas. The same is true of designers who can incorporate full lifecycle costings into their design, reduce carbon emissions and utilise recyclable and recycled materials.

Link

For more on these technologies, see pages 266 and 272 on.

Key term

Flash flood – sudden flood in a local area due to heavy rainfall.

Activity 11.4

Junhui is a project manager. He is planning the construction of a regeneration project in an area where unemployment is very high. He is making a list of employment opportunities that this project will create for the local community during its construction.

Identify two opportunities that Junhui could include in his list.

Commercial benefits

A sustainable project with green spaces is more valuable, as these spaces make the development more appealing. Additionally most funding from the government and banks is linked to sustainability goals.

Greenfield and brownfield sites

Brownfield sites are sites where construction work has already been carried out.

This means that using a brownfield site might involve the costs of:

- demolishing existing structures and disposing of the waste
- disposing of special waste such as asbestos
- decontaminating the site.

Construction on brownfield sites will improve the landscape of the area. Most such sites are in urban areas, so house building may reduce car use as public transport is more readily available in urban areas.

Greenfield sites are sites where no construction has taken place before. When any building is added to such sites, green space is reduced and the volume of traffic increases, as more people will travel from their homes here to urban areas. This will cause congestion and pollution.

Just checking

1. List two advantages of designing and constructing a project using sustainable approaches.
2. List three training opportunities created as a result of a sustainable development.

Designing for sustainability

Introduction

In this topic, you will develop an understanding of the reasons for designing for sustainability, how it reduces the environmental impacts and reduces operational costs of construction, and how it supports sustainable development for communities.

Using sustainable materials

Remember

Embodied energy is the energy needed to produce a material, from extraction to its point of use.

When designing a domestic, public or commercial building, sustainable materials should be part of the design. At this early stage, designers can specify low embodied energy materials such as timber, straw bales, stone, slate, reeds for thatching and hemp for insulation. Ways to reduce reliance on limited fuel and materials can include:

- specifying a local source to reduce transportation costs and local pollution
- specifying modular dimensions so that materials do not need cutting, meaning wastage is reduced. Modular dimensions are the sizes of building components readily available in the market.

Modular and prefabricated buildings can reduce the wastage of materials.

Using design and technology solutions

- Designers can specify natural ventilation. Space and water heating can be achieved by using energy-efficient equipment which uses less energy. Such equipment will also generate fewer emissions (meaning less pollution), and therefore is more sustainable.

- Various solutions are available to save water, such as push-type taps, low volume flush toilets, and shower and tap flow restriction devices. Regular equipment maintenance also saves water.

- By specifying double and triple glazing, recycled glass mineral wool, sheep's wool, **hemp** and **flax**, buildings can be insulated so that less heat and noise escape.

- The building's orientation can be chosen to maximise natural light – in the UK this is south-west. A curved road layout with south-facing houses maximises the warmth and light the homes receive during the movement of the sun. Low-energy halogen lights should also be used as these save on energy.

- By providing weather-stripping materials made from vinyl, foam, metal or a combination of materials, for use on doors and windows as well as automatic external door closers, the air leakage from a building can be reduced, avoiding loss of heat.

- Building components can be made in a factory. Due to the controlled conditions there, material wastage is reduced. This technique is called prefabrication.

- Designing the **density of homes** so they are not too compact, because providing open green spaces and including social community areas will mean that residents do not feel cramped and too close to their neighbours.

- The use of **thermal mass** in buildings will absorb and emit heat.

Key terms

Hemp and flax – widely grown plants that have excellent insulation properties. Hemp can be mixed with lime to produce insulation products. Flax can be used as an insulation material and as strips for sealing joints around doors and windows.

Density of homes – the number of homes built over an area. The larger the number of homes, the higher the density.

Thermal mass – the ability of a material to absorb, store and release heat in line with the heating and cooling cycle of a building.

Activity 11.5

Nandita is an architect and is involved in designing a housing project. Her client wants the project to be sustainable.

Explain why Nandita might include two named features in a sustainable house.

Codes and regulations

For a building to be certified as sustainable, certain requirements need to be met. Some requirements are compulsory due to government regulations, while others are voluntary codes.

Building Regulations 2006, Part L

The Building Regulations are split into various parts. Part L deals with fuel and power conservation. Some of its requirements include:

- each building needs to have a certificate of energy performance
- each building needs to have a minimum **U-value**
- air leakage in building is specified.

Key term

U-value – this measures the loss of heat from a building element such as walls, floors and roof. These are used to specify insulation standards in buildings.

Link

For more about U-values, see *Unit 1: Construction Technology*.

Other parts of the regulations deal with resistance to the passage of sound and making buildings damp proof.

Table 11.2 Acceptable U-values in a new building (from Building Regulations, Approved Document L)

Element of building	Highest acceptable U-value
Roof	0.20 W/m^{2}K
Wall	0.30 W/m^{2}K
Floor	0.25 W/m^{2}K
Windows	2.00 W/m^{2}K

Code for Sustainable Homes 2006

This code uses a scoring system to rate a new home's sustainability. Each sustainable feature of the building is rated and the whole building given a rating of one to six stars. The code takes into account features such as:

- waste management
- biodiversity
- use of sustainable materials
- sound insulation
- daylighting, or using natural light rather than artificial light as far as possible.

▶ Transport

For a sustainable project, carbon emissions due to the use of transport could be reduced by providing:

- cycle tracks to encourage less use of vehicular transport such as cars
- mass rapid transport links (trams, bus routes) to encourage use of mass transport
- measures such as designated 'two people' or '2+' car lanes, which are priority lanes for vehicles with two or more passengers
- vehicle parking.

The construction process itself can create carbon emissions from the plant and vehicles used on site. Regular maintenance and servicing of these vehicles will help to reduce this pollution.

Why is it so important to consider transport from the outset of any development?

Case study

Long Meadow is a development of terraced housing and apartments and is an example of sustainable construction. It was constructed on a greenfield site using Hemcrete with 300 mm solid wall. The timber used was guaranteed to be from Forest Stewardship Council (FSC) certified sources and had a high proportion of recycled materials. Houses have dual-flush toilets and the Sustainable Urban Drainage Systems (SUDS) approach has been used.

The project achieved the following U-values:

- 0.08 W/mK (floor)
- 0.10 W/mK (roof)
- 0.19 W/mK (external walls)
- 1.2 W/mK (windows).

The designer used standard sizes for all components so that materials are used efficiently. The project provided low-cost houses for people working in the town so that they do not have to live outside the local area. The project lasted for a year and created many training and employment opportunities.

Using the details given above, answer the following questions:

1 Do the U-values achieved fall within the limits set out in Part L of the Building Regulations?

2 Identify how energy and water is saved on this development.

3 Would this development provide social and economic sustainability?

Remember

When looking at U-values, remember that lower numbers are better.

TOPIC   B.2

▶ Sustainable materials

Introduction

Construction of buildings involves using and dealing with lots of different materials. Using materials that are sustainable is a key feature of any sustainable building. In this section, the range of sustainable materials available is discussed, along with their advantages and disadvantages, how they are used effectively and how they reduce the environmental impact of developments and buildings.

It is important for designers and manufacturers to think ahead. For instance, a building's demolition should be considered in its design, and a material should be made so it can be recycled at the end of its useful life.

In sustainable developments, natural or recycled materials should be used as much as possible. Using materials that produce low carbon during manufacturing and that therefore have low embodied energy is essential.

Recycled and crushed hardcore from the demolition of existing structures on brownfield sites should be kept on site for use as a fill material. Alternatively, blocks can be made from this waste material.

Case study

Beddington Zero-Energy Development (BedZED) is in the south London borough of Sutton. It is a high density, compact urban development for mixed use, with 82 units and approximately 284 residents. For this development, 52 per cent of the construction materials were sourced in a 35-mile radius of the site.

Give two reasons why you think this approach is sustainable.

▶ Timber-based products

Timber is a natural material and is very popular for using in structural frames. It can be very sustainable as we can harvest and regrow it repeatedly. In the UK, the **Forest Stewardship Council (FSC)** certifies whether timber is from a sustainable (renewable) source or not.

There are a number of timber-based products available for use in the structure of a building, as well as for cladding and insulation. These include:

- cedar boarding and shingles
- recycled particleboard sheets
- engineered eco-joists
- engineered timber joists
- Structurally Insulated Panels (SIPS).

Link

For more information about SIPS, see *Unit 1: Construction Technology*.

▶ Roofing materials

Roofing materials such as thatch are gaining popularity. Thatching is a traditional method using vegetation such as straw, which is laid in layers to protect the inner roof. The layers help to shed rainwater off. As this type of roofing is based on natural and renewable resources, it is considered sustainable.

Reconstituted roofing slates are made from crushed slates and are good at resisting extreme weather conditions.

▶ Insulation products

Recycled and natural products are sustainable and include:

- recycled glass mineral wool
- sheep's wool insulation
- hemp
- flax.

Did you know?

- Plastics are not generally considered sustainable, as they need a lot of energy to produce. However, most plastics can be recycled and therefore could be used.
- Metals like steel are long-lasting, so they do not need to be replaced frequently. Metals can also be recycled at the end of their useful life. For instance, when the old Wembley Stadium was demolished, 96 per cent of the aluminium was reclaimed and recycled.

Assessment practice 11.2

Which one of the following is not a sustainable material?   [1]

- ☐ **A** Cedar wood
- ☐ **B** Cement
- ☐ **C** Sheep's wool insulation
- ☐ **D** Structurally insulated panels (SIPS)

Sustainability in Construction

UNIT 11

Just checking

1 Identify three sustainable materials and describe the advantages of using these materials.

2 Identify three materials that can be recycled.

3 Identify where these could be used after recycling.

TOPIC B.3

▶ Alternative energy sources

Introduction

The construction industry is adopting a wide range of alternative energy sources that are sustainable and reduce our reliance on fossil fuels. This section discusses the characteristics, applications and advantages and disadvantages of using renewable sources of energy and water heating.

▶ Photovoltaic roof tiles and panels

Photovoltaic (PV) tiles and panels are becoming more and more popular, especially for new developments. These panels absorb sunlight or natural daylight and convert it into electrical energy. The system is connected to the main electricity supply. A building with photovoltaic panels will use energy from the panels first. Any surplus energy can be sold back to the electricity company, or if there is a shortfall, the rest of the energy can be supplied by the electricity company.

As photovoltaic tiles depend on daylight to produce energy, these should be installed on south-facing roofs, clear of any trees or other shading.

▶ Ground source heat recovery

Below the ground, there is a lot of heat energy, which can be used to heat buildings and water.

To make use of this heat, pipes are buried into the ground. These pipes contain water and antifreeze. Heat is absorbed by this mixture and passes on to a heat pump called a ground source heat pump. The pump then provides energy to heat the water and radiators.

▶ Air source heat recovery

Heat from the air can be absorbed and used to heat water and radiators using an air source heat pump. These pumps work like refrigerators in reverse. Refrigerators take heat out of the inside, while air source heat pumps take heat in from the outside. One disadvantage of this method is that these pumps need electricity to run.

 Did you know?

The UK government has set a target to reduce total UK CO_2 emissions by at least 80 per cent by 2050.

Key term

Photovoltaic (PV) – photo means light and voltaic means electrical potential. Photovoltaic materials are able to produce electricity when they are exposed to light.

271

▶ Combined heat and power units

Both heat and electricity can be generated using combined heat and power or CHP units. These units provide heat energy and some electricity. One disadvantage is that the units need gas or LPG (liquefied petroleum gas) to run.

▶ Small-scale wind turbines

These can be used to provide electricity for homes. The **turbines** use wind energy and convert it to electricity. A wind turbine has large blades. The wind moves the blades, and these drive a turbine which generates electricity. The stronger the wind is, the faster the blades will move and the more electricity can be generated.

Photovoltaic cells and wind turbines do not have to be used only on roofs or in wind farms – they can have a variety of uses, including street lighting.

▶ Solar hot water panels

Solar panels absorb sunlight and convert this into energy, which can be used to supply hot water for domestic buildings. The energy is enough for domestic needs during summer months as there is enough sunlight. During winter months in the UK, boilers or immersion heaters can be used to give extra heat.

As sunlight is free, these panels provide heat energy at no cost other than the initial installation.

▶ Biomass fuelled heating systems

These systems use wood pellets, chips or logs to fulfil the heating needs of a building. There are two types.

- A stove provides heat to a single room and can also be used to provide hot water by having a back boiler.
- A boiler is connected to the central heating and hot water system to provide heat to the entire building.

Activity 11.6

Ali is a building services engineer. He is working on a housing project and has been asked to design services so that the minimum possible energy is used in operations.

1 Identify three alternative energy sources Ali could use.
2 Describe two advantages of using each of these sources.

▶ Sustainable techniques

Introduction

The design and construction of buildings needs to take a sustainable approach, and the construction industry is adopting a wide range of sustainable techniques.

▶ Straw bale construction

This method of building uses straw bales to construct a house and take the load of the building's structure. They can also be used as in-fill alongside other building types such as timber frames. The advantage is that straw bales:

- are locally available
- have good thermal insulation
- have little impact on the environment as they are a natural material.

However, the walls have to be thicker than normal, with the average size being 500 mm thick. With an external finish added to the wall, it might reach a thickness of 700 mm. This means that less space will be available inside for rooms.

Another downside of this type of construction is that the straw bales have to be kept very dry. If moisture penetrates the straw bales, they lose strength and the building becomes damp.

▶ Timber-framed construction

Timber is one of the most common construction materials. Timber-framed construction is a method of building where a series of beams and columns are connected to form a frame. This is like the skeleton of a building, which supports all the building loads.

The frames are made off site with a high level of accuracy and quality, and are then brought to site for assembly. They can therefore be constructed faster than conventional structures.

Why do you think timber-framed construction is sustainable?

▶ Green roof technology

Green roofs are living structures. They are constructed by providing a number of layers on the actual or structural roof. The layers provide water-proofing and root protection. The top layer is the growing layer, where vegetation such as **sedum** can grow.

These roofs can improve the quality of air in city centres. They also give good thermal and sound insulation, and have low embodied energy. However, the plants on these roofs need regular maintenance and the roof adds weight to the structure.

 Key term

Sedum – a small hardy plant that is good at resisting extreme weather conditions.

▶ Sustainable Urban Drainage Systems (SUDS)

When rainwater falls on land, it drains off naturally into nearby streams and rivers. This is called surface water. Rainwater also soaks through the ground to top up the water below ground (groundwater).

When buildings, pavements and roads are constructed on greenfield sites, the natural surface water's route through the ground surface is blocked. This means that the natural drainage is disturbed. As urban areas are built up, water can move too quickly on these man-made hard surfaces and reach streams earlier than it would otherwise. This can cause floods.

Because land is covered by roads and pavements, rainwater is no longer absorbed by the soil to top up the groundwater. This can result in a shortage of water for the communities living there.

These changes, which might happen due to the construction of new developments, can be managed using the Sustainable Urban Drainage Systems (SUDS) approach. This is a system of managing surface water so that the natural flow pattern is maintained and water resources are protected. This is achieved by:

- saving or holding the water for use
- slowing down the flow of water so that there is no flooding
- letting water go down into the ground
- improving the quality of water.

These systems include a number of different structures, shown in Table 11.3.

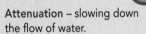

Key terms

Attenuation – slowing down the flow of water.

Permeable – a material that allows water to pass through.

Retention – holding the water before passing it on.

Detention structures – used to slow down the flow of water.

Table 11.3 SUDS structures, features and benefits

SUDS structure	Features and benefits
Green roofs and rainwater harvesting	These help to slow down the flow of water as well store it for later use. These therefore act as a means of **attenuation** and storage.
Permeable surfaces	Water soaks into the surface before reaching groundwater, which helps to control the flow of water at the source.
Swales	These are shallow channels to collect and move water.
Channels	These are used to move water as well as to remove silt and oil. This improves the quality of water.
Filter strips	Water passes over a strip of grass, which removes silt and debris, and improves the quality of water.
Soakaways	This lets the water soak through a layer of materials before becoming part of the groundwater. A soakaway is like a large void or hole filled with gravel. It holds water and then lets it go to the groundwater or to another SUDS structure.
Retention and attenuation structures	Retention structures are like ponds which store water while **detention structures** are for attenuation or slowing down the flow of water. Both help to reduce flood risk.

Rainwater harvesting

Rainwater can be stored for use in gardens, irrigation, flushing toilets or for drinking purposes. The rainwater is stored before it flows over large areas of the ground so its quality is still quite good. Systems to collect and reuse rainwater are simple and cheap to install. Water butts are commonly used in houses for this purpose.

However, larger systems involve more space and money. A large tank in the back garden can collect rainwater for use in the garden or the house. Such large systems are called rainwater harvesting.

Rainwater harvesting provides free water, which means less water is needed from the mains. This method also slows down the flow of surface water and therefore helps to reduce the chances of flooding.

Grey water recycling systems

Grey water is the used water from showers, baths and handbasins. It does not include waste water from toilets. Water from kitchen sinks, washing machines and dishwashers is also normally included. This water can be reused or recycled to flush toilets, in the garden or for washing purposes. It is not used for drinking purposes.

Grey water recycling systems reduce the water demand in a house. This means that less water from the mains is needed.

Thinking about sustainability from the start means that sustainable solutions can be built in, such as this water butt.

▶ Passive stack ventilation

All buildings need a supply of fresh air to make sure that people living inside are in a healthy and comfortable environment. Fresh air also helps to control **condensation** and to make sure heating appliances continue to work safely and efficiently.

Most new buildings are designed with very few ventilation openings, resulting in less supply of fresh air. Activities in a house such as cooking and drying clothes create a lot

of moisture. Without a good supply of fresh air, this moisture will not be removed and will cause unhealthy living conditions, such as increased humidity levels where there is more moisture in the air, making it difficult to breathe. This unwanted moisture can be removed by providing ducts in the ceilings of kitchens, utility rooms and bathrooms leading to the roof. The warm air will automatically move from a high temperature inside the building to a lower temperature outside. This system is called passive stack ventilation. It is suitable for houses and blocks of flats of up to four storeys.

 Key term

Condensation – the most common form of dampness in a house. It happens when warm moist air comes into contact with cooler air or a cold surface.

▶ Sun shading

A building in the UK with south-facing windows and glazed areas can get the maximum light, reducing the energy needed for artificial lighting. Such a building will also gain a lot of heat from the sun during the winter months. This means less energy is needed to heat such a building.

However, during summer, the sun is at a high angle, which can result in buildings gaining unwanted heat. **Louvre** screens stop buildings gaining heat during summer by blocking the sunlight, which means less energy is needed to bring the building to a lower temperature. This in turn reduces emissions from both heating and lighting. Louvre screens can be made of timber, such as cedar wood, or metal, such as aluminium.

Key term

Louvre – a set of angled slats fixed over a door or window. They allow air and light through.

Activity 11.7

1 Lisa is an architect and is always interested in designing buildings that use suitable construction methods and techniques. She is currently designing a block of flats in a busy city centre where the traffic is heavy and air quality is poor. She is making a list of the choices she has to include in the design. Help Lisa finalise her choices by completing the following table.

Choices	Advantages	Disadvantages
Type of structure		
Improving air quality inside and outside of the building		
Saving water resources		
Maximising the use of natural sunlight		

2 Lisa is working on another project, which is to be constructed on a large greenfield site. The project involves the construction of 200 houses and a sports complex. The project will need the construction of roads and drainage as well. She is aware that there have been floods recently and does not want her project to make this worse. Describe two measures Lisa can take to provide a sustainable drainage system.

Assessment practice 11.3

Your local college has been constructed using a large south-facing louvre screen. The screens are made of cedar wood.

Explain two reasons why using these screens might be a sustainable technique. [4]

▶ Sustainable site practices

Introduction

Construction activities can result in environmental pollution due to wastage of materials, pollution such as dust, and loss of wildlife and natural features such as trees. This section looks at construction site practices that can minimise these effects.

▶ Storing materials correctly to prevent damage

One of the common reasons for material waste is incorrect storage, resulting in damage. Once damaged, material is not suitable for use and has to be replaced. Needing extra materials means that more energy is used, which could have been saved.

Materials that can be stored in the open include bricks, blocks and aggregates. Materials that are likely to be affected by weather should be stored in a shed and include cement and timber. They should not be stored directly on the ground, as ground moisture might damage them.

▶ Use of silt traps on temporary drains

Temporary drains are constructed on site to dispose of water. Dust can get into these drains or be mixed into the water flowing into the drains. This is called sediment. Silt traps are used to catch this sediment. These traps can be like a small pond where water is stored, allowing the sediment to settle down before the water is finally allowed through the drains.

▶ Dust reduction

Construction activities generate a lot of dust, which causes pollution in the environment on and around the site. Dust can be reduced by using water spray to damp it down. Regularly sweeping the roads and cleaning the wheels on plant and vehicles also reduces dust. Dust suppression equipment can be used, which uses a water jet to settle the dust.

▶ Segregation of waste

When you separate your rubbish into waste and recycling you are segregating the waste. As in a house, site waste should be segregated. For example, separate bins can be provided for general waste and for waste to be recycled. This reduces waste.

▶ Recycling materials

Recycling means that instead of throwing away the waste material, it can be reused. For example, you can use waste paper to make more paper. If materials are not recycled, they are put in landfill, and contractors have to pay landfill tax to do this. On the other hand, making new materials by recycling old ones needs less energy than starting again, and therefore the embodied energy of recycled materials is low.

Remember

Materials should be stored close to where they are to be used, to save time and energy in moving them.

Did you know?

A Site Waste Management Plan (SWMP) has details of how waste will be handled on site. All construction projects in England with a value of more than £300,000 must have a SWMP.

On a construction site, a variety of waste is generated, and each type of waste is recycled differently.

- Crushed hardcore can be used for filling low-lying ground or under floors.
- Large timber pieces can be re-sawn or remoulded to make new products.
- Plastics and metals are heated so that they can be remoulded to form new products. Metals such as steel are widely used in construction and these are made using a large quantity of recycled material.

Correct storage of fuels and chemicals

Fuel, oil and lubricants are stored on most construction sites. A spillage of these materials can pollute the ground. Such materials should be stored in lockable areas having bund walls.

Materials that can catch fire or which are hazardous include paints and thinners. These should be stored in lockable sheds for the safety of all site users.

Providing water and heating onsite

Workers' on-site welfare facilities need water and heating. Rainwater storage and harvesting can be used for non-drinking purposes. Heat pumps and solar panels can provide an efficient way of heating welfare areas.

The local environment

Construction activities can also disturb natural habitats. If wildlife is present on site, these should be relocated to a new home nearby that has the same features as the original one. Experts called chartered environmentalists can offer guidance about the type of wildlife and the features needed. This will reduce the impact of construction activities on the natural environment.

Protective fencing around trees

Trees are a valuable natural feature and help to maintain the quality of air. A site that is sustainable is one where construction activities such as excavation or movement of plant and machinery do not damage any trees. This can be ensured by building protective fencing around any nearby trees during construction.

Remember

A bund wall is a structure built to hold any spillages.

Did you know?

Trees on a site might be protected by law. These trees will have a Tree Preservation Order (TPO), which means that cutting any part of them is not allowed without the local planning authority's consent.

Activity 11.8

Fatima is a site manager. She is planning for the construction of a project and is thinking about the possible site practices that are sustainable. She will need to store a variety of materials on site. The project is on a site where there are a lot of trees. An initial survey suggests the presence of wildlife, which may be affected by the construction activities. She does not want dust pollution on her site.

What should she consider in her planning to achieve the following?

- Protect trees
- Recycle materials
- Manage waste
- Minimise disturbance to wildlife
- Reduce dust pollution

WorkSpace

▶ Samantha Martin

Site manager

I am a site manager with a local construction company. At the moment, I'm managing the construction of a development that will add 300 houses to the local community. The project is really challenging, as we want to reach demanding sustainability goals by using sustainable methods and materials. Our site is part of the Considerate Constructors Scheme.

The local community were involved in the design of the project and were really interested in the sustainable aspects, as well as the possibility of job opportunities for people living in the area. As part of my job, I keep them informed of our progress. We have regular meetings so they can raise any issues or concerns. Last week, we agreed on a better time of day for materials to be delivered to the site, which was great progress.

So far, the project has met all its targets. We've been able to achieve this success thanks in part to my knowledge of sustainable approaches. This knowledge really helps to understand the way that the physical, social and economic aspects of sustainability interact. Honestly, I think that everyone in the construction industry today should be interested in sustainable construction approaches, because these methods are the future.

Think about it

1 What other job roles need knowledge of sustainable construction techniques?

2 Why is knowledge of social and economic sustainability important?

3 Do you agree with Samantha that it is important for everyone in the construction industry to be interested in sustainability? Why?

How you will be assessed

You will take a paper-based examination. The examination paper will have a maximum of 50 marks. The number of marks available for each part of a question will be shown in brackets, e.g. [2], with the total for each question being shown at the end of the question.

There will be different types of question in the examination:

A Questions where the answers are available and you have to choose the correct answer(s).

Tip: Always make sure that you read the instructions carefully. Sometimes you may need to identify more than one correct answer.

Examples:

Which **one** of the following is an appropriate method of involving the local community in a construction project? [1]

A	A street party
B	Nothing – they do not need to be involved
C	Local residents' committees
D	Meetings with estate agents

Answer: C

Which **one** of the following statements best describes embodied energy? [1]

A	The energy used to produce and install a material
B	The energy used to transport the material
C	The energy required to recycle the material
D	The energy required to maintain the material

Answer: A

B Questions where you are asked to produce a short answer worth 1 or 2 marks.

Tip: Look carefully at how the question is set out to see how many points need to be included in your answer.

Examples:

Construction activities can cause environmental pollution.

State **two** sources of pollution. [2]

Answers: Plant and machinery, and dust from excavation.

Identify two methods used to conserve water. [2]

Answers: Grey water recycling and rainwater harvesting.

C Questions where you are asked to provide a longer answer – these can be worth up to 8 marks.
Tips: make sure that you read the question in full, and answer all of the parts of the question which you are asked. It is a good idea to plan your answer so that you do not forget anything and remember to check your answer once you have finished.

Example:

A construction firm is planning to construct a large office block which is intended to achieve low carbon emissions. The designers are considering a number of solutions to achieve this goal so that the building has a minimal impact upon the environment.

Advise the construction firm by suggestion some solutions, giving reasons for your suggestions. [8]

Answer: The building should use as little energy as possible, because lower energy use means fewer emissions and less pollution. The designers should specify very efficient heating systems, because these will require less energy to run. The building design should also provide adequate ventilation for areas where computers and printers are used, because running at a cooler temperature is more efficient.

Energy can also be saved by providing good insulation, such as triple glazed doors and windows or natural and recycled insulation materials in the walls and roof space. To avoid any extra heat loss, weather-stripping materials as well as automatic external door closers could be used.

The designers could further reduce carbon emissions by specifying prefabricated building components. This reduces material wastage on site during the construction process.

Electricity use can be minimised by orientating the building to achieve maximum sunlight. If required, the building could also have a curved road layout. Low-energy lights should also be used as these save even more energy.

Finally, water can be saved easily by using push-type taps and low-volume flush toilets.

Hints and tips

Use the time before the test – make sure that you have got everything you will need. Check that your pen works and that you read the instructions on the front of your examination paper. Try to make yourself feel comfortable and relaxed.

Keep an eye on the time – the examination will last one hour. You should be able to see the clock in the examination room so that you will know how long you have got left to complete the paper. Allow roughly one minute for every mark on the paper, so that a question worth 5 marks takes you about 5 minutes to answer.

Read the questions fully – it is easy to misread a question and then write an answer which is wrong. Always check you are doing what you have been asked to do.

Plan your answers – when answering longer questions, spend a minute or two writing down the key points that you want to include in your answer. If you are being asked to evaluate, remember to include positive and negative points in your plan and answer.

Check your answers – once you have answered all of the questions on the paper, you will probably have a few minutes to spare. Use this time to check your answers, especially the longer ones. Fill in any blanks which you have left. Try to answer every question on the paper.

Make sure you have completed the front of the paper – once you have finished, check that you have filled out the front of the paper.

How to improve your answer

Read the two student answers below, together with the feedback. Try to use what you learn here when you answer questions in your examination.

 Question

> You work with a firm of architects who are designing a new housing development. The design team wants to explore various sustainable construction methods and techniques and choose the ones most suitable for the project.
>
> You have been asked to evaluate the advantages and disadvantages of straw bale construction and green roofs. You need to provide one advantage and one disadvantage of using these methods. [8]

 Student 1's answer

> Advantage of straw bale construction – uses natural material.
>
> Disadvantage of straw bale construction – large wall sizes.
>
> Advantage of green roofs – living structure.
>
> Disadvantage of green roofs – weight.

Feedback:

Although the advantages and disadvantages listed are correct, the student does not attempt to explain the advantage of using natural materials in terms of impact on the environment. The student mentions large wall sizes, but does not explain why this might be a disadvantage. This means that they get 1 mark for each advantage and disadvantage, rather than 2 marks.

The student has stated that an advantage of a green roof is that it is a living structure, but without any further explanation this will only achieve 1 mark. Similarly, the disadvantage of weight is very vague and would not achieve any marks. This student will achieve 3 marks in total.

 Student 2's answer

> One advantage of straw bale construction is that it is done using a natural material, and its use has little impact on the environment. It is also locally available across the UK, so it requires minimal transportation. One disadvantage is that, because it is a lightweight material, the walls have to be thicker. This means that there is less space left inside the building for use.
>
> An advantage of green roofs is that they contain plants and vegetation. This means that even buildings in a busy city centre will provide green space, which will improve the area's air quality. One disadvantage is that, because these roofs are constructed using a number of layers of materials including the growing layer, it adds extra weight to the roof structure.

Feedback

This student has identified one advantage and one disadvantage of both straw bale construction and green roofs. They also clearly state their reasons. This learner will achieve 8 marks in total.

Assess yourself

Question 1

The Considerate Constructors Scheme (CCS) aims to: [1]

A Improve the image of the construction industry

B Improve standards of training in the construction industry

C Promote social sustainability

D Make buildings more aesthetically pleasing

Question 2

Construction on brownfield sites is considered to be more sustainable than construction on greenfield sites. Give **three** reasons why it might cost more to construct on a brownfield site. [3]

Question 3

An architect is designing a large housing development and wishes to make use of alternative energy sources.

Evaluate four alternative sources of energy suitable for a housing project. [8]

For further practice, see the Assessment Practice questions on pages 259, 270 and 276.

Introduction

Working in the construction sector is an exciting and challenging career, from the teamwork aspects of producing an iconic building like the Olympic Stadium in London, to restoring buildings like the Liverpool Docklands Warehouses. All of these challenges need the right people with qualifications, experience and training in their area. Many different sectors make up the construction industry. These range from the design of structures by architects to the organising of the projects by contracts or project managers. There are hundreds of different roles and careers in construction, as the sector also covers a major portion of the supply chain that services it. In this unit we will explore the different roles and responsibilities, and the professional associations that support these.

When a project first takes shape, a smaller number of roles are involved. The client commissions the project, while the designers produce the drawings, specification and details. The production team contains all of the operatives, craftspersons and supervision, followed by the facilities team who will run, operate and maintain the building for a client.

The opportunities for someone starting out on a construction career are numerous and worldwide. To prepare you for this, the unit examines the sources of construction vacancies, career pathways, the production of a curriculum vitae and preparing for a formal interview. You need to plan each of these aspects carefully to make sure you are on course for the final career you want to follow.

Assessment: You will be assessed by a series of assignments set by your teacher/tutor.

Learning aims

In this unit you will:

A examine the job roles and responsibilities in the construction industry

B explore approaches for gaining employment in the construction industry.

At the moment, I'm applying for jobs as a trainee construction administrator. I want to be a construction administrator because it's an exciting and challenging career, as no two days are the same. This unit has given me a really detailed insight into the construction industry and how it operates, which helps when I'm applying for jobs.

Cerys, *17-year-old aspiring construction administrator*

The Construction Industry

12

Assessment Zone

This table shows what you must do in order to achieve a **Pass**, **Merit** or **Distinction** grade, and where you can find activities in this book to help you.

Assessment criteria

Level 1	Level 2 **Pass**	Level 2 **Merit**	Level 2 **Distinction**
Learning aim A: Examine the job roles and responsibilities in the construction industry			
1A.1 Outline a craft and an operative job role in the construction industry.	**2A.P1** English Describe a managerial, craft, and operative job role in the construction industry and the skills and qualifications required. **See Assessment activity 12.1, page 297**	**2A.M1** English Compare the skills and qualifications requirements for an operative, craft, managerial and professional position in the construction industry, including professional membership where appropriate. **See Assessment activity 12.1, page 297**	**2A.D1** English Discuss how a combination of skills, qualifications and experience enable progression from craft roles through to managerial or professional job roles in the construction industry, considering two different progression routes. **See Assessment activity 12.1, page 297**
1A.2 English Outline the function of a professional association in the construction industry.	**2A.P2** English Describe the function of a professional association in construction and the progression opportunities provided by achieving professional status. **See Assessment activity 12.1, page 297**		
1A.3 English Identify health and safety responsibilities for an employee in a craft role in the construction industry, relating to current regulation and legislation.	**2A.P3** English Describe the health and safety responsibilities of an employee in a craft role and a supervisor for a construction project, relating to current regulation and legislation. **See Assessment activity 12.2, page 300**	**2A.M2** English Explain the main health and safety responsibilities of an employee in a craft role, a supervisor and a construction manager. **See Assessment activity 12.2, page 300**	
Learning aim B: Explore approaches for gaining employment in the construction industry			
1B.4 English Identify sources of construction vacancies and opportunities with guidance.	**2B.P4** English Describe sources of construction vacancies and opportunities. **See Assessment activity 12.3, page 306**		

Assessment criteria			
Level 1	Level 2 **Pass**	Level 2 **Merit**	Level 2 **Distinction**
Learning aim B: Explore approaches for gaining employment in the construction industry			
1B.5 English Create a covering letter and a CV with guidance.	**2B.P5** English Create a covering letter and a CV in response to a given job description: • with appropriate formatting • with no grammatical or spelling errors • that follows document format conventions • with content relevant to the job description. **See Assessment activity 12.3, page 306**	**2B.M3** English Create a covering letter and a CV in response to a given job description: • with content that matches the applicant's relevant skills and attributes to the requirements of the job description. **See Assessment activity 12.3, page 306**	**2B.D2** English Evaluate a CV and letter of application against that of another applicant, for a job description. **See Assessment activity 12.3, page 306**
1B.6 Identify potential questions in preparation for an interview with guidance.	**2B.P6** Develop answers to potential questions in preparation for an interview. **See Assessment activity 12.3, page 306**	**2B.M4** English Analyse given recruitment information and materials to prepare for potential questions at interview. **See Assessment activity 12.3, page 306**	

English / Opportunity to practise English skills

How you will be assessed

This unit is internally assessed by the use of two or three assignments set by your tutor or teacher. These will cover a range of assessment criteria for this unit. The assessments will contain a scenario to help you focus on what to include with your written evidence in support of the grading criteria.

The assessments will contain an opportunity to work towards a merit and distinction level award for your final grade. You will need to extend many of the topic areas in order to achieve these higher grades. Make sure that you meet the assessment deadlines in order to receive positive feedback from your assessor. The unit specification will give you additional guidance as to the evidence requirements for each grading criterion.

▶ Construction career pathways

Introduction

Deciding what direction or pathway to take is one of the hardest decisions you will have to make in your life. In order to help with this decision, you need to get as much information about your chosen career as possible.

In this topic you will examine the different career paths that are available in the construction industry.

Discussion

In groups, discuss what sort of jobs there are in the construction industry and what you need to do to get these.

▶ Design

The built environment offers a fantastic opportunity for people to express ideas, themes and cultures through architecture. To work in design, you must have some creative skills in sketching and drawing, and be interested in producing structures that people will see and admire.

Architecture and design have several different careers and levels. The job areas involved in design can be broken down into the following roles.

Architect

An architect is appointed by a client to commission the design of their building. The architect is responsible for taking a design brief from the client, which sets out what they want built, then turning this into a design that the client likes. You have to be able to interpret a client's ideas and concepts, and turn them into a realistic drawing that they can understand. Often a 3D model is built as this is the best way of expressing the final design.

Architects may design one-off buildings or whole new housing developments – for example, the development of Milton Keynes and the infrastructure layout of the roads and estates there.

The Gherkin, or 30 St Mary Axe, is an **iconic** building in London. What do you think makes the Gherkin iconic?

Key term

Iconic – very famous or popular. In construction, this is usually used to refer to a building that is instantly recognised for its design and location, like the Sydney Opera House.

Take it further

Research a leading architect like Norman Foster (who designed Wembley Stadium) or Zaha Hadid (who designed the London 2012 Olympic Aquatics Centre). Find out how they became an architect.

An architect acts as a client's representative on the site and will check quality, issue instructions, payment certificates and revised drawings, and monitor progress until a building project is finished. It is a career with great responsibilities as you are producing a building that has to be completed on time, to budget and to the required standard of quality.

Architectural technician or technologist

An architectural **technician** or technologist works at a level below the architect. They help with the production of drawings, filling in details and preparing materials specifications. They work as an assistant to the architect and act under the architect's instructions, and they are especially good at computer-aided drafting (CAD). Technologists are very useful to the architect as they let the architect concentrate on the overall design.

What sort of qualities do you think an architect needs to have?

Interior designer

This is a designer who specialises on the design of the interiors of buildings. A good interior designer can use their skills and natural light to create a sense of space, and pick colours that make the spaces feel warm and attractive for occupants. An interior designer may coordinate their work with the architect to ensure that this works with the architect's dimensions and floor to ceiling heights.

Consulting or structural engineer

Consulting engineers are needed for the structural design of a building, to make it stand up safely on its foundations for its serviceable life. They create the supporting structure for the architect's design to be placed on. Consulting engineers are also responsible for the foundations that the building sits on, making sure the ground can support the weight of the building. Another term often used for this role is 'structural engineer'.

> **? Did you know?**
>
> The arch over Wembley Stadium is the world's longest unsupported roof structure and was designed by structural engineers.

Building service engineer

Building service engineers are responsible for the services in a modern building. This covers water supplies, the heating of a building, its artificial lighting, air conditioning and electrical needs. Movement around a building in terms of lifts and escalators is also part of this role, along with fire detection systems and alarms.

Activity 12.1

In groups, discuss the following questions.

1 How will you decide what career to enter?
2 What major decisions do you need to make now or very soon?
3 Where can you find information about construction careers?
4 Do you want to follow a professional career pathway to take one of the roles described above?

▶ Finance

Quantity surveyor

Construction projects have to be run on time and kept to the client's budget. This is why the quantity surveyor's role is important. The quantity surveyor who works for a client will:

- prepare the client's budget
- prepare the **tender** documents for getting a price for the work from a contractor
- take care of the payments to the main contractor
- prepare the final costing for the work.

Quantity surveyors who work for main contractors will deal with:

- placing orders on subcontractors
- financial management of the project
- valuation of **variations**
- preparation of the final account.

Estimator

The estimator is responsible for pricing construction work for a company. They receive the tenders, which then have to be priced. This involves asking subcontractors for quotations for specialist parts of the work, and getting plant and material rates from hire firms and builders merchants. The estimator normally has two or three weeks to put together the price for the work, which is submitted as a tender to the client. To do this you have to be good at mathematics, and able to read and understand drawings so you can get **quantities** from them.

Commercial cost surveyors

This is a very similar role to the quantity surveyor, but they may not be professionally qualified to the Royal Institution of Chartered Surveyors (RICS) standards. They deal with all the commercial costs on projects just as a quantity surveyor would.

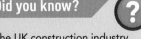

Key terms

Tendering – the process of getting a competitive price for the client's proposed building project.

Variations – the alterations or changes that may have to be made during construction due to design changes, client's alterations or errors.

Quantities – the amounts of materials needed from suppliers.

Did you know?

The UK construction industry employs over 2 million people.

Just checking

1 Describe the role of architectural technologist.
2 Describe the role of a quantity surveyor.
3 Describe the role of an estimator.

Construction supervision

Once the tender has been won by a construction company, the estimator passes it over to the production team. This team will consist of the following different types of personnel, depending on the size of the building contracted.

Site engineer

The site engineer is responsible for the setting out of the building and its external works so it meets the dimensions shown on the architects' plans.

Planner

The planner produces a contract programme, schedule or Gantt chart, which is used to monitor and plan progress on site.

Site manager

The site manager is responsible for the day-to-day running of the construction site, organising labour, plant and materials.

Site agent

This is a very similar role to the site manager. The only difference is that the site agent may just be employed for that contract and then move on. A manager tends to be directly employed.

Construction manager

This person organises a number of contracts that the site managers are running, obtains the services of subcontractors, works with the architect and makes sure progress is monitored and maintained. This role is also known as the contracts manager.

General forepersons

These operate below the site manager and are specific to different areas – for example, brickwork and joinery.

Gangers

Gangers supervise ground workers constructing foundations and concrete works.

These people are responsible for the supervision and management of the building while it is constructed, the organisation of resources on site, and the health and safety management of all workers. They produce the building project on site by directing the workforce to construct it in line with the architect's drawings and **specification**.

Take it further

Browse the job categories on an online construction job site and explore what options are available for the management of construction sites.

Key term

Specification – the written details of all of the components and materials for the building that have been given by the architect or designer.

Activity 12.2

What sort of skills do you think these job roles need? List two or three skills for each role and then compare with others in the group.

▷ Construction

Craftspeople and general operatives are the people who physically construct a building. They lay bricks, pour concrete, and fix floor joists and roof trusses. They can work for a contractor directly or be self-employed.

What qualities do you think a successful craftsperson will have? How could you develop these qualities?

Craftsperson

Craftspeople are often 'time-served', meaning they have followed an Apprenticeship route to gain appropriate qualifications in their trade area. Typical craft roles include:

- **bricklayer** – responsible for laying brickwork and blockwork for the external walls
- **carpenter and joiner** – responsible for making things like window frames and staircases
- **painter and decorator** – responsible for the overall aesthetics of the finishes
- **plasterer** – responsible for applying plaster finishes to a smooth finish and standard
- **roofer** – responsible for the roof tile finishes to the roof trusses fixed by the carpenter.

General operative

General operatives are often semi- or non-skilled, but very good at manual skills such as excavation, materials handling, and lifting and moving. General operatives may have extra skills and responsibilities relating to:

- finishing concrete
- laying drainage pipework
- foundation groundwork.

▷ Safety in construction

Health and safety is a legal requirement on a construction site. Everyone has to be included and work safely to avoid any accidents.

The Health and Safety Executive (HSE) is the government's safety organisation that inspects construction sites for safety. They also investigate major and fatal accidents, and carry out prosecutions for people or companies that do not follow the regulations.

Health and safety officer

The health and safety officer in a construction company has a responsible role involved in risk assessment, safety training and site inductions. They also write the safety policies for the company, and monitor their use and review. The health and safety officer often acts as a 'trainer', providing on the job training, inductions and safety talks on site as part of their role as a health and safety specialist.

Construction Design and Management Regulations co-ordinator

Another important and responsible role is that of the Construction Design and Management Regulations (CDM) co-ordinator for a project. They are responsible for checking that the construction company supplies a health and safety plan at commencement, and a health and safety file for the building when it is finished.

Value, use and maintenance of buildings

Buildings are valuable and have to be maintained to prevent any deterioration and loss of value.

Estate agent

Estate agents are responsible for buying and selling homes, businesses, land and any other structure. You can commission them to sell your house, and they produce details for publicity purposes and negotiate with potential buyers on your behalf.

Facilities managers

Once a building has been completed and handed over to the client, it has to be used and maintained in a safe and serviceable condition for the occupants.

Facilities managers are responsible for running the centre or commercial building, making sure it is safe for the public, ensuring the security of occupants, maintaining of all operating equipment, and cleaning and waste disposal, among many other duties.

Activity 12.3

The facilities manager who looks after a large television centre has a very busy job. They have to maintain a newly built complex, which has just been handed over by the contractor.

As the facilities manager, you would have to know a great deal about the systems and services that each building requires.

- How would you learn this?
- Where could you find information about each system?
- What facilities on site would need maintaining in the first year?

Maintenance direct labour

These are the operatives who are directly employed as employees by the company that owns the buildings to be maintained. They are a general maintenance crew who will deal with any daily reported health and safety issues to keep visitors and occupants safe – for example, changing light bulbs.

Contracted services

This covers the parts of facilities management that are subcontracted out for a set time – for example, the maintenance of a building's fire alarm system, the cleaning of all of the fire detectors, and the testing and inspection of all firefighting equipment on a large site. Contracted services allow specialist help to be brought into a building to help maintain and extend its serviceable lifespan.

Building surveyor

A building surveyor is responsible for the surveying of a building to work out its defects and the scheduling of maintenance to protect and extend its life. Building surveyors may also be responsible for the refurbishment of buildings, measuring and producing drawings, and carrying out property valuations for owners and people planning to buy a house.

▶ The professional pathways

▶ Gaining professional status

The starting point in a professional career is at school with some good grades in GCSEs. You can then either take A levels or a BTEC National qualification to gain entry on to a university degree course.

This degree should be specific to the professional field that you want to pursue and must be a degree approved by the professional association you want to join. Only approved degrees meet the professional standards required by each institute. When you have finished this study, you will need to get a graduate position with a professional firm or company to obtain some experience for the professional interview.

The professional interview is conducted at the association that you wish to join and covers your experiences, training and development that you have done to gain full membership status. When you have done this successfully, you may add the professional association's letters after your name and advertise using their logo.

Case study

Ellie is 16 and has to make some important decisions about how she plans to qualify in her chosen career, engineering. Some learners go to university and take a full-time degree, while others work and learn at the same time.

- What are the advantages of working and learning at the same time?
- Would working and learning at the same time make you more motivated to study?
- What would you miss if you chose not to be a full-time student at university?
- Which option gives you better job prospects?

Each professional must become a member of their representing professional association. Each of these associations has its own membership rules and entry qualifications. For example, to become a full member of the Royal Institution of Chartered Surveyors (RICS) you would need an association-recognised university degree, along with the needed number of years' experience.

The professional institutes

A professional institute is a recognised association covering a particular specialist area. For example, the Royal Institute of British Architects (RIBA) covers architecture and the design of buildings. To join, you must have the required qualifications and experience. The RIBA gives official recognition for its members of professional status as well as setting a minimum standard for membership. Professional associations are able to offer several services to their members such as professional indemnity insurance and continuing professional development.

Table 12.1 outlines several of the major professional associations that operate in the UK.

Table 12.1 Some professional associations in the UK

Specialist area	Institute	Short name
Construction management, estimating and planning	Chartered Institute of Building	CIOB
Land, building, quantity, surveying, estates management, project management	Royal Institution of Chartered Surveyors	RICS
Architecture and design of buildings and structures	Royal Institute of British Architects	RIBA
Electrical and mechanical installations, access systems, water supply and heating, fire detection and air conditioning	Chartered Institute of Building Services Engineers	CIBSE
Highways, roads, concrete works, harbours, foundations and railways	Institution of Civil Engineers	ICE

Activity 12.4

Deciding about your future career in the construction industry can seem like a huge choice. To help you make informed decisions, you should review your current skills and what you will need in the future. This will help you to find the pathway that really interests you.

Complete each of the sentences below to analyse your own skills and interests.

- My strengths are…
- My current skills include…
- I need to work on improving my…
- My ideal route to entering a construction career would be…
- The area that really interests me is…

 Take it further

Examine the website of a professional institute and find out the entry requirements to gain full membership status.

▶ Responsibilities of personnel in the construction industry

Introduction

Each role in the construction industry has very different responsibilities. In this topic you will find out about these responsibilities.

▶ The designer

A designer is responsible for the overall design of a building . This must meet the needs of a client's brief, be constructed in the set time and be of the required quality. The designer has to develop a client's brief and produce an approved sketch design drawing. These sketches are then developed into working drawings that are prepared for planning permission, and then into full construction drawings that will be used to get a price for the work. Planning and getting Building Regulations approval are important legislative responsibilities that the designer has to take care of so the client's project can proceed. The designer usually follows the document titled the RIBA Plan of Work. This is a work plan that outlines the roles and responsibilities of everyone involved with a project, from the initial brief through to the handover at the end.

A designer is also the client's or employer's representative on site. They have to make decisions about any information needed on site about variations to the design, materials specifications or issues on quality. The designer usually leads the monthly progress meetings with the contractor on site and is also responsible for distributing all contract drawings and documentation.

▶ The financial management team

The financial aspect of a contract is normally handled by a quantity surveyor. At the briefing stage of a project they will be responsible for the initial cost estimate of the architect's design concept so a client can make an informed decision on the budget. During the tendering stage they are responsible for the tender document production that a contractor will use to give a price for the client. They control the contract costs from agreeing interim payments and the calculation of the final account for the project.

Quantity surveyors deal with the financial payment and agreement with subcontractors, and the measurement and valuation of any variations to the project. They will also produce financial reports for clients on a monthly basis, so spending can be monitored.

▶ The construction manager

Site managers are responsible for the day-to-day running of the whole site and everyone working on it. This will involve using subcontractors on site, who will do some of the specialist work as part of the **construction programme**. Construction managers need to make sure that all the materials needed arrive on time and the skilled labour is available. Good organisational and people management skills are therefore essential. Health and safety is especially important, ensuring that everyone on site is kept safe and away from any construction hazards.

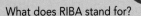

Remember

What does RIBA stand for?

Did you know?

The professional association for construction management is the Chartered Institute of Building (CIOB).

Key term

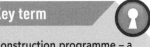 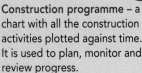

Construction programme – a chart with all the construction activities plotted against time. It is used to plan, monitor and review progress.

The facilities or maintenance manager

This important role starts when a building is handed over to a client and is occupied by the workers. The building will then need to be maintained and managed so it is safe to use and operate. The maintenance team will do day-to-day repairs that are reported as well as planned maintenance.

Managing the maintenance of a building also includes:

- lifecycle costing – this involves examining the costs of a building over its whole life, including its maintenance costs
- energy management – this involves reducing the energy costs of a building to the lowest possible level.

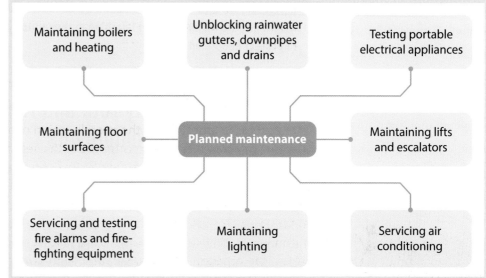

Figure 12.1 Planned maintenance is a vital part of the lifecycle of any development. Without it, the building will not be able to fulfil the needs of its occupants

---

Assessment activity 12.1 *English*

1 You have been asked to prepare a recruitment leaflet for potential apprenticeship applicants. Produce a short A4 leaflet that describes each of the following roles in construction and outlines the skills and qualifications needed:

- managerial
- craft
- operative.

2 You have been asked to join the RIBA as a student member. Describe the function of such a professional association and what progression opportunities full membership could bring.

3 Copy and complete the following table to help with a careers event planned at your company, which is looking to recruit trainees locally. Make sure that your description in the boxes forms a comparison between roles.

4 The construction recruitment officer needs help in producing the following recruitment advice pamphlet for your new drive on finding people who want to progress in an organisation. Discuss how a combination of skills, qualifications and experience make it possible to progress from an operative to a manager, and from a graduate to a professional role.

Level	Skills needed	Qualifications	Professional membership
Operative			
Craft			
Managerial			
Professional			

Health and safety requirements

Introduction

Health and safety in construction is vitally important. This is because we use many temporary structures during a building's construction, such as scaffolding. Falls from height are the major cause of fatalities in the industry and every precaution must be taken to protect people on site.

Health and safety role and responsibilities of employees and employers

Both employers and employees are responsible for maintaining health and safety in the workplace. Organisations that employ over a hundred employees may have a dedicated health and safety manager to help them do this. This person should be suitably qualified and will be in charge of implementing health and safety throughout the company. This will involve following new legislation, carrying out safety inspections and audits, arranging training for employees and maintaining safety records.

It is vital to have a clear health and safety plan in place on a construction site? Why do you think this is?

Safe site management

Health and safety management of a construction site covers aspects such as:

- all personnel responsibilities for hazards and risks and their control, using suitable measures to reduce any risk to an acceptable level
- method statements that plan the operations to be carried out
- site inductions to make everyone aware of the risks posed by any site hazards
- policy statements that detail a company's commitment to health and safety, which everyone must follow.

Activity 12.5

Health and safety regulations have a big impact on construction work on site.

Using a search engine, find out what different regulations apply on a construction site using the following subheadings:

- waste management
- noise
- chemicals
- heights.

Remember

Communication is vital to keeping everyone informed about hazards, risks and the control measures used to reduce them to an acceptable level.

Roles and responsibilities

Health and Safety at Work etc Act 1974 (HASAWA)

This is the Act of Parliament from which all of the safety regulations have been developed in the UK. It requires that the following responsibilities must be accounted for:

- duties on employers to provide a safe place of work, a duty of care, safety systems of work, policies, information, instruction and training, competent persons, cooperation and coordination, health surveillance, work equipment, personal protective equipment (PPE), reporting and recording, safety representatives and insurance

- duties on employees to take care of themselves and others, cooperate, report any unsafe features, and not misuse or interfere with any safety equipment

- duties on manufacturers, suppliers and designers of equipment to make sure it is safe to use and free from risks, adequate information is given and the CE mark (showing it conforms to European directives) has been applied.

What is this employee entitled to receive from their employer? What responsibilities do they have?

Construction Design and Management Regulations (CDM)

These regulations were brought in to prevent and reduce the large number of serious and fatal accidents that can occur on a construction site. They place duties on the persons listed in Table 12.2.

Table 12.2 Roles and responsibilities

Role	Responsibility
Designer	To make sure their design reduces hazards and risks with its use and maintenance
Client	To make sure all are competent and adequately resourced, project welfare facilities are suitably arranged and all pre-construction information is given
Principal contractor (the main contractor on a site)	To plan, manage and monitor the construction phase of the project, along with site rules, to provide a safety plan, site inductions and competence checks consultation, and ensure suitable welfare facilities are provided and maintained
Contractor (the sub-contractor who may be working under the principal contractor)	To plan, manage and monitor all their own work, carry out competence checks, provide training, information and welfare facilities
CDM coordinator	To advise and assist the client, notify project to the HSE, coordinate health and safety of design, liaise, distribute pre-contract information, prepare/update health and safety file for the project

Control of Substances Hazardous to Health (COSHH)

These regulations examine the use of any chemical substances used on a construction site. Any chemical used must have its safety data sheet examined in order for a risk assessment to be carried out on its use. The risk assessment may identify potential hazards of the substance and a set of control measures that may be needed for its use. The following controls are recommended by the Health and Safety Executive (HSE).

- Change the harmful product or substance and use a safer one.
- Use a safer form of the product, e.g. paste rather than powder.
- Enclose the process so that the product does not escape.
- Get rid of emissions of the substance near the source.
- Have as few workers in harm's way as possible.
- Provide personal protective equipment (PPE) such as gloves, coveralls and a **respirator**. PPE must fit the wearer.

Key term

Respirator – a PPE device that fits over the nose and mouth. It filters air entering the lungs to get rid of impurities.

Manual Handling Operations Regulations

These regulations concern the movement of materials around the construction site by hand. Supervisors need to be aware of any mechanical handlers that can be used to avoid manual handling. The Regulations state that if any manual handling is to be done, **employees** must:

- follow the system of work that has been set out, to reduce any risks from manual handling
- use any equipment that has been supplied
- cooperate with the employer
- inform them if any hazardous handling activities occur
- take care not to put others at risk.

Employers must:

- avoid manual handling by employees so far as is reasonable practicable
- doing a risk assessment
- reduce the risk from manual handling so far as reasonable practicable, as discussed in other units.

Activity 12.6

The Health and Safety Executive (HSE) has many downloadable guidance documents about each of the Regulations that have to be applied to construction operations and processes.

You are using a lot of jack hammers and compressors on site. The site manager has been told to sort out the correct procedures for this type of work. Look at the legislation regarding the use of vibrating machinery and create a presentation.

Assessment activity 12.2   *English*

1 You are working on a local housing development. The 'toolbox talk' on your site is about health and safety responsibilities. Describe the health and safety responsibilities of:

- a craft role employee
- a supervisor.

Make sure that you refer to current regulations.

2 The supervisor on site has asked you to help sort out who is doing what, as things are getting very confused on site. Explain in some detail the main health and safety responsibilities of an employee in a craft role and a supervisor, so everyone on site knows what they are doing.

Construction recruitment

Introduction

There are lots of different construction vacancies. If you work hard at studying for qualifications and getting work experience, you will maximise your chances of being recruited by an employer. In this topic you will explore your options.

Apprenticeships

An Apprentice works with an employer as well as attending training at a local college. This route lets you work and learn from more experienced craftspeople while gaining your qualifications.

The construction industry has its own sector skills council, the Construction Industry Training Board (CITB-ConstructionSkills). They oversee the development of Apprenticeship programmes and run the Construction Apprenticeship Scheme (CAS) in the UK. This scheme offers a structured training for apprentices.

Case study

Sadiq is considering applying for an Apprenticeship. He wants to start work in the construction industry so that he can start earning a wage, but he also wants to continue his studies. He thinks that an Apprenticeship is right for him because it would give him the chance to learn on the job from the craftspeople and professionals that he will work alongside. He will also work towards a level 3 qualification like a BTEC National.

There are many different construction-related Apprenticeships available in the UK covering everything from the crafts through to civil engineering.

1 How would you find out about them?
2 How would you find a suitable position?
3 How would you apply?

Discussion

Discuss in groups the kinds of job opportunities that are available and the different ways you might access them.

Remember

An Apprenticeship does not guarantee a job at the end. You will have to demonstrate commitment and the right attitude and behaviour to be offered a job at the end of your training.

Did you know?

Apprenticeships can take between one and four years to complete.

College and school links

Schools, colleges and training centres often form strong links with local employers. This can give you the opportunity to gain work experience with local employers. Networking is very useful for those wanting to start in the industry, as personal recommendation goes a long way with potential employers.

Local careers guidance services can also give information about jobs in construction.

Family connections with relatives who have their own companies and businesses in construction are also a good way to start in the industry.

Did you know?

The 'milk round' is the nickname for employers' visits to universities in the UK.

Activity 12.7

Consider the following questions.

1 Where in the world would you like to work? And in which profession?

2 How will you achieve this?

3 What do you need to do now?

University recruitment

Many major employers recruit from universities and attend their open evenings, trying to attract the best candidates for their vacancies. This is a great way to join an organisation as a graduate trainee or an intern.

Many organisations sponsor graduates to do some research on a higher degree in support of the company that is offering the scholarship. Often this leads to employment with the company after graduation.

Recruitment agencies

It is good to register your curriculum vitae (CV) with recruitment agencies, so that any opportunities can be emailed to you. Often companies will supply a personal profile to the agency for the type of person they are seeking.

Agencies also work at the craft levels, supplying skilled labour on a daily basis to construction sites. This is often a useful method of working for an employer using short-term contracts.

Website searches and advertisements

The internet has created lots of opportunities for employment. Any organisation can use its own website to recruit and advertise its vacancies, along with an online application process. Training organisations, employers, careers guidance organisations and sector skills councils all now have a web presence so you can contact them and gain an entry into the industry.

Bricklayer

Manchester | **£12.50 – £13.00 per hour**

Contractor looking for reliable bricklayer with five years' site experience to work on a number of housing sites in the Manchester area. Must have own tools and transport.

Apply for this job

Figure 12.2 What qualities do you think your covering letter and CV would need to show if you applied for this job?

Professional journal advertising

Many professional associations publish a monthly news journal for their members. In the back of these journals is often an opportunity to advertise for vacancies among the professional network. There are also opportunities at regional continuing professional development (CPD) events, where there may be discussions about vacancies.

Press advertising

Industry magazines and other publications often feature jobs sections, so you can browse them for vacancies that you would be interested in. Many magazines also have companion websites, which often have a job search function. Some examples include *Construction News* and *Building Magazine*.

Regional and local newspapers will also provide advertising for employers to recruit prospective employees. As they are local, they give an idea of the current vacancies in your own area.

▶ Direct applications to companies

Direct applications to a construction company are another way to find a job. Companies will often take a certain number of graduates or trainees per year and will have a detailed selection process in order to pick the best candidates.

A direct method is one of the best ways to find work as you are dealing direct with the company. You should research the company to learn as much as you can about it. This will make your application stronger.

Just checking

1 Where would you find about doing an apprenticeship?
2 Where else could you look to find job vacancies and opportunities?
3 What could you do to add value to your application?

▶ Applying for jobs

Introduction

Applying for a job vacancy is a very important process. First impressions can make a huge difference. A well-presented covering letter and CV go a long way to getting a foot in the door of an organisation. Taking the time to hand-deliver your application in person is always a great way of introducing yourself to an organisation.

The application must be written correctly, have no spelling mistakes and be grammatically correct so it reads well. A professional-looking CV is the best first impression you can give an employer.

▶ Research the opportunity

When you find a construction vacancy you are interested in, you must always research the company advertising it. This will give you information that you can use to support your application letter. Knowing relevant information about the company will also make you seem well informed and interested during the application process, especially in interviews.

The purpose of covering letters and CVs

First impressions are very important when you are applying for jobs. You would not turn up to an interview in shabby clothes, so make sure that your covering letter gives just as good a first impression as you do.

Most applications need a covering letter. This is the first impression you will make on an employer, so the letter must be professional. A covering letter often accompanies a completed application form and gives a little bit more information about why you are applying for the position, to make an employer want to meet you. Badly written letters will not encourage an employer to offer you an interview.

The letter needs to:

- be well presented and laid out correctly
- use correct spelling and grammar
- have an introduction
- explain why you have applied
- explain your skills and sell yourself
- show your motivation for the position.

You can find many examples of covering letters on the internet. Take the time to look around and find out which style suits you best.

Dear John,

Iam writing to you to ask you for a job at your company, and I think that you would be stupid not to take me on.

I have attended my local college and obtained my BTEC National in Constructtion. I am advised that you are looking for a traionee site manager and I would like to be considered for the post.

I am currently undertaking work experience with the Local Authority Highways department and feel civil engineering is the career I want to follow.

I enclose my C.V. highlighting the units and the gardes obtained at college along with my work experience to date.

I am available for an interview Monday to Friday after 3.00pm

Thank you,

Stuart Preston

Figure 12.3 What sort of first impression does this covering letter give?

Activity 12.8

One of your friends has just finished a level 3 qualification in construction and is applying for a trainee site manager position. They have asked you to check their covering letter. Figure 12.3 is a copy of their letter. Read it and then think about the following questions.

1 Imagine you are an employer. What would you think about this letter?
2 Would you start the letter 'Dear John'?
3 Are the spelling and grammar correct?
4 How would you improve this letter?
5 What is missing from the letter?

Take it further

Look for a suitable template online that you could use as a basis for your covering letter. Download it and add some details so you have a useful starting point for any job application.

The features and layout of a CV

A curriculum vitae (CV) contains your details and previous work history. A good CV should include basic content about you as listed in Table 12.3.

Table 12.3 Basic parts of a CV

Your contact details	Give your address, home and mobile telephone numbers, and email address.
Personal profile	You can use this to reflect your skills, aspirations in life and personal goals.
Qualifications	List all your qualifications gained in date order, any professional memberships and training courses you have done.
Education	List where you studied your qualifications.
Previous job roles or experience	Give a full history, in date order, of where you have worked, what your roles were and your responsibilities.
References	Give two people whom a potential employer could contact for a reference about you as a person. They may be asked what you are like and how you would cope with the new job. These people are your 'referees'.

There are thousands of CV templates online that you can use to give an effective introduction about yourself to a potential employer.

Activity 12.9

1. Use the skills assessment you completed in Activity 12.2 to help you write your personal profile. Remember to think about what an employer will want to see in a potential employee.

2. Do some further research using the internet or careers guidance from your school or college to find an eye-catching CV template. Fill in your details and any other information, remembering to make it brief and informative as well as well formatted and well written.

 # Proofreading covering letters and CVs

You should check very carefully that the spelling and grammar are correct on your CV. Use the computer's spell checker and a dictionary to make sure the English you have used is accurate and correct.

Just checking

1. What would you write in a covering letter to go with an application form?
2. What would you put in your CV?
3. Would you list any work experience in your CV?
4. Would you include referees?

▶ Preparation for interview

Introduction

Congratulations – you've got an interview! Now you need to prepare. Interview preparation is about more than being dressed smartly. Planning well for an interview helps you stand out as a motivated individual.

▶ Research the company or organisation

First, find out as much as you can about the company. Use this information to support your application. It will also be useful in discussing their business during the interview. It shows that you are keen and motivated. Research the company's strengths – you need to be aware about what they are good at doing, and refer to this when you talk to them.

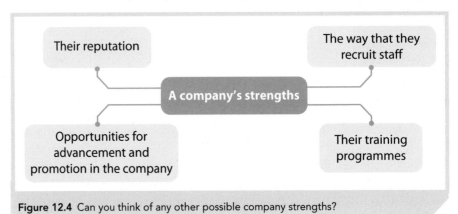

Their reputation

The way that they recruit staff

A company's strengths

Opportunities for advancement and promotion in the company

Their training programmes

Figure 12.4 Can you think of any other possible company strengths?

▶ Preparing your responses

You need to be prepared for any difficult questions they will ask you so evaluate your own strengths and also your weaknesses. You will need to anticipate what questions they are likely to ask.

Prepare to be asked if you have any questions for your interviewers. Always prepare these questions well, as this will be the last thing they remember about you when they make a final decision.

Assessment activity 12.3 *English*

1 You are starting to look for work after finishing at college, and are struggling to find a job. Describe the sources of construction vacancies.

2 You have been asked to send in your CV after contacting a local construction company. Evaluate your CV by proofreading and correcting it.

3 When you have completed this CV, evaluate it against someone else's. Give yourself positive as well as critical feedback.

4 You have been called for an interview. Develop a set of questions that you think the employer might ask.

WorkSpace

▶ Dinesh Kulkarni

Assistant site manager

I work as an assistant site manager for a large construction company. When I finished my level 3 qualifications, I looked for work as a site manager, but I found that as I had no experience, I didn't get asked to any interviews.

I decided the best thing to do was to ask for some work experience on a site with a local company I knew. They agreed to give me a period of six months. This let me add specific site management experience to my CV. I was then able to apply for vacancies with bigger national companies, as they could see that I had work experience as a site manager.

While I was at college I worked on my covering letter and CV as part of my 'employability skills'. This gave me a clear understanding of what was needed and how to sell myself to an employer.

My position now will give me an ideal opportunity to move up to being a full site manager, and then I want to become a project manager or contracts manager once I've got enough experience. My current employers are thinking about a day release course that would allow me to attend a degree in construction management at university.

I've learned from all this that working hard and getting qualifications and experience will benefit you in the long run.

Think about it

1 How did Dinesh deal with the problem of not having experience?

2 How will you find the job that you will enjoy when leaving your studies?

3 What can you do now to make yourself stand out to an employer?

Unit 1: Construction Technology

1 **C**

2 Drinking water and toilet facilities

3 Flat roofs

These can be considered as aesthetically pleasing and can provide interesting features in the building design. These roofs are also popular for their ease of maintenance and for the fact that they provide flat recreational areas where people can relax.

However, these roofs are not very good at draining water, and this can result in 'ponding' or the build-up of standing water. The roof surface also needs treatments such as solar reflective paint and extra hardwearing surfaces, and these can be costly over the lifecycle of the roof.

Pitched roofs

These roofs are also considered aesthetically pleasing and can create more floor space or storage space in loft areas. These drain water well due to their slope and require less maintenance.

However, the initial cost of constructing a pitched roof is higher than a flat roof. They also take longer to build and are more difficult to access for maintenance.

Unit 11: Sustainability in Construction

1 **D**

2 Demolition of existing structures and disposal of the waste; disposal of special waste such as asbestos; decontamination of site.

3 **Photovoltaic tiles and panels** – Photovoltaic (PV) tiles and panels are becoming more and more popular, especially for new buildings. These panels absorb sunlight or natural daylight and convert it into electrical energy. As photovoltaic tiles depend on daylight to produce energy, these should be installed on south-facing roofs, clear of any trees or other shading.

Ground source heat recovery – Below the ground, there is a lot of heat energy. This energy can be used to fulfil the heating needs of a building, such as hot water and heating radiators. However, the cost of installation can be high depending upon the location and the depth required.

Small-scale wind turbines – These can be used to provide electricity for homes. The turbines use wind energy and convert it to electricity. However, location has to be studied to ascertain its suitability.

Solar hot water panels – Solar panels absorb sunlight and convert this into energy, which can be used to supply hot water for domestic buildings. As sunlight is free, these panels provide heat energy at no cost other than the initial installation.

A

Adjacent – next to or touching something. For example, the houses either side of a terraced house are adjacent to it.

Aesthetics – the appreciation of beauty or the appearance of something.

Affordable housing – low-cost properties that are built within a development that buyers (particularly first-time buyers) can afford to purchase or rent.

Aggregates – an aggregate is a mixture of pieces of crushed stone and gravel. They are used in making concrete as well as more generally in construction activities.

Air entraining – a chemical product that forms thousands of bubbles. These trap air in the block, which makes it a very good insulator.

Amp – the measure of the amount of current flowing within an electrical circuit.

Attenuation – slowing down the flow of water.

B

Biodiversity – this is made up of two words: biological and diversity. It means the variety of living organisms on the planet.

Bitumen – a black sticky by-product from oil refining.

Boat level – a small short level used for awkward areas where a large level is not practical.

Bond – an arrangement of bricks and blocks. The term is also used to describe how various courses of brick or block work are joined together.

Brownfield – a site that has already been built on.

Bucket handle – a joint that is rounded, forming a concave shape to the mortar joint in the brick wall. It is the most common joint.

Building line – this is an imaginary line along a street that all building fronts must keep behind. It is set by the local authority.

Building services – the services of water, gas, electricity and communications that have to be designed for a building.

Built environment – the buildings and other structures constructed by humans.

Bunded or **bund wall** – a structure that is built to hold any spillages.

Burr – rough-sawn edges.

Buy-to-let – when someone buys a property to rent out rather than to live in themselves.

C

Capillary action – the absorption of liquid into the pores in a porous material.

Carbon footprint – the amount of carbon dioxide released into the atmosphere as a result of human activity, such as the construction of a building.

Ceiling rose – the unit used in lighting that fixes directly to the ceiling.

Cladding – a covering or coating on the outside of a structure.

Condensation – the most common form of dampness in a house. It happens when warm moist air comes into contact with cooler air or a cold surface.

Conductors – materials (for example, copper) that allow electricity to flow through them.

Coniferous – these are trees that have cones, such as pine, larch and fir. Timber used from these trees is also called softwood.

Constraints – limiting factors.

Construction programme – a chart with all the construction activities plotted against time. It is used to plan, monitor and review progress.

Consumer unit – the unit where the meter and isolation fuse feed into the domestic circuit. It has all of the fuses, residual circuit devices (RCDs) or miniature circuit breakers (MCBs).

Continuity – the completion of a circuit without any breaks in the conduction of electricity.

COSHH – the Control of Substances Hazardous to Health Regulations 2002.

Cross-lining – hanging lining paper horizontally.

Cross-sectional – in a cross-section view. This means imagining that you can see through the object, as though it has been cut in half.

Current – the amount of flow of electrical charge, which is measured in amps.

Cutting in – painting a neat line between surfaces that touch each other – for example, the line between the wall and ceiling or where the skirting board meets the wall.

Cutting wheel – a hardened steel wheel that is gently rotated and tightened against the copper pipe and slowly cuts through it.

D

Deciduous – these are trees whose leaves fall during the year. Examples include oak, beech, ash and walnut. Timber used from these trees is also called hardwood.

Deflection – the distance a structure moves or changes position under stress.

Degradation – when a material is exposed to sunlight, water and wind, it starts losing its strength, shape or appearance.

Delamination – when the two layers of wallpaper separate. This can be caused by over-soaking the paper or using a seam roller too much.

De-nib – removing any bits or plaster splashes from a surface.

Density – mass per unit volume, measured in kilograms per cubic metre (kg/m^3).

Density of homes – the number of homes built over an area. The larger the number of homes, the higher the density.

Detention structures – used to slow down the flow of water.

Double glazing – this is a technology used to make windows less likely to lose heat. A double-glazed window is made of two panes of glass with a narrow gap in between them. The air is sucked out of this space to create a vacuum. It is difficult to transfer heat through a vacuum, so a double-glazed window loses less heat.

Dry lining – the edges of plasterboards are taped and filled over. The whole area is then painted. When using this technique, there is no need to skim the surface with plaster.

E

Eco-tourism – responsible tourism to a natural environment. It does not damage the natural environment and the wellbeing of the local community.

Elasticity – the ability of a material to recover its shape and size completely when the deforming force is removed. Even steel is elastic.

Embodied energy – the energy needed to produce a material from extraction to its point of use. It is also known as embedded energy, as it is the energy contained by or embedded in each brick, tile or piece of timber.

End grain – this is the grain at the end of a piece of timber when the timber has been cut.

Evaluation – bringing together all the relevant information and using it to form a conclusion about something.

Excavation – digging up the ground to reach the right level below ground to lay the foundations.

F

Fabrication – another word for manufacturing.

Facing bricks – bricks with a decorative face to provide an attractive wall.

Feasibility – the possibility of being able to do something.

Ferrous – containing or made of iron.

Ferrule – a metal band that secures the filling (bristles) of a paint brush to the handle.

Fixing – the method used to secure a copper conductor into its terminal block using a screw.

Flange – a projecting flat rim for strengthening, guidance or attaching to something else.

Flash flood – sudden flood in a local area due to heavy rainfall.

Flexible – changes shape easily.

Flux – this helps the soldering process by stopping the cleaned copper from oxidising and stopping the solder from bonding to the copper.

Fly tipping – dumping waste illegally (usually done to avoid paying to dispose of the waste).

Former – this is the radius part of the pipe bender, which holds the correct diameter pipe in position as it is bent around the former. This gives the correct radius for the pipe that is being bent. Normal-sized formers are 15 mm and 22 mm.

Fossil fuels – non-renewable fuels such as coal, oil, gas or peat.

Foul water – the used water that comes from toilets, sinks and showers.

Fungi – (singular: fungus) these are micro-organisms such as moulds.

Fungicide – added to paste to prevent mould growth. It is especially important when hanging vinyl papers because these are non-porous and can take a long time to dry out.

G

Gauge – in screws, this is the diameter of the screw's body, or shank.

Gauge – the depth of a brick or block plus one bed joint. For example, a brick is 65 mm depth + 10 mm = 75 mm gauge.

GDP – this is the value of the total amount of goods and services produced by a nation in one year.

Grades – the grade depends on the size and quantity of abrasive particles on the abrasive paper.

Gradient – the slope.

Greenfield – a site where no construction has taken place before.

Grey water – waste water from bathing, dishwashing or using washing machines. It can be recycled to be reused in other areas of the house, but is not used for drinking.

Grommet – in electrics, a rubber ring that fits within the steel back box where the inlet has been formed and protects the cable from any sharp edges that could cut the cable insulation as the cable is pulled through.

H

Habitable – suitable to be lived in or occupied.

Hardcore – materials such as broken bricks, stone or concrete, which are hard and do not readily absorb water or deteriorate.

Hazards – things that have the potential to cause harm, such as a naked flame.

Heat capacity – the heat needed to raise the temperature of an object by 1°C.

Hemp and **flax** – widely grown plants that have excellent insulation properties. Hemp can be mixed with lime to produce insulation products. Flax can be used as an insulation material and as strips for sealing joints around doors and windows.

Hierarchy – a ranking system according to the importance of each item listed in relation to the other items.

Hot work – work that will need equipment that generates a lot of heat.

I

Iconic – very famous or popular. In construction, this is usually used to refer to a building that is instantly recognised for its design and location, like the Sydney Opera House.

Identification – in this context, this means looking at and accounting for all the people who may be affected by a hazard.

Impedance – the opposition of a circuit to the passage of electricity.

Imperfections – when a surface is not totally flat and smooth – for example, with dents, chips or scratches.

Impervious – not allowing water to pass through.

Incineration – a method of waste treatment where waste is burned and is converted into ash and gases.

Industrial action – protest action taken by the employees of a company or organisation, such as striking.

Infrastructure – the basic structures needed for the operation of a society, including roads, buildings and power supply.

Insulation – the plastic covering that surrounds the copper conductors in an electric cable.

Integrated – to become a part of something.

Intercept – where one thing interrupts or cuts off something else. In the equation for a straight-line graph, it is where the line cuts the y-axis.

Intumescent paint – paint that is intumescent swells when heated. This makes it fire resistant, as when it is heated up by fire, it expands and becomes a thicker layer on top of the painted material. This slows down the transfer of heat to the painted material.

Inverse operation – doing something (e.g. an equation) the other way around.

J

Joint box – used to connect two or more electric cables together safely.

K

Kelvin – this is an alternative measure of temperature used in scientific study. Zero kelvin is equal to a temperature of –273 °C and is the coldest temperature possible. Its symbol is K.

Key – this is what allows a previously painted surface to bond with the next coat of paint.

Knotting – a preparation liquid substance or solution of shellac and methylated spirit. It is applied to knots in timber to stop the resin leaking out and damaging the paint film.

L

Latent heat – the energy needed to change the state of the material.

Lateral restraint – when sideways movement of building elements is stopped.

Leaf – the part of a door or window that is hinged. A double leaf door features two hinged doors.

LED – light emitting diode. LEDs are a different way of giving light. They do not get hot as they do not use a filament within a bulb, so they last a lot longer than an ordinary bulb.

Limit of proportionality – the greatest stress a material can sustain without deviating from Hooke's law.

Load – the weight pressing down on one element of the building or structure, such as a load-bearing wall or a floor.

Local plan – this is a legal document that every local authority in the UK uses to set out their local planning policies in the area under their authority. It defines where residential and industrial developments can be built, and any planning application is checked against the plan.

Louvre – a set of angled slats fixed over a door or window. They allow air and light through.

M

Make good – prepare a surface to be painted.

Malleable – able to have its shape changed by flattening, bending or denting out of shape.

Manually – by hand.

Mass – the amount of matter in a body, measured in kilograms (kg).

Mitre – a piece of wood that has been cut at an angle.

Mortar – a mixture of cement, sand, lime and water. It is used to join bricks and blocks together.

Mortise – a square or rectangular hole in timber.

Musculoskeletal injuries – injuries affecting our muscles and bones.

Musculoskeletal – to do with the human frame and muscles that function to give movement.

N

Noise – this is any unwanted sound. Noise should be avoided wherever possible.

Non-combustible – does not burn.

O

Olive – a metal ring or fitting tightened under a threaded nut to form a seal.

Opacity – a paint's ability to hide a surface underneath.

Open coated – when the abrasive particles are spread out and less concentrated.

Operating pressure – the pressure of the water within the pipe that normally would be produced when in use. Your tutor will set the operating pressure that the test rig's starting pressure will be set from.

Orange peel – this occurs when a long pile roller sleeve is used on a smooth surface. It leaves the surface slightly textured, like an orange.

Orientation – the direction that a building faces.

Outlet – this could be a fused outlet where the cable from the appliance is directly wired into the ring main.

Outline planning permission – this is provisional planning permission for a development that outlines details such as how many houses can be built and what size they can be. The outline must be converted into full planning permission in order to proceed with any building project.

Oxidisation

Oxidisation – the interaction between oxygen molecules and all the different substances they may come into contact with – for example, copper. Oxidisation can be destructive, and when copper oxidises it turns green and then black. This oxidisation has to be removed in order to allow the pipework to be joined using a soldered joint.

P

Paint system – all the coats of paint on a surface.

Parallel – parallel lines run alongside each other and are always the same distance apart. They will never cross.

Performance – how well a building provides a comfortable, safe environment for its occupants.

Permeable – a material that allows water to pass through.

Perpendicular – the pipe is cut at 90° to its length, or cut 'square' across its length.

Photovoltaic (PV) – photo means light and voltaic means electrical potential. Photovoltaic materials are able to produce electricity when they are exposed to light.

Pile length – the length of the material used for the roller sleeve. Long pile sleeves are used for heavily textured or rough surfaces. Short pile sleeves give the best finish on smooth surfaces.

Pi (π) – approximately 3.14159.

Pipe rig – a small-scale assembly of pipes and fittings in a framework to test your skills at bending, jointing and cutting accurately.

Plant – machinery used in the construction process, such as bulldozers and excavators.

Pointing – filling the joints in brickwork with mortar to improve appearance and weather proofing.

Polarity – the direction of a magnetic or electric field.

Porosity – a surface's ability to absorb moisture.

Porous – a porous material has a lot of pores or air pockets. These allow air or liquid to pass through the material.

Prefabricated – 'pre' means 'before' and 'fabricated' means 'made'. The term describes the parts of the building made in a factory and brought to site for assembly only.

PVC – a type of plastic. PVC is short for polyvinyl chloride.

Q

Quantities – the amounts of materials needed from suppliers.

R

Ratio – the proportion of one thing to another. For example, if a ratio of water : cement is 1 : 2, there is twice as much cement as water.

Render – a type of plaster finish used on external as well as internal walls. It can improve a building's insulation.

Respirator – a PPE device that fits over the nose and mouth. It filters air entering the lungs to get rid of impurities.

Retention – holding the water before passing it on.

Risk assessment – a process of identifying the hazards, the people who might be harmed, a risk rating and the control measures that must be used when doing the work.

Risks – these result from hazards, such as someone burning themselves with the naked flame.

Roofing battens – strips of wood fixed to rafters, used to attach roof tiles to a roof.

Roofing felt – a protective layer between the actual roof structure and the building. It is made up of waterproof materials.

Runs – a length of pipe in a run from one point to another.

S

Screed – this is made from cement and sand to provide a level surface before a floor is laid.

Seasoning – treating natural timber so it is not affected by changes in moisture.

Sedum – a small hardy plant that is good at resisting extreme weather conditions.

Sensible heat – the heat that can be measured by a thermometer.

Setting out rod – a 1:1 drawing of the frame you are going to make.

Shingles – a roofing material, generally made of cedar wood.

Size – a coating applied to a surface to make it less absorbent. Thinned-down wallpaper paste can also be used for this job.

Sleeving – a separate sleeve that fits over the exposed earth conductor and covers up all of the copper conductor.

Soffits – the undersides of eaves.

Solder – this is a metal that melts at the temperature of the blowtorch. It fills the gaps between two copper surfaces and bonds to them, forming a watertight joint.

Specification – the written details of all of the components and materials for the building that have been given by the architect or designer.

Specific heat – the amount of heat needed to change one unit of the mass of a substance by one unit of temperature.

Stable – when a structure can keep its balance without moving.

Statutory – something that has to be done by law.

Stretcher – the dimension of a brick along its length, normally 215 mm.

Stripping – removal of the outer layers of plastic insulation that surround the copper conductor.

Surface water – water that runs off roads, roofs and gardens.

Sustainability – preserving resources for future generations and minimising the impact of construction activities on the natural environment.

Sustainable Urban Drainage Systems (SUDS) – systems that make sure water is drained off in a sustainable manner.

T

Tendering – making a formal offer (tender) to carry out work for a stated fixed price.

Tendering – the process of getting a competitive price for the client's proposed building project.

Tenon – a rectangular shaped part of timber that fits exactly into a mortise.

Termination – the final terminal that an electrical cable is connected to.

Thermal efficiency – how efficiently a building uses heat energy.

Thermal insulation – insulation against heat loss.

Thermal mass – the ability of a material to absorb, store and release heat in line with the heating and cooling cycle of a building.

Thermal resistance – this is measured as an R-value. This shows the ability of a material to reduce heat loss because it resists the movement of heat through it. Increasing the thickness of a material increases its R-value.

Tolerance – this is the amount of error that is acceptable in an object that is fit for purpose. If a joinery firm makes a lot of window frames that turn out to be the wrong size, the tolerances they have used are too broad.

Turbine – a machine like a wheel. It extracts energy from water, gas or air and converts it into another form, such as electricity.

U

uPVC cladding – a covering made of uPVC (unplasticised polyvinyl chloride).

Useful life – the length of time that a building fulfils the needs of the people who live or work in it.

U-value – this measures the loss of heat from a building element such as walls, floors and roof. These are used to specify insulation standards in buildings.

V

Variations – the alterations or changes that may have to be made during construction due to design changes, client's alterations or errors.

VDE – Verband der Elektrotechnik (the Association for Electrical, Electronic & Information Technologies) is one of the largest technical and scientific associations in Europe, and is a brand name for tested electrical tools.

Volume – the amount of three-dimensional space an object occupies.

W

Wall tie – a component used to join the two halves or skins of a cavity wall.

Wet scrubber – a device that removes pollutants from gases.